THE UNEXPECTED JOY OF SPONSORSHIP: *AN AA SPONSOR'S HANDBOOK*

An AA Sponsor's Handbook

GAIL ANDREA S
Peripatetic Publishing,
A Virginia Company

An AA Sponsor's Handbook

An AA Sponsor's Handbook

First published 2013

Copyright 2013 Andrea S
ALL RIGHTS RESERVED

Printed in the United States of America. No part of this book may be used, reproduced or transmitted in any manner whatsoever without written permission except in the case of brief quotations embodied in critical articles and reviews. While every effort has been made to ensure the accuracy of the content of this book, the author assumes no responsibility or liability for errors made herein.

First Edition Published by: Peripatetic Publishing, a Virginia Company

The Unexpected Joy of Sponsorship/Andrea S.

ISBN *978-1-492-38318-5*

I dedicate this book to my sponsees, and my sponsors, to my friends, to Alcoholics Anonymous, and to my family, especially my grandchildren, who have never seen me drunk.

I love you all.

An AA Sponsor's Handbook

Credo: I Believe

Emily Dickinson said 'Behavior is what a man or woman is, not what he or she thinks, feels, or believes.'

I've long since left the fantasies of drunkenness and childish daydreams behind. What I do is what I wanted to do; who I am can be determined by that which I do.

Sponsorship, for me, is neither teacher-student relationship, nor illuminator of enlightenment. The sponsor and sponsee are two travelers on a spiritual path, walking together towards a better life.

I want to talk about the gifts of the Program of Alcoholics Anonymous, and perhaps a spark of what is possible in this book. My sponsees and I have sallied forth from a starting point of pain and ignorance, losing our egos and our false pride, and receiving strength and self-awareness, the ability to practice transcendent principles, and the capacity to help others achieve what we have been so freely given.

A sponsor is a person who listens and who cares, about you, your sobriety and your life. She is a person who shares enough of her life, no matter how shameful or embarrassing, so that you feel comfortable with her. In the truest sense of the word you meet her, rather than use her.

Hopefully, this will be an important relationship of mutual respect that will do more than save your life. You will, perhaps for the first time, have a wonderful life worth saving.

TABLE OF CONTENTS

THE 'RULES' 28

Some of what I learned in AA (WILAA): 29

Introduction 30

Carrots and Sticks 30

AA funerals 31

CHAPTER ONE: WHY I WROTE THIS BOOK 33

My Experiences 34

The process of AA 35

The benefits of going where you don't want to go, or meaningful service positions 36

The gifts of Alcoholics Anonymous 39

A magical moment in sponsorship 42

CHAPTER TWO: TO THE SPONSOR 46

WILAA: Sponsorship is all about the Steps 48

CHAPTER THREE: THE ROLE OF A SPONSOR 50

Humility 53

My journeys with 'chronic *relapsers* and how I got burnt out 55

Relapse Prevention 56

A little bit on gratitude 60

You should know the difference between Big Book Rehabs and all the rest 61

A practical suggestion for sponsors: learn about community services 64

CHAPTER FOUR: CARRYING THE MESSAGE, NOT HAVING TO DO IT ALL 65

Important practical considerations 69

Talking with the newcomer (or someone who has relapsed) 73

The notebook 78

Picking a rehab, health care professionals and types of treatment: this is your life we're talking about 81

I always ask my new sponsee to look in the *Big Book* if she's getting conflicting messages 83

What you need to do to stay sober 84

CHAPTER FIVE: A GOOD PLAN OF RECOVERY 86

It's good to have a game plan, early on 86

You always need a game plan, even if you've been sober forty years 87

A sample list in later sobriety 87

It helps if the sponsee creates her own prayers and promises for each Step 88

Putting Recovery First 90

A very good question to ask sponsees 91

Knowing what the Big Book says 92

My boring story 93

Lest we forget: we're here to stop drinking 96

The Alcoholic's Creed 98

CHAPTER SIX: THE LIE OF SELF-RELIANCE 103

For take-charge marines 103

Inadequate coping mechanisms 106

The process of Alcoholics Anonymous 108

I stopped asking why and started asking how 108

What does it take to see? 110

CHAPTER SEVEN: THE NECESSITY OF FORGIVENESS IS WOVEN INTO EVERY ASPECT OF THE TWELVE STEPS 113

I dwell in a world where my ego is checked, my instincts are functioning properly, and I feel vaguely at peace 114

CHAPTER EIGHT: MY JOURNEY THROUGH THE STEPS AND WHAT I LEARNED 120

A little more about self-sufficiency, and there's always a little more to say about that 120

Spiritual fitness 125

CHAPTER NINE: WHEN AM I READY TO SPONSOR SOMEONE? 131

Why I needed time in Alcoholics Anonymous to be a good sponsor 131

The three years when I was sponsoring chronic relapsers 132

So why do I feel guilty about not doing more in AA? 134

I was so busy trying to change what I could not change, that I had no time or energy to change what I should have been changing. 135

Sponsorship is more than conveying information 136

CHAPTER TEN: THE URGENCY OF NOW 138

Practicing the presence of God 139

I work diligently with sponsees so they can find their outside help. It generally isn't me. 141

CHAPTER ELEVEN: TALKING ABOUT THE TWELFTH STEP IS ANOTHER WAY OF TALKING ABOUT BEING A SPONSOR 142

Part one of the Twelfth Step: 'Having had a spiritual awakening as the result of these Steps. 142

Part two 'Carrying the message' 143

More on when someone is ready to be a sponsor 144

Somebody said that you can't do Twelve Step work wrong. Sure you can. I see it all the time 145

Part three: Practicing these principles in all of our affairs 147

We each have our own higher power 149

Principles of the Twelfth Step, which I, particularly as a sponsor, attempt to practice always 149

CHAPTER TWELVE: THE SPIRITUAL INVENTORY 151

Finally: If God were truly in my life: What would my life be like? What would I be like? 152

CHAPTER THIRTEEN: SOME QUESTIONS I'VE BEEN ASKED ABOUT BEING A SPONSOR 153

Basics of Sponsorship: When do we start working the Steps? 156

When is it time to say good-bye? 158

When a sponsee relapses 163

If she's tried to do the work 164

It's not time to say goodbye 164

Examples 165

CHAPTER FOURTEEN: HOW DO I NOT GET INVOLVED IN THE SPONSEE'S LIFE? WHY + 167

Usually love is about addition 171

CHAPTER FIFTEEN: DO I EVER REFUSE A REQUEST FROM SOMEONE IN AA? 177

Who I don't sponsor 178

CHAPTER SIXTEEN: GOD AND RELIGION 181

The three places I've found large numbers of people who believe that nothing is more powerful than they: AA meetings, psych wards, and Capitol Hill 183

God is either everything or nothing 183

CHAPTER SEVENTEEN: THE VISION THAT SAVED MY LIFE: I HAVE MET GOD AND HE IS GOOD. 189

CHAPTER EIGHTEEN: A VERY SHORT DISCUSSION OF THE STEPS: 197

Steps One, Two, and Three 197

Step Four 198

Step Five 198

Step Five and a Half 198

Step Six 198

Step Seven 199

Step Eight 199

Step Nine 199

Step Ten 199

Step Eleven 199

Step Twelve 200

CHAPTER NINETEEN: THE STEPS IN MORE DEPTH BEGINNING WITH STEP ONE 201

Step one-'We admitted that we were powerless over alcohol-that our lives had become unmanageable.' 201

The alcoholic is 'different in mind, body and spirit' from normal drinkers 206

More of my story 208

Here are the Principles of the First Step 209

CHAPTER TWENTY: STEP TWO. 'Came to believe that a power greater than ourselves could restore us to sanity.' 210

More of the process of AA 214

Principles of the Second Step 217

CHAPTER TWENTY-ONE: STEP THREE 218

Step Three helps me see that I can't 'just say no.' The Big Book is very clear: I'm not in charge. If I want to change, I'll have to do a lot more than want to change 221

The Set Aside Prayer 221

The Third Step Reality Check 223

Third Step Prayer: 227

Make sure you make this prayer with 'complete abandon.' 227

The principles of Step Three: 228

CHAPTER TWENTY THREE: MORE ABOUT THE THIRD STEP 230

The difficulty with decisions. Three Ladies 230

The actor in a play 233

CHAPTER TWENTY-THREE: THE FOURTH STEP: Made a fearless and thorough inventory of ourselves. 235

Helping someone do a Fourth Step 236

Cheat sheets 239

Are there three columns or four? 240

Proposal for a new kind of therapy 240

The Bankruptcy Theory of the Fourth Step 241

Some results of this Step 242

Business inventory 242

We just don't have the sizes that will sell. We've got to get rid of damaged goods, even if we like them and they're our size. 243

The Resentments Inventory 244

The Fourth Step Prayer in its entirety 245

The Second Column 245

The Third Column 246

The Fourth Column (or not 246

To get rid of fear 247

Reflections on the Fourth Step 249

The Sex Inventory 250

The Fourth Step resentment list 252

Last but not least 253

The Principles of the Fourth Step 256

CHAPTER TWENTY-FOUR: STEP FIVE 258

Part One: Doing a Fifth Step 258

The pathology of me 258

Part Two: The second aspect of the Fifth Step is hearing it 261

So what's a sponsor to do? (Less than you want to) 262

I need to be a sponsor as well as sponsee to get the full benefit of the Steps 262

Principles of the Fifth Step 263

The need for external things disappears in this spiritual experience. I experience joy 264

CHAPTER TWENTY-SEVEN: STEP FIVE AND A HALF 265

What I learned 265

What I practiced 266

CHAPTER TWENTY EIGHT: STEP SIX 267

Step Six is the rallying point 271

Principles of the Sixth Step 273

CHAPTER TWENTY-EIGHT: STEP SEVEN 275

The Seventh Step Prayer 279

Principles of the Seventh Step: 280

CHAPTER TWENTY-NINE: ENTERING THE WORLD OF THE SPIRIT-THE EIGHTH STEP: 281

What is an amend or an amends? 282

The idea of a living amends 283

The purpose of Steps Eight and Nine: to help me become of maximum service to God and others 283

Forgiveness entails being honest about the harm that was done to me, otherwise it isn't forgiveness 284

The way to make amends 284

The index card method 285

Forgiving someone is letting go of the hurt and moving on. This is the Step where I enter the world of the Spirit 287

The price of admission to the world of the Spirit is releasing my anger and forgiving the other person 287

Do I put myself on the list? 287

The method of the index cards: Don't procrastinate 288

WILAA: When making an amends I do not go with anger, but I also don't proceed with an attitude of shame. As a child of God I crawl before no man. 289

We must, one more time, forgive 290

Martin Buber and the Concept of *I and Thou* 290

Principles of the Eighth Step 293

CHAPTER THIRTY: STEP NINE. 295

The questions you can't answer but have to 297

Steps Four and Nine set me free 301

Principles of the Ninth Step: 303

CHAPTER THIRTY-ONE: STEP TEN 304

Basic Tenth Step Directions 305

I say, 'Thy Will (not mine) be done'; that's a prayer too 306

No one graduates from AA 307

Some Promises 307

Directions 308

Mother Teresa on carrying the vision of God's will into all of our affairs 311

Principles of the Tenth Step: 313

CHAPTER THIRTY-TWO: STEP ELEVEN. 315

'After my review I ask God's forgiveness.' 316

After this prayer for forgiveness, I ask what corrective measures should be taken 317

'Upon awakening…' 317

'We ask God to direct our thinking 317

'We think about the twenty-four hours ahead.' 318

The rest of the morning mediation 319

There are a number of promises associated with Step Eleven 319

The Rest of Step Eleven 320

In the evening I go over my day 321

In the morning, during prayer, meditation, on my morning walk or in the shower, I receive one of a set of responses 322

The problem comes when I think I'm a magician and can cure the person's psychological problems 324

Improving conscious contact with God 325

The spirituality of the Steps is not separate and apart from life 325

The maintenance of my spiritual condition becomes more difficult and easier as I proceed. 327

I can eat only at McDonald's or I can partake in the banquet of life 328

Principles of Step Eleven: 329

CHAPTER THIRTY-THREE: STEP TWELVE. 330

What I've experienced in meditation has its own reality. 333

Steps Ten, Eleven and Twelve anchor me 333

There are three part of the Twelfth Step 334

Part one 334

Part two: 334

Part three 334

Principles of the Twelfth Step: 335

CHAPTER THIRTY-FOUR: A SHORT SET OF QUESTIONS FOR THE SPONSOR AND SPONSEE TO TALK ABOUT 337

A very good set of short questions for someone who has been around for a while and would like to do more work 337

Create a new prayer and promise that would help you practice the Steps. In no more than a page, explain the Step to a newcomer. Also, in as much detail as you can, tell how you practice the Step in your daily life 337

Actually there are some wrong answers 338

Step One 338

Step Two 339

Step Three 340

Step Four 341

Why do you tell God first, then yourself and then another person the exact nature of your wrongs? Have you internalized the Fourth Step method and do it in spite of yourself? 342

Step Five and A Half 343

Step Six 343

Step Seven 344

Step Eight 344

Step Nine 345

Step Ten 345

Step Eleven 346

Step Twelve 347

CHAPTER THIRTY-FOUR: THE TRADITIONS. A VERY BRIEF DISCUSSION 349

TRADITION ONE: 'Our common welfare should come first; personal recovery depends upon AA unity.' 349

TRADITION TWO: 'For our group purpose there is but one ultimate authority-a loving God as he may express himself in our group conscience. Our leaders are but trusted servants; they do not govern.' 353

TRADITION THREE: 'The only requirement for AA membership is a desire to stop drinking.' 355

The cost of AA membership 356

An important question: 'Who dared to be judge, jury, and executioner of his own sick brother?' 357

TRADITION FOUR: 'Each group should be autonomous except in matters affecting other groups or AA as a whole.' 358

TRADITION FIVE: 'Each group has but one primary purpose-to carry its message to the alcoholics who still suffers.' 360

TRADITION SIX: 'An AA group ought never endorse, finance, or lend the AA name to any related facility or outside enterprise, lest problems of money, property and prestige divert us from our primary purpose.' 363

TRADITION SEVEN: 'Every AA group ought to be fully self-supporting, declining outside contributions.' 365

TRADITION EIGHT: 'AA should remain nonprofessional- but our service centers may employ special workers.' 366

'TRADITION NINE: 'AA as such ought never to be organized, but we may create service boards or committees directly responsible to those they serve.' 369

TRADITION TEN: 'Alcoholics Anonymous has no opinion on outside issues, hence the AA name ought never be drawn into public controversy.' 371

TRADITION ELEVEN: 'Our public relations policy is based upon attraction rather than promotion: We need always maintain personal anonymity at the level of press, radio and films.' 372

TRADITION TWELVE: 'Anonymity is the spiritual foundation of all of our traditions, ever reminding us to place principles over personalities.' 377

SOME STEP WORKSHEETS 380

Step One: We '...admitted we were powerless over alcohol-our lives were unmanageable.' 380

A NICE WAY TO BEGIN 380

Some questions 380

Are you able to distinguish the true from the false 381

Admission 382

Powerlessness: 382

Unmanageability 382

Acceptance 382

The most important question of all 383

Some more questions 383

Principles you practice as part of the First Step 384

STEP TWO: 'Came to believe that a power greater than ourselves could restore us to sanity.' 385

More questions: 387

Another reality check 388

The principles of the Second Step: 390

Step Three: 391

Things to write about 391

And write out the Principles of this Step please. 393

Step Four: Made a searching and fearless inventory of ourselves.' 393

Last question: What's wrong with taking responsibility for your life and making sure you do things right? 395

Step Five: 'Admitted to God, to ourselves, and to another human being the exact nature of our wrongs' 395

Last Questions 398

Step Five and a Half 399

To a sponsor 399

How do you practice Step Five in your daily life? 400

Step Six: 'Were entirely ready to have God remove all these defects of character.' 400

What would it take to make you happy? 402

Step Seven: 'Humbly asked Him to remove our shortcomings.' 403

The Seventh Step Prayer 404

To write about 404

What do you want most in the coming year? 406

STEP EIGHT: 'Made a list of all persons we had harmed and became willing to make amends to them all.' 406

STEP NINE: 'Made direct amends, wherever possible, except when to do so would injure them or others.' 408

What is forgiveness? Is your forgiveness of me the same as God's forgiveness of me? 409

Principles of the Ninth Step 409

STEP TEN: 'Continued to take personal inventory and when we were wrong promptly admitted it.' 409

STEP ELEVEN: Sought through prayer and meditation to increase your conscious contact with God, praying only for knowledge of His will or the power to carry it out. 412

This is the Program, folks. Each Step brings us closer to practicing the presence of God 413

Don't nag God 413

Wait before acting 414

STEP TWELVE: 'Having had a spiritual awakening as the result of these steps, we tried to carry this message to alcoholics, and to practice these principles in all our affairs.' 415

Your spiritual awakenings as a result of each Step 415

A few more Twelfth Step Questions 416

Practicing these principles in all of our affairs 418

CHAPTER THE LAST: AFTERWORD 427

Resources: a mere beginning 428

Some great websites to download AA speakers 428

A SHORT BIBLIOGRAPHY 429

The *Wilaa's* one more time 431

THE 'RULES'

- First and foremost: **DPDT: Don't preach; don't teach**.
- **When doing the Steps with a sponsee, don't ask her to do anything you wouldn't do.**
- **Don't expend more energy on a sponsee's sobriety than she does.**
- **Don't take anything a sponsee says or does personally.**
- **Always look for the sponsee's strong points, never her weaknesses.**
- **Do your best to tell the truth, and make sure you know which truth you are telling.**

(To the Reader: sponsees are known as pigeons, babies, sponsees and sponsorees. What word you use depends on where and when you got sober.

Some of what I learned in AA (WILAA):

It's better to step on a sponsee's toes than walk on her grave.

When someone tells me I don't understand, the odds are I do.

Living the principles of the Steps is necessary if I want to carry the message. I am a visual aid.

Coffeemakers make it.

Unsolicited advice is always judgmental.

My relapse prevention is working the Steps. My trigger is breathing. I can't work on myself. It would be like performing brain surgery on my own brain. I often don't know what the next right thing is. I couldn't do it if I did. For a long time I concentrated on not doing the next wrong thing.

Silence is golden except when it's yellow.

(More *WILAA's* are spread through this book.)

Introduction

I decided to write a book to share my experiences in AA, as a member and a sponsor. I wanted to tell you how AA kept me sober and gave me a life worth having, done solely and simply according to the *Big Book of Alcoholics Anonymous.* It was a lot easier that way. Except for one occasion, I've never wanted to have a drink since the day I came into AA.

Carrots and Sticks: If you read the *Big Book* you'll find a lot of carrots and a lot of sticks. The carrots are promises, often florid, often extravagant. Being 'rocketed to a fourth dimension of existence,' could send you to AA or away from it, but those of us who have stuck around have, indeed, been rocketed to a life we never thought possible. Shame and guilt disappeared. Old friends reappeared. New ones became a large part of the landscape of our being. Instead of being lost and abandoned, overwhelmed and terrified, we felt comfortable and at ease.

Happy? Maybe. Joyful? Almost always. We became the people we always wanted to be without even trying. We didn't actually change. We were just more of what was good about us and less and less about the fear, selfishness, dishonest, resentment, anger and self-seeking that had seemed to define us. And that was a very good thing.

The sticks in the *Big Book* are actually far less terrifying than those that drunks and drug addicts face in real life. Dying isn't necessarily so bad. Living with the overwhelming compulsion to use substances that can only make us feel less terrible is far worse. Feeling the agony of failure and the remorse of always doing wrong to others and to ourselves, on a minute by minute basis, is hell on earth. Then there are all the physical consequences that attend the substance abuser.

AA funerals

Some actors in Hollywood look amazing, twenty or thirty years younger than their stated age. Not so the drug raddled alcoholic, whose face is a road map of pain, and whose body is a fetid, rotting bundle of bones and skin. No names; only memories of photos in newspapers and magazines. Their funerals are testaments to a wasted existence. Few attend, except for some indifferent hangers on and some gloating victims of the deceased's abuse.

I've seen a lot of AA funerals. Some are filled with the casualties of the person who died, where guilt abounds. If only they had done more, they think, but whatever they did would never have been enough. They couldn't stop their loved ones from drinking, or dying. Nobody could.

I've seen beautiful deaths and healing funereal ceremonies, where friends and loved ones come to celebrate the wonderful life of one who gave so much and took so little. I've felt the spirit of these marvelous human beings as they stop one more time to kiss those they loved before they move on to yet another heaven or an eternal, blessed, peaceful sleep.

CHAPTER ONE: WHY I WROTE THIS BOOK

I think AA is getting very watered down. I wrote this book to get back to the fundamentals found in *The Big Book* of Alcoholics Anonymous. This is a handbook for sponsors. I talk about my experiences as a sponsor: how I've done it and what it's done for me. In the beginning I sponsored so I would stay sober. I was carrying the message.

From the beginning of my sobriety I learned as much about the *Big Book* and AA as I could. I used my knowledge to help me lead a better life and find God. The idea, always, is to help others use the tools of the Program to move along a spiritual path.

I hope this book will help readers learn a little more about sponsorship, themselves, and their Higher Power. That will, I think, make anyone a better sponsor and have more confidence that they're doing just fine.

Every day you're sober is preparation for being a good sponsor, or at least it should be. If not, you need to do a little more work. You might even need a different sponsor, one who gets you into the *Big Book* and into service.

In the beginning I used the program to become a happier person. After a while, I saw that my true purpose was not only to stay sober but to help another alcoholic achieve stay sober. Every day that you're sober should be helping you become a better mentor, friend, and sponsor. If you're not doing that, well, get started.

My Experiences: I don't know how many women I've sponsored. A hundred if you include the ones I sponsored for a few days. Of the ones I've spent time with for at least a year, I would say about forty.

Sponsorship was the major type of service I did, although I did get involved in other activities as well. Mostly, it was a pleasant learning experience.

Almost all of the women I've sponsored for a period of time have stayed sober. This had nothing to do with me. I told them what I did and encouraged them to do likewise. Those who did, did so because they wanted to stay sober, or at least wanted to stop hurting. My ladies started the Steps at our first session together and found service positions soon after that. I gave out work sheets and each sponsee and I met weekly to go over them. Sometimes they didn't do any work, and that was fine, for a while.

After that we had 'the talk'. Then they did work or we both moved on. Except in the very beginning, I never 'fired' anyone. I just said I would be available if they wanted to go through the Steps. Some came back and that was good. Some left and both of us were quite relieved.

The high success rate was high because the women were not a random sample: the women were highly motivated. I think my way is a good way to sponsor someone. It works very well. I'm simple and I'm mostly clear. You can check out what I say by reading the *Big Book* of Alcoholics Anonymous.

Sponsorship, service and God were the transformative forces in my life. I have a lot of wonderful memories and a feeling that I've been useful.

The process of AA

The process of Alcoholics Anonymous means I slog through sponsorship exactly as I trudge the road of happy destiny. I learn by taking women through the Steps. I learn by internalizing percepts, not by memorizing them. The idea is to be able to see and show others how to see as well.

It took me a while to realize that Alcoholics Anonymous wasn't theoretical. I was busy teaching what I had read. I was preaching the value of the *Big Book*. I was inadvertently breaking the **DPDT (Don't Preach, Don't Teach) Rule**. In Alcoholics Anonymous we share.

When I perform selfless acts that are helpful and appropriate, I'm at peace. I try to live my life according to spiritual principles. Sometimes life has been difficult. Sometimes it's been painful. The end result has been a feeling of ease and comfort, a feeling I've been searching for my entire life.

If you ask me why I love AA, it's because of that feeling of being useful, that feeling of ease and comfort, and the ability to live peacefully, surrounded by friends and family who love me. It wasn't that way when I came in to AA. I'm so glad it is now.

The benefits of going where you don't want to go, or meaningful service positions

All of my sponsees take meaningful service positions. These are the hard ones that you don't want to do, and do, week after week, month after month: the jails, mental institutions, women's shelters, and detox units. They're part of recovery. Everyone, including me, did them in California, which is where I got sober. That's what my sponsees did. It's a big reason most of them stayed sober.

I had to overcome a lot of barriers in these institutions. The only way to do that was to speak from the heart. Being honest, gut level honest, takes practice and courage. I had to lay myself out before an often hostile audience. I was able to do that, despite my pride, my fears, and my need to be special, because I wasn't trying to win anybody over or have them like me. I just wanted to carry a message of strength and hope. AA allowed me to move beyond learned behaviors and neurotic needs.

A good example: Many years ago, I dragged myself back from a family celebration in another state. I had been at a party where I came as close to drinking as I had ever been in my then thirteen years of sobriety.

I was supposed to lead a meeting in a jail forty miles away that evening. I didn't want to go because I had driven a few hundred miles to get home and I was tired. I didn't want to go because I had nothing positive to share. I didn't want to go because, one more time, I was an inadequate loser who couldn't get it right.

I didn't matter much to one part of my family. That's just the way it was, and not because I used to drink too much and embarrassed them. The children had never seen me drunk. They just didn't value me. It's very difficult not to be valued by people you love.

I didn't want to go to the jail, but I went. Jail meetings were challenging. The women were perceptive. They didn't think a white, middle class lawyer had anything to teach them. They were right. I had nothing to teach them. Fortunately I wasn't there to teach them anything. I was there to share my experience, strength and hope. I was there to show my respect for them as recovering alcoholics and maybe, even, to give them some of the love so freely given to me by members of AA.

I went to the jail and apologized. I told them how depressed I was and that the only reason I came was because I couldn't get a last minute replacement. I admitted I was down because I loved my family and I wasn't important to them.

I explained that I had always talked about the Program and the Steps and how to practice them. I did a lot of practicing. It made no difference. I wanted that drink. I should have been stronger.

I had been a few inches from taking a glass of Champagne and a few drinks away from getting drunk. I told them that I snuck away from the party, packed my bags and drove back home in the middle of the night. I didn't want to drink and I wasn't going to. I was running away because that was the best I could do.

I cannot describe all the ways the women comforted me. They talked about bridges they had burned because of their drinking and drugging. Some of them despaired of having their children talk to them again. I'll never forget one beautiful women of about forty who told us that she had been allowed to go to her daughter's high school graduation. Her family treated her the same way mine treated me.

She knew she was going to drink or take drugs, said goodbye, and came back to the jail a day early. 'I thank God that I had a jail to come back to, because I don't want to drink or drug again,' she said.

Can you imagine? Can you just imagine?

That's a gift of the Program. It teaches me I tend to exaggerate and paint a very gloomy picture of my life, without seeing how much worse other people have it. I've learned not to take myself so seriously.

I told the women that at least they had behaved badly because they were drunk or high. Their families were very hurt by their behavior and didn't want to experience any more disappointments. My family just didn't like me, not because of the drinking I had done but because I was me. The women in the jail could get sober and they would get their families back. I was sober and it made no difference.

They were better off than I was.

The gifts of Alcoholics Anonymous

This was an important lesson for me. I could be useful. I could use my experience to communicate a message of depth and weight, hope and encouragement. I was sure that that the meetings in the jail were monitored and our words recorded. The inmates believed that as well. That tended to have a chilling effect at the AA meetings.

Not this time. We were not newly sober women with one woman who'd been around a while. We had things to say and didn't care who heard us.

We were sisters in sobriety. We knew there was an answer to our problems that we could find in the rooms of AA, whether in a Church basement, a jail or at the Salvation Army.

I learned that I didn't have to be perfect. My failings were my greatest gift. The ladies at the jail meetings could hear me because I was just like them. I wasn't Miss AA super star, just another drunk with a lot of problems.

Sometimes the best thing to do is run. I know the *Big Book* tells us that there will come a time when alcohol is not a problem and that we'll recoil from it like a hot flame. Most of the time I've found that to be true. When I was desperate, I was a little ashamed that the best thing I could do was run. Sobriety was more important than looking good, so I ran.

I ran. I think that's when I truly became a member of AA. I think that's when I truly had a message worth giving.

I've gone to a lot of different meetings in a lot of different places. That means I've heard a lot of good things and met a lot of good people. The tapestry of my recovery is rich, deep and wonderful. I have lovely memories of fine and generous men and women. That's all good, but the best times I've had are when I just had nothing to give and that nothing was the best thing I could give.

I want to take credit for the successes of my sponsee, but I can't. Over and over I see how AA functions in my life. The sponsee is the one who does the work. I'm just a messenger. I study, I learn and I make suggestions. I can't take credit for any of it and I don't want to. I don't have to be special. I don't have to be brilliant. I just carry a message. I'm one more worker among workers, one more drunk among drunks. The best message I have is not that I know it all but that I don't.

I came to the meeting because I met my obligations. I call that part of the Third Step: making a promise and keeping my word, no matter that I am sure I can't do a good job. It's not about me, after all.

So my message was that when I hit a bottom in sobriety and had no answers, I could weather what faced me, hopefully with some dignity and grace, but if not, I still didn't have to take a drink.

The women at that jail meeting would be released. They could come to any AA meeting and know that the well-dressed success story sitting next to them had the same problems and the same solutions; they knew that they were worth as much as somebody with a million dollar job or home, and that they could provide the help and strength someone else needed so desperately. They learned it at the jail that Sunday night, and so did I.

A magical moment in sponsorship

I'd like to think I had something to do with the magic, but, no, all I could do was repeat what was in the *Big Book*. My sponsee Lindsay (not her name) was two months sober. She was a slim, pretty and very intelligent woman but, as she said, 'a little bit bossy'. She came to our breakfast meeting very upset. We were supposed to be doing the Third Step.

Her husband had been looking for a new job and asked her to stop asking what he was doing and wondering how things were going. Above all, he wanted her to stop giving him advice. He was the lawyer. She had been a teacher. She really didn't know much about what he did at work or how well he was doing. She knew she had been 'a little over the top' and agreed to keep out of it. She asked him to promise to give her flowers if he heard that he'd got the job.

He promised. He got the job. She didn't get the flowers. And it was her birthday. She went off on him.

'Did you do this in front of your children?' I asked.

'Not at first but then I did. I just couldn't stop.'

'Well, you can't act that way, no matter what he did. I think you owe him an amends.'

Her problem was that he didn't hear her. She felt she didn't matter to him.

I knew those feelings. I've had them often. Instead of identifying with her and telling her how horrible her husband was, I stopped. It came to me. She had to buy him flowers. I told her so.

'You don't understand. He promised to buy me flowers,' she said.

WILAA: When someone tells me I don't understand, the odds are pretty good that I do.

'No. I do understand. Don't you think you're being a spoiled brat? You have to do this. You have to make this amends.'

'I'm on the Third Step,' she said. 'Not the Ninth.'

Funny, I thought.

'I feel this so strongly, in my gut. I can't even say why,' I told her. 'Just do it.'

She grumbled, muttered, and left. One of Lindsay's best qualities was, and is, her honesty. She might not like what I was saying but I knew she heard me. I was pretty sure she would buy the flowers.

She not only bought flowers, she bought peace lilies, symbolic of promoting peace and harmony. She gave them to her husband telling him, among other things, that she was wrong and that she loved him.

She says that's when she became a member of AA.

Not very long afterwards, her husband was diagnosed with cancer. They had no insurance because he was on his new job and the health insurance hadn't kicked in. They had three young children and she was very frightened.

She cried herself to sleep only after he went to sleep. She was able to be there for him and for her children. He told her afterwards that she was a rock and sustained him through the whole ordeal.

It's many years later and he remains cancer free. They have a very strong marriage and Lindsay appreciates her husband each and every day. I am sure he appreciates her just as much. In fact, I know it.

That's the beauty of AA. That's the beauty of Sponsorship. When I was first sober, I would have listened to Lindsay's complaints, not wanting her to think I didn't care. I wouldn't have had the courage to say what I felt but it wasn't about me. I was just doing what I had been taught: talk to her about the solution, not the problem. If you harm somebody you have to try to make it right and, by the way, you have to forgive him.

The results can be very dramatic. Consequences are not always so spectacular and not always so immediate but I'm not in this for the consequences. A sponsor carries the message. If it works out, I don't take credit. If it doesn't work out, I don't feel guilty. I do my best and am grateful for the opportunity to be useful.

CHAPTER TWO: TO THE SPONSOR

I'm a sponsor for a lot of reasons. My primary purpose is to stay sober and help another alcoholic achieve sobriety. Does that make my sponsoring people selfish? Yes and no. The exercise of the solution eradicates the problem of egocentricity. Self-reliance and selfishness are removed in the act of being helpful, i.e., unselfish.

I'm also expressing my gratitude for my sobriety and the warmth and caring which alcoholics extended to me when I came into AA by paying forward, helping others as I'd been helped. I know that:

> 'Practical experience shows that nothing will so much insure immunity from drinking as intensive work with other alcoholics. It works when other activities fail. This is our twelfth suggestion: Carry this message to other alcoholics! You can help when no one else can. You can secure their confidence when others fail. Remember they are very ill.' *The Big Book of Alcoholics Anonymous*. (All quotations come from the *Big Book*, except where otherwise indicated.)

A body in motion stays in motion. When I am acting selflessly, it is self-perpetuating. After a while, I automatically behave as I should. I sponsor because it has become ingrained in me. It is part of who I am. I think it's the best part of who I am.

I know that newcomers are very ill. This makes not taking things personally a lot easier. I pass on what I've experienced and observed, not mouth platitudes and opinions based on neither logic nor fact. I love it when I go to a meeting and hear someone talking about solutions and find it's a sponsee of one of my sponsees.

Seeing women grab onto the Steps and observing the changes in their lives as they go from troubled, selfish individuals to kind, thoughtful and helpful members of society is a fantastic reward of Alcoholics Anonymous. I love being given the opportunity to facilitate these miraculous transformations.

And if people don't get it and move on, I don't take it personally. I carry the message. I'm not responsible for the people getting it. If they get it and move on, I try not to take it personally. I usually do an inventory over it though, to make sure I'm not being obnoxious. Sadly, time in the program may smooth some rough edges, but they do reappear.

One of the reasons sponsorship is so important is that it brings out the best in us.

I believe that being a sponsor is an obligation and an honor. It's difficult sponsoring people who are very new. It's tough to sponsor people in long term treatment facilities or who are chronic relapsers. Most sponsors want to do the right thing. It takes a lot of experience to know what the right thing is. It takes time and effort. I have to keep my reality testing skills in good order because I can always lapse back into the 'cannot distinguish the true from the false' mode where I think I have all the answers.

I have noticed that I can find opportunities for inventories in all of the Steps, another sign of the genius of the founders of Alcoholics Anonymous.

The slogans are great, but I have to use them carefully. I guess that means I have to listen to what I say and say what I mean. I have to leave my sheep mentality behind. I'm more likely to be too analytical and miss the wisdom of the catchphrase. 'Love and tolerance is my code' is often misunderstood. It doesn't mean I have to accept the unacceptable. The *Big Book* tells us that God gives us brains so that we may use them. *I help a sponsee use her brains- not borrow mine.*

WILAA: Sponsorship is all about the Steps

We talk about personal problems in relationship to the solutions offered by the Steps. Otherwise I'm a would-be lay therapist, guru or substitute mother.

A sponsor takes someone through the Steps. I believe I first have to learn what the Steps are, what they mean, and how to practice them in my daily life. I also have that set of rules I've devised that I try to follow.

I try to tell no one the sponsee's secrets, or even what she and I talk about. I try not to judge the sponsee or make her feel terrible but I won't sugarcoat her behavior either. Minimizing problems doesn't help. I work on understanding how things are; how the sponsee acted without meaning to harm people; and how she sometimes did things out of hatred and ill will. I remember that she is 'very ill.'

I'm available for her when necessary, but not on call every minute of every day. I set appropriate boundaries and demonstrate how to abide by boundaries by abiding by them myself. I'm willing to share my life with the sponsee, as appropriate, so that we are true partners in our spiritual journey.

I'm not a banker, lawyer, therapist or chauffeur. And neither should the sponsee be. I have a good working knowledge of the *Big Book* and the ability and experience to proceed.

CHAPTER THREE: THE ROLE OF A SPONSOR

For me, there are only two kinds of sponsors-the ones who go by the *Big Book* and those who don't. I go by the Book. And when I say 'go by the *Big Book*,' I'm not just talking about what I tell people the book says or even what I think it says. It's not about what I say. It is about what I do.

More rules for me: I try to practice Steps Ten, Eleven and Twelve on a daily basis. I've learned to have patience when dealing with newcomers who think they know more about staying sober than I do. I've learned to ignore thinking which isn't logical and the manipulations of people who are very passive aggressive. I learn how to deal with outright lies.

I, mostly, don't take things personally. I do get tired of people thinking they're getting over on me. I might make a little comment to suggest I'm aware of what's going on or I might not. That depends on the circumstances, the sponsee, and how long she has been sober.

I've stopped trying to best others verbally. In my day I was quite good at it. I sometimes regret that AA strongly discourages such behavior. It might move things along a lot faster. I do my best to be kind and loving but sometimes it's very difficult. I remind myself that I hold myself to very high standards but that it is not up to me to hold others up to those standards.

(That's quite different from my pre-sobriety days when I excused my bad behavior but expected everyone else to behave well.)

I've learned to be very clear before I begin sponsoring someone. That helps a newcomer decide if I'm the right woman for her. That way the sponsee and I eventually know when the time has come to end the relationship.

I don't gossip or discuss anything that comes up in my contact with sponsees, although I might give a general idea of some aspects of it with my sponsor if I need help. I don't gossip about other people with my sponsees. Nothing distances a sponsee more than hearing me talk about another sponsee. I really try not to gossip at all.

I also want to learn more and never rest on my laurels. I go to workshops, do more reading, and talk with my sponsor-whatever it takes.

I've read the Chapter to Wives in the *Big Book*, which has a lot of practical advice. I just substitute me for the wife and the sponsee for the drunk. I hated this Chapter when I first read it. Bill wrote it even though he pretended to be a wife. Lois, his wife, wanted to write it but Bill wouldn't let her. I guess Bill thought she had enough to do being the sole breadwinner of the household, cooking, cleaning and taking care of the alkies that stayed in their home.

I don't have to be perfect. I need on the job training. I have to have done the Steps and be reasonably sane. I owe my sponsee courtesy and civility. I make sure that I know what's important, and what's important isn't me.

I keep the sponsorship relationship in the forefront. I know when my little plans and designs are particularly inappropriate. I know when hers are.

I listen and choose my words carefully. I have to make sure I'm not giving mixed messages. I must be aware of my facial and bodily gestures, my tone of voice and the way I dress so that sponsee feels comfortable.

If I'm asked to lead a meeting or speak, I make sure that I am fairly dressed up. It's an honor to do these things, and I want to make sure I convey that.

I try to be on time. I expect the sponsees to be punctual as well.

I remember what the sponsee has said and the names of the important people in her life.

I don't take phone calls when I'm doing step work with sponsees, unless there's an emergency. That hasn't happened very often.

I actually keep a word file with my sponsees' weekly assignments. That way at least one of us remembers.

Most importantly I pay attention. I have a good memory and remember the details about my sponsees, the names of the people in their lives, and a lot more. It's one of the reasons I felt comfortable sponsoring a number of women at the same time.

WILAA: There's no Sponsor of the Year Award.

Humility

I was at a meeting at a sobriety club. A man spoke and said that he had been sober for seven years, had a substance abuse counselor certificate and worked at a rehab. Then he drank. He ended up jobless and homeless. He was sleeping in his car and now had about two months of sobriety.

The topic of the meeting was humility. He raised his hand and shared that he knew all about humility. Why that very day he had to humble himself. He didn't like it but he had to humble himself. He related that he had gotten a job at the animal shelter down the block and had been working there three week.

He related that he was having trouble lifting a large dog onto the examining table. The head of the shelter was walking by. She was a veterinarian who'd worked at the shelter for thirty years.

'I had to humble myself,' he said. 'I had to ask her for help.' That didn't sound like humility to me.

Isn't it in the natural order of things that someone who's been working in the shelter for thirty years would know a lot more than a guy who'd been there three weeks? His asking for help wasn't humility.

He thought it was humility because he felt should know everything and not need help. He had very high and quite unrealistic expectations of himself. That was arrogance, not humility.

I drove him to his car after the meeting. It was filled with stuff. Only the driver's seat was clear of what looked like rubbish, but were his treasured possession. That was a lesson for me. I never thought living in a car was romantic, but I didn't know it was so grubby.

I never saw the man again. I doubted if he stayed sober but he may have learned humility somewhere along the way. If so, his chances were as good as mine. If not, then not.

My journeys with 'chronic *relapsers' and* how I got burnt out

I don't hold myself to such high standards as the man who lived in his car but I try to keep learning.

I got very stale when I was about seventeen years sober. I knew what everybody was going to say and do. I'd heard it all before. Following a friend's advice, I started going to different meetings.

I began attending meetings at a local shelter, detoxes and various long term treatment facilities, including one which consisted primarily of court ordered patients, most of whom had just been discharged from jails or prisons. I did that for more than two years and ended up with a lot of sponsees. That's what I call being in the trenches. That's where I've been for a lot of my sobriety.

I told the women I met about the Program. Many of them wanted me to sponsor them. I was a hot item. I think it meant something if I sponsored them. I tried to talk to the ladies about the worksheets I gave to them and about AA in general. They weren't interested.

Part of it wasn't their fault. Their counselors told them they needed to work on relapse prevention. They had to find their triggers and avoid them. They had to work on themselves. They had to do the next right thing. These ideas have contributed greatly to the watering down of AA. I wish someone would turn off the faucet.

Relapse Prevention

My relapse prevention is working the Steps. My trigger is breathing. I can't work on myself. It would be like performing brain surgery on my own brain. I don't automatically know what the next right thing is. I couldn't do it if I did. For a long time I concentrated on not doing the next wrong thing. That was a lot more doable.

My ladies could have read the *Big Book* or even searched the Internet for commentaries on the Steps. They chose not to. Instead they listened to what I said, shook their heads and smiled. The look on their faces told me they thought I was speaking in tongues.

I couldn't understand why the women trusted their counselors, many of whom weren't even in recovery. I think the women chose to avoid confrontations and do what their counselors told them to do. This was particularly ironic because they never did what they were told in any other part of their lives.

I tried to point out that the rehabs weren't about getting people better but about having them graduate from their programs. That's how they justified their existence and the payments they received. It was a numbers game. It was fine if the graduates came back repeatedly. The counselors may have believed what they taught. The psychiatrists probably did believe in what they were doing even though their results were abysmal.

Statistics can be made to prove or disprove anything, if you're clever enough. Most of the statisticians did not differentiate between people in AA who followed the precepts of the *Big Book* and those who did not. If not, their methodology is flawed and their conclusions defective.

I spoke with the women I sponsored about our work together. Mostly they thought I was very demanding and the worksheets too much like school. They told me they had too much to do in their facility and no time for extra work. They implied, or flat out said, that the professionals they met were better trained and knew more than I did about getting and staying sober.

Few of these professionals dealt with anyone who had more than a year or two of sobriety, but no matter. They had a very short term view. Even there, I believe, they had a stake in the venture: namely, to keep getting their paychecks.

The idea that patients' time consuming and expensive activities would result in sobriety and would no longer be needed was implied but not examined. Of course it wasn't. This is very different from AA, where its members learn techniques to deal with every aspect of their lives, now and in the future; techniques which are useful, quick and free,

I've sponsored plenty of people in these facilities who had no trouble finishing step work. It's all about how you spend your day. You can make phone calls, smoke, watch TV, and socialize with other 'clients' or you can do AA activities. I've tried to have sponsees do an analysis of the way they use their time, but that was too much work for them.

AA helps you see but a lot of people don't want to look.

I tried to go over the Steps with these women who so wanted me to be their sponsor but it was like talking to a wall. They couldn't get the powerlessness because the health care professionals and the counselors were telling them they had to take responsibility for not drinking. Why listen to me? I was just an AA nut.

Maybe so, but I had been sober a long time, and my life was very lovely. Could the health care professionals say the same? The patients, clients, or whatever you called them, had no idea of what was going on in the lives of those they trusted to treat them. It wasn't therapeutically significant. It wasn't professional.

In AA, sponsor and sponsee share their lives. That's part of the treatment plan. Each party grows healthy as they trudge their way into a better life. If I don't share my failures how can I transmit hope? If I don't share my problems, am I not just being one more judgmental woman showing them how they are doing it wrong?

I tried, repeatedly and often. I gave them little passages to read. I tried metaphors and little stories. I tried whatever I could to explain that they, because of their brains, their bodies, their genetic makeup, their early upbringing and their later experiences, could not just say no. Not to drinking. Not to overeating. Not to overdramatizing or underthinking. Not to feeling bad or good or angry or in despair. They just didn't have that power. They didn't have that control.

The ladies felt, with the support of their therapists, that they just had to do things a little better, especially if they drank. It is an interesting concept in therapeutic matters that when all else fails blame the patient.

I laid it out for them as plainly as I could. We tried workshops. We listened together to others, the ones who got sober and the ones who couldn't get sober. They thought they had heard it all. They thought they had seen it all. They didn't see how the percepts of AA related to their lives.

The problem was I could explain it to them but I couldn't understand it for them.

Sometimes all you can do is plant a seed. If the ground is hard and there is no water or sun, the seed will not germinate: The flowers will not bloom. The soil was barren. I kept thinking it wasn't impossible for flowers to grow, but someone had to do some watering. I gave up. It was someone else's turn.

You know, it was very good for me. I became convinced that I didn't know anything. My other sponsees got sober because they wanted to, not because of anything I said. I guess I was becoming a little bit humble. I also learned about boundaries. I carried the message. I didn't have to carry the mess.

A little bit on gratitude

When my grandchildren were little, they had Barbie dolls. The New York contingent had about a hundred dolls, with dresses, hats, and shoes. They threw the dolls, usually naked, into boxes and never looked at them again. The southern contingent had six Barbie's and one Ken. This was to some extent because their mother disapproved of the structurally impossible dolls on philosophical grounds. Nonetheless they accumulated their meager supply. Every morning they brought them down to breakfast, dressed and groomed. At night, the dolls accompanied the girls as they heard their bedtime stories.

WILAA: Gratitude is an action word.

My grandkids tired of the dolls after a while, but while they had them they took good care of them because they appreciated them.

WILAA: Gratitude elevates the soul; a sense of entitlement destroys it.

You should know the difference between Big Book Rehabs and all the rest

I love facilities which are *Big Book* oriented. I love hard core AA. It's a lot better than not reading the Book but I don't want to break the **DPDT rule**. I can't reconcile 'sharing' with an insistence on doing recovery just one way.

When I was newly sober I was sure there was only one way to do the Steps and practice the principles of AA. I was wrong. All around me I saw people who demonstrated all of the principles of the Steps in their daily lives. They didn't quote the *Big Book* or use the buzz words that have become so common.

They may not have been sponsoring many people. That might have been because they have other responsibilities: a large family, a demanding career, a need to paint, or write, or play sports.

There are a lot of sober alcoholics leading great lives with substantial years of sobriety. I always keep that in mind when I want to get on my soapbox.

I try not to judge or reject. I may not like what I see. Tough on me. Love and tolerance is my code, even though I don't want it to be.

Hard core messages work only when you're preaching to the choir. If you want to convince 'middle of the roaders' to get more involved with the Program, sternly telling them they're doing everything wrong won't work. To add insult to injury I've heard a few young hard core fanatics with a month or so of sobriety and not much of a story, tell an old timer, with years of hard living on the streets or in penitentiaries, that he isn't really an alcoholic anyway. (Because if he were, he couldn't stay sober the way he has for the last thirty years.) I kid you not.

On the other hand, I've met people in AA with ten years or more who have never read the *Big Book*, worked the Steps or cared about leading a principled life. Good for them. They are either not alcoholics or very much loved by God. These people can do a lot of harm when they sponsor people, for obvious reasons.

Recently I heard that a woman, let's call her Edna, described to me as 'really into AA, just like you. She sponsors lots of people and has lots of service positions...' who wanted to hand out flyers for a dance at the rehab she had attended ten years before.

There was a problem. Several of the old timers said she couldn't do that. This was AA, not ANB (the name of the Rehab). Edna was furious. The old times called a group conscience. The group voted with the Fifth Tradition: the message of a treatment center is not the same as the message of AA. Besides, what about the Sixth Tradition? Doesn't that apply as well?

Edna didn't understand. ANB got and kept her sober. Wasn't it the same as AA? What was the matter with all these old fogeys?

They told her she could put the flyers on the desk and people could read them. She could hand out the flyers after the meeting. She couldn't make her rehab part of AA.

Her response? She stormed out of the meeting, handed back the meeting check book, for she had been the treasurer of the meeting, and didn't appear at the meeting ever again, after weekly participation for ten years.

I wonder about her ability to sponsor anyone: she never listened to what the old timers were saying. She just insisted she was right and they were annoying. She rejected the Traditions because they didn't allow her to do what she wanted. Singleness of purpose: wasn't ANB trying to keep people sober just like AA?

Her sponsees walked out with her.

Edna started another meeting at the same time a few blocks away. So much for Tradition One. She had no idea that the message of the treatment facility was not the message of AA. Isn't the message that you don't drink and go to meetings, find your triggers and, get it, take responsibility for your drinking? If you think that's the message of AA, please get a new sponsor.

Sometimes I wish there was an AA police.

A practical suggestion for sponsors: learn about community services

It's a good idea to attend meetings at the local shelters, detoxes, and rehabs. You can meet some of the counselors. That way you know what's available for newcomers and can sometimes facilitate admission to one of the places that are more difficult to get into.

It's also good to know about the local food bank, food stamps, and county services, from medical and dental to educational opportunities.

Going with a sponsee to the food bank because she doesn't have a car and bringing the boxes of food to her apartment or group home is an eye-opener. You realize you don't have it so bad.

CHAPTER FOUR: CARRYING THE MESSAGE, NOT HAVING TO DO IT ALL

I know the sponsor should take someone through the Steps but a few practical solutions can literally be life-savers.

I've given up jawing away at someone: When someone cannot stop drinking but doesn't see her powerlessness I don't hit her over the head with a two by four. It won't convince her and will be unpleasant for us both. If she has a hundred excuses why she can't go to a detox or a rehab I agree with her and move on.

That's part of the rule of not devoting more time or energy on someone else's sobriety than she does.

I was at a meeting when a woman came into the sobriety club where it was held. She was drunk and raving about one of the members. Thinking a new prospect had entered the club I walked out of the meeting and spoke with her. I told her I would drive her to a hospital where she could detox. She didn't want to do that. She wanted to talk about her boyfriend. I said fine and went back to the meeting.

The *Big Book* tells us not waste time on the person who doesn't want to be sober. I take that to mean not to work with someone who doesn't want to practice the Program. Every time I tried it, it didn't work.

If I agree to sponsor someone, I mentally agree to stay in the relationship for at least six months, if at all possible. It's a unilateral agreement. If I think I can't do that I refuse to be her sponsor. Better now than two months later. I pay attention to what the prospective sponsee says and does. There may be so many red flags that I just shouldn't do it.

I will sometimes ask my sponsor what to do, but by this time, I have a pretty good idea of when a sponsor relationship with someone is impossible for me.

I was a person who did as little as imaginable as seldom as possible. Sponsorship changed all that. This I do with all my heart. I don't change my approach because I am criticized for it. Lately I've felt people think that AA has passed me by. On the other hand, I think AA is getting derailed

A story about some problems I have in AA and how I deal with them: At my home group, (and I urge you to have a home group, whether sponsor or sponsee) a skinny blonde woman with a million years of sobriety shared that 'everyone was entitled to their opinion.'

She stared at me to make sure everyone knew she was talking about me. 'Some people feel bad because they don't do what she did. She's a Step Nazi,' the lady said, shaking her well coifed head and smirking at me so no one could miss who she meant.

'If somebody told me to do the Steps in my first year, or in my first five years, I would have been out the door.'

I had an image of her stuffed into a tight Storm Trooper uniform at Bergen Belsen carrying a whip sometime during the Second World War. Ironically, she was forcing her opinions upon me. Everyone could have their opinions as long as they agreed with hers. She was far more of a Nazi than I would ever be, aside from the fact that I'm Jewish.

I don't think love and tolerance was her code. For me, it's more of a goal but at least I'm in the same ball park and the same game. Restraint of tongue and pen is foreign to me and requires a lot of energy.

I have to think before I speak, and be willing to say nothing at all. And when I'm disturbed I know there's something wrong with me. It's something I have to look at. So I was looking at myself. I didn't share. I thought about my experience, strength and hope.

My experience was that she was an idiot. My hope was that she would kindly shut up. My strength was that I didn't say a word.

I didn't want a newcomer to take her comments for truth. If I pointed this out to her at the meeting, I would be confrontational. The situation would be unpleasant, which would be far worse for a newcomer to observe. Here's the thing. I might be correct but I wouldn't be right.

I've learned to quit the debating society, to stop making points so that people think I'm smart, and above all not to care if everything isn't made exquisitely clear immediately. So if people thought I was an old fossil, or an SS officer blabbing about yesterday's news, so be it. I didn't even give a sardonic smile when Blondie spoke.

My knitting days: I started knitting at meetings. It kept me calm. I used to make blankets since they required no concentration. One day I went to my daughter's house. Her dog, a black lab named Nellie, was lying contentedly on a blanket I'd made for my son-in-law, at his request. Apparently, he didn't want it.

I smiled to myself and said, 'Oh well.' The 'Oh well' concept is a short form Step Ten and far better than a temper tantrum. I admit I used to be filled with rage. Five years of sobriety and knitting cooled that to mild annoyance. I'm even better now. I don't knit any more.

I do get annoyed when I hear people explaining 'where I'm at today.' Aside from lacking any relationship to a grammatical sentence, we all know where the person is, at an AA meeting wasting everyone's time.

I also wonder what a sponsor is thinking when she tells a sponsee that she must share at every meeting, and talk about what's bothering her. What does that have to do with recovery or the Steps?

Important practical considerations

How I begin the sponsor-sponsee relationship: After we agree to become sponsor and sponsee, the woman and I meet at some quiet place. I ask the sponsee to do two things:

Make a list of ten things she will do before she takes that drink.

Write fifty good things about herself. (Most are lucky to write five. I said I had a nice smile, thick hair and was intelligent.)

A good assignment for a new sponsee who doesn't know the names of the people who share or speak at means and doesn't have a clue as to what someone shared is have them write the name of one person who said something she liked and what it was. She should do the same with someone she didn't like.

She should also write down one idea that she thought was great and one that she hated.

For people who have trouble with writing things out, the woman can jot down the people's names, and a few words about the things said.

Sometimes it's not only newcomers who aren't listening. I learned this when I was about fourteen months sober. For two months, I talked about moving and how uncomfortable I was to leave everyone and everything I knew, except for my daughter and her husband, who lived in the new town.

At my home group, I said this was the day I was leaving. At least four people came up to me and asked me why I hadn't said anything before.

Another 'Oh Well' moment: It's one reason why I don't get nervous when I speak before a large crowd. Odds are very good nobody's listening.

I have to look at AA and see what things work. People sponsor differently. Also different people need different kinds of sponsors. Sometimes newcomers are too foggy to do any Step work. Sometimes people are so defiant that a gentle set of talks is all they can manage. I have occasionally sponsored that way. Many women with a lot of time do. I've seen the sponsees stay sober and the sponsors stay sober too. The thing is I respect my sponsees and don't want to think they're not up to doing any step work so get off the 'too foggy' train as soon as possible.

Often, though, the sponsors are in the 'loving until the sponsee can love themselves,' mode because they don't have a grounding in the *Big*

Book. That's one of the reasons I wrote this book, but so far I don't think any of the people who aren't into the *Big Book* have read it.

Who am I to criticize the way someone else sponsors, even though I want to?

I try not to intrude on the sponsee's family or friends. It can lead to serious, and rightfully so, distrust of me and my motives. In the early days of AA, people would speak with the spouse of the drunk and find out all about them from their family. I don't do that. I've observed a few people who tried it but it always ended badly. I meet with the person and find out what she's like. I ask for a little of her story. I tell a little of mine and how I do the Steps.

When I'm thinking of how to say something that my sponsee can hear, that isn't phony and isn't abrasive, I am learning how to be a better person. It takes a lot of concentration to listen and a lot of energy to exercise restraint.

I try to find out all I can about the sponsee. I remember once learning that a young woman had been a resident of a school that was shut down for the many abuses it inflicted on its students. I thought she was exaggerating and was probably a little…nutty. I bought the book on Amazon and read it before we met again.

She actually minimized her experiences. She was very grateful and surprised that I took the trouble to read the book. I was her third or fourth sponsor and none of the others had even found out that she went to the school or that that a book had been written about it. Reading the book helped me to understand this woman and see how brave she was.

Usually there aren't books to explain things. That means the best way to learn about a sponsee is by listening. If I'm talking, I'm not learning.

I always ask the new woman if she's been in AA before. If not, I tell her the first time she tries to get sober is the easiest. I have a lot of friends who came in and stayed in. I did. It's a lot easier that way. The more times you relapse, the harder it is to get sober.

If the person says this isn't her first dance and she knows what to do, I ask her what it takes. Generally the relapser thinks it's going to meetings, not drinking, and having a network.

I ask what medications she's taking, what dosages, who's prescribing them, and how she is monitored plus what physical ailments she might have. These facts are essential. Two of my sponsees had sponsored a woman with juvenile onset diabetes. Neither one of them troubled themselves to learn about the ramifications of this, but were both sure the woman needed a psychiatrist and different, or more, or some meds. When I learned of the woman's condition, I realized they both had it wrong. A sponsor must know a lot about the disease a woman has and how it influences her life. You might want to read up on diabetes to understand why this is so.

I never substitute my judgment for that of a licensed health care professional, but I like to know what medications are being given, and how the sponsor is being monitored. I also check for drug seeking behavior.

Like they say, the monkey's off my back, but the circus is still in town. Good for someone to check to see what's happening with the meds, which might mean the sponsee needs a second opinion.

Talking with the newcomer (or someone who has relapsed)

Sometimes a woman says, quite seriously, 'I know the most important thing is not drinking no matter what and going to meetings and getting a sponsor.'

I ask how can she 'not drink' when she can't stop drinking. I also ask if that's in the *Big Book* and if it's in the Steps.

I ask if the woman had a sponsor the last time and followed her advice, if she's sponsored someone, and what spiritual principles she followed on a daily basis.

Here's where I get that old I'm speaking in tongues feeling.

Within ten or fifteen minutes, I have a pretty good idea if the person wants to be sober or is just going through the motions. I explain that I sponsor by meeting once a week and going through the *Big Book*, using a series of questions specifically designed for her. Phone calls are not mandatory for 'checking in' although she can call to say hello and to talk. I want a sponsee to call when she has genuine questions or feels a need for a conversation. I'll call back within a day. If she says it's urgent, I do my best to call back as soon as possible.

I explain that in AA we talk about personal problems in relation to how we can solve them using the Twelve Steps of Alcoholics Anonymous. I indicate that I am not a therapist, attorney, chauffeur, or banker. I believe that I'm not supposed to function in any of those capacities. Of course there are times when we just chat and times when I tell the woman it's time for some outside help.

What I explain is that 'The Steps are a group of principles, spiritual in nature, which, if practiced as a way of life, will remove the obsession and desire to drink and make us happily and usefully whole.' (*The Twelve and Twelve*, Forward)

I respect the concepts of confidentiality and tolerance. I promise not to talk about her or our work together. I explain that I have trouble with lateness and an inability to show up after we've agreed to meet, without at least a prompt phone call. I believe in love and tolerance but I won't accept the unacceptable.

I tell her I hope that she doesn't complain about me. I want her to talk to me about what's bothering her, even me. I won't hold it against her. I believe in being direct and honest and hope she will be too. I tell my new friend that there are a lot of things she can do even in earliest sobriety: Come to meetings early and stay late. Say hello to the newcomer and talk to new people rather than the ones from your treatment center. Become part of the group. Get telephone numbers from people you think are relatively sane and tuned into the Steps. Oh yes, and call them.

I suggest that she stick to the topic of the meeting. If it's on a Step she isn't up to, she should say so, and pass. I want her to forget about impressing anyone. She doesn't have to be witty, funny or clever-just honest.

The best shares aren't when someone's done something perfectly and solved a tricky problem. Honest.

In AA, when you expose yourself and your problems, when you lay yourself out and speak from the heart, and talk about how you are dealing, imperfectly, with a problem, you are heard, understood and loved.

The one who gets it perfectly and talks about it wants some applause. So let's give it to him and his ego and get on with the meeting

If it's a big meeting, I tell her to keep her share very short. Give everyone else a chance. Spirituality is indeed a three minute share.

I ask her to listen and identify with the speaker and see how she is the same, not different.

I stress the need to avoid being slimy. She might want to declare a moratorium on sexual relationships for a bit. She won't die from a little celibacy.

I let her know that 'One day at a time' means she doesn't have to quit forever. It also means she should stay in the present. It's better here.

I lay out the Program and give her a sheet describing the Twelve Steps very briefly. (You can find it further on in this book.) I explain that she needn't always complete assignments in a week. Some of them are fairly long, although most are not. Sometimes she might not feel like doing the work. I would hope that she would do her best to do it anyway. I understand that she should get sober in her time, not mine, unless the plan is not to get sober at all. I explain that this is the way I sponsor, however, and if she is not comfortable with weekly assignments, she might decide I'm not the sponsor for her.

Two questions which come up: The first is sponsoring friends. I try never to do that but my sponsees do become my friends and that is fine. The second is sponsoring people of the opposite sex. In many areas there aren't enough women who have the time to sponsor according to the *Big Book*. I have a male sponsor right now. I am an old woman, who has left 'relationships' behind and it is working well.

During my meeting with a prospective sponsee I talk about some of the suggestions in the Chapter *Working with Others* in the *Big Book*. For example, 'Burn into the consciousness of any man that he can get well regardless of anyone. The only condition is that he trust in God and clean house.' I'm don't 'burn' anything but I'm pretty firm.

Sometimes I talk about the need for believing in a power greater than yourself and for leading an honorable and honest life. I talk about being an atheist when I came in and not thinking I was an alcoholic but that made no difference: I stayed sober.

I believe that sponsor and sponsee walk day by day on the path of spiritual progress in a true partnership and say that is my goal for each person I sponsor.

I talk about what I did to stay sober and ask each new sponsee to think about what she's willing to do. I also ask her what she doesn't want to do. I tell her that I would like her to devote as much time and energy to her step work as she does to other matters in her life. I have learned not to take it personally when a sponsee does work that took her about three minutes.

It always happens: At some time in the sponsor relationship I find I have to ask one question: What is the sponsee willing to do to stay sober and what isn't she willing to do? In the beginning most sponsees are willing to do a lot. As time goes on, the response is silence. That speaks quite loudly.

The notebook

I want each sponsee to keep a notebook. She writes all assignments in there, inserts emailed assignments and puts her answers in as well. That includes what she's willing to do to stay sober. It worked for me.

It's a very good habit to practice.

The notebook has another function. Here are worksheets, research and thoughts, some AA memories and more, all in one place. It's a good way to learn to be organized and it makes sponsorship a lot easier for the sponsee down the road.

I ask the sponsee to respect my time and peace of mind, be punctual and complete assignments in some mutually agreed upon time. I tell her that if she agrees to do this, we can go ahead. She might write down all that she agrees to do in her notebook and sign it.

I've sponsored women in women's shelters and two who were homeless. They had no trouble keeping a notebook.

Doing a time check to see what a sponsee is really doing with her time: I'm pretty flexible. I don't expect someone to do everything immediately or completely, but I'd like the sponsee to try to do as much as she can as completely as she can. If she says she doesn't have time, I ask her how she spends her day, including how much time at the computer and on her phone. I indicate I mean for recreation and not work. If there's a choice between step work and Angry Birds, the former is a better one.

I talk about meaningful commitments. The brain works best if you're acting well. It tends to turn to mush if you don't. Often rehabs (and sponsors) tell people they should 'just work on themselves' and save service work for later. That is foreign to me and not in the *Big Book*.

That's what people hear at treatment centers. What's happening these days is that people go to rehabs and then enter an aftercare program. It all sounds great. They have a therapist, a psychopharmacologist, a therapist for group, a counselor for problems, perhaps a nutritionist or an exercise coach. Some even have a life coach. The rehab leaves no stone unturned. Sometimes this generates a lot of income for the facility. I have noticed that in the last few years, the patients are getting a lot of modalities of treatment and a variety of medications.

It was AA wisdom in my early days that it took a year of sobriety before a treating physician could get an accurate picture of the patient before making a diagnosis. That said, some people require medication immediately and should get it.

The newcomer is proud of being proactive and doing everything she can to stay sober. She's looking at her triggers, her needs, her wants and her responsibilities in daily life. She dutifully attends AA meetings, gets a sponsor and does step work as best she can.

The one thing most people don't question is whether the various therapies conflict.

Sometimes I wonder about the choice of medication. In the last year two women I knew were prescribed Wellbutrin and each had a seizure. It is apparently a well-known side effect of the drug. I spoke with a Board Certified Neurologist who was incensed. "There are many other drugs that are far better and don't have this side effect."

That means a person who goes to a treatment center needs, sometimes, to check what medications she is receiving. This adds a wrinkle to trying not to be self-sufficient. Sadly, sometimes you have to be an advocate for yourself and check on your doctors. That's why it's good to have a sponsor, who can reassure you that being self-protective is not being self-sufficient and might be necessary.

Putting that aside, the main conflict is between being in control and acknowledging that self-sufficiency doesn't work. You either can stop drinking or you can't. AA says you can't do it on your own. The rehab is giving you a lot of 'tools' to help you work on yourself. If you're truly powerless over alcohol, do you think those tools will work?

One definition of an alcoholic is someone who can't stop on his own. For heavy drinkers, the rehab might very well work. By definition, one who can't stop on his own, can't stop on his own.

Picking a rehab, health care professionals and types of treatment: this is your life we're talking about

Checking the rehab, the professionals, and the methods of treatment before making the decision to use it or them is very important. Let's be real and let's be logical. Getting some help from a member of Alcoholics Anonymous is a great idea. If you don't know a member, you're your local Intergroup.

You want to know what agendas the medical staff, counselors and institution have. Do you feel comfortable following the advice of your counselor and sort of, kind of, or even totally, being in control? Who can fault you for doing everything you can? Isn't that what they talk about at AA meetings, namely, going to any lengths to stay sober? Find out exactly what you are agreeing to do before moving forward.

Here's the problem, it's that old puppy struggling with a newly waxed floor. There's a lot of activity but the puppy isn't going anyplace, and isn't in control. It's taking a shotgun and shooting at the moon. It won't get you sober but will keep you busy. You'll spend a lot of money and think you'll stay sober. If you're not an alcoholic it could work.

Usually the director of the rehab will confess he's not sure which of the many things you're doing is working, but at least you're doing a lot. Something should work, even though your life is spinning out of control. Your family doesn't see you. Stress in all areas of your life increase. You just don't have enough time because you're going to all kinds of meetings and therapy sessions. Your pocketbook is getting thinner and you still want to drink. You just might want to take a drink to relax.

Besides, will you have to do this for the rest of your life?

As for AA, leading a principled life costs nothing and has a lot of benefits, and probably would reduce stress. You might see the need for self-examination and being useful to others. AA seems to be promulgating a way of life that has benefits whether you're an alcoholic or not, and one which you probably have sought before.

One more rant on the statistics of recovery. Is it like the Zen of sobriety? What is the sample being studied? Does the scientist differentiate between the individual sent to AA by the Court, the one handed an ultimatum by his boss, and the person who wants to get sober because his life is too painful? Does the scientist differentiate between the person who attends meetings sporadically and the one who concedes in his inner most soul that he is powerless over alcohol, and that there is a power greater than himself?

In short, does the scientist understand the difference between one who plays at recovery and one who tries to practice the principles as best he can in his daily life? Of this group, what percentage stays sober?

Does the scientist know what the process of Alcoholics Anonymous is when making his calculations? I think not, primarily because I've never seen distinctions in regards to the above conditions, distinctions necessary if one wishes to assess the efficacy of the Program.

I always ask my new sponsee to look in the *Big Book* if she's getting conflicting messages

That was what I did when I first got sober and it's what I do now. One reason I didn't want to do the therapy, medication, etc., route, is that I had tried it and it didn't work.

What you need to do to stay sober

The burn, the principles, and some mechanics: I explain that if, after a month or so, a sponsee attends no AA meetings, does little or no Step work, and makes no attempts to follow the principles of the Program, the best thing is to stop the relationship. It's pretty simple: If this, then that; if not this, then not that.

Experience has taught me that this works best for me. At times I would wait a year, or two, or three, before I gave up. I didn't want a woman to feel abandoned. That didn't help the sponsee and it didn't help me.

WILAA: People who are intensely afraid of being abandoned often act in ways that make it impossible for other people to stick around.

It's up to me to make the *Big Book* more accessible to people who are very emotionally impaired or who have trouble reading. It's up to me to simplify the written Step work. There are some people who are so disturbed that it requires a lot more time and patience but I've found that the most disturbed people I sponsored were often the most anxious to get well and did the most Step work.

Over the years I've agreed to sponsor some of the 'unsponsorables,' the ones with special problems that nobody wants to sponsor. Someone has to do it and I've done my share.

I learned to be very careful with these women, to have strict rules, no calling before eight AM or after 8PM, no coming to my house, and no machine gun telephone calls. The women responded well to the disciplined approach. I think I sponsored most of them for about six months and then they moved on.

CHAPTER FIVE: A GOOD PLAN OF RECOVERY

I always talk about the Program of AA as giving a plan of action for recovering from alcoholism. My sponsee and I talk about what's important. I suggest we pick five items that would be helpful and set up a schedule for doing them on a regular basis.

Now this might sound very rigid and time consuming, but it should be a five minute discussion, jotting down a few words.

It's good to have a game plan, early on

In the beginning, it's about going to meetings, listening carefully at AA meetings, trying to make sense of AA and its members, doing Step work, reading literature, doing your best to be honest, and maybe praying or meditating. I often ask the newcomer to make a note of one thought she found helpful, and one she might have thought was misleading, or not according to the *Big Book*. She might want to look to see if she arrived on time, stayed until the end of the meeting and talked to other people she saw.

Setting up a weekly schedule: I believe that she shouldn't try to do everything all the time, but setting up a weekly schedule is a good idea.

You always need a game plan, even if you've been sober forty years

As time elapses, and the sponsee is working through the Steps, the items change, not because the earliest actions should be abandoned, but because the sponsee is doing them automatically.

I periodically go over this plan with my sponsees.

A sample list in later sobriety

Prayer

Meditation

Service

Reading of AA conference approved literature and other literature as well

Taking a principle of one of the Steps and practicing it daily, and writing a few sentences about it.

Making a checklist of practices performed regularly.

Some other things the Sponsee thinks are necessary for recovery.

Some things I think are either distractions or absolutely deal breakers.

I have done this myself and find it useful. No matter how much I study or sponsor others, I always find something I have, for no apparent reason, stopped doing. That's part of the elusive nature of the *Big Book* and Step work. When I talk about being eternally vigilant, I mean that I'm keeping my plan for recovery in mind.

Usually, when a woman I sponsor is very uneasy or off the beam, it is because she has taken her plan of recovery for granted and stops doing the thing or things that are uncomfortable for her. She is very rarely doing all, or any, of Steps Ten, Eleven and Twelve.

I have to say most people do the steps in a not very disciplined way and fare very well. That doesn't work for me. It's too easy for me to spin out of control. I'm just not organized enough to rely upon what I've done before.

It helps if the sponsee creates her own prayers and promises for each Step

One early assignment I give each sponsee is to find the prayers associated with many of the Steps and write them in her notebook. I also want her to find the promises associated with many of the Steps and write them in her notebook as well. We work on this together because it is a lot for a newcomer to do. When she starts sponsoring, she's familiar with the prayers and the promises and knows where to find them.

Take a look at http://friendsofbillw.net/twelve_step_prayers

When she gets upset, I ask her to find a prayer and a promise that keep her going. I also ask her to turn the promises into questions. That gives her an idea of how successfully she's practicing the specific Step- and to do at least one of these a week.

I encourage the sponsee to use the prayers of the Steps to help deal with problems and to facilitate change; e.g. The Fourth Step Prayer ('Please save me from anger...') is very useful. I tell her that using the promises of the various Steps as reality checks keep her centered. Of course that means that she's familiar with them. If she's not, you need to do some work.

> (For example: The Third Step Promise found in *The Big Book of Alcoholics Anonymous*: '…we will be less and less interested in our little plans and designs and more and more interested in...' becomes 'Are you less interested in your little plans and designs and more and more interested in…'.)

If a person only talks about her little plans and designs and has no interest in what she can give to others, the reality check makes it clear: she needs to do more Third Step work.

It might mean it's time for her to do a Fourth Step Inventory, or, if she's done that, do another one, or hit hard on Steps Ten, Eleven and Twelve.

I have to use my experience and judgment as to what I think will work for her. A big one is that I ask all my sponsees to put recovery first.

A note to the reader: I am not writing down the promises and prayers because I think it is important for each reader to find them for him or herself. Please try to do so now.

WILAA: Anything that doesn't move me closer to sobriety takes me further away from it. I try to put recovery first. I have to be sure I don't get off track. I've seen too many people who could never make it back.

Putting Recovery First

> **Believing that my primary purpose is to stay sober and help an alcoholic achieve sobriety, and acting that way at all time.**
>
> **Promising to do AA with all my heart and soul.**
>
> **When choosing an activity, making sure I consider my primary purpose: is the activity helpful or a distraction?**
>
> **Acting responsibly, honorably and well. Acting with love and kindness.**
>
> **Following the directions of my sponsor.**
>
> **Living life according to the percepts of the *Big Book*. Anything else is ego. Not letting prestige, money or relationships seduce me from my goal.**

Here are some things that women I know have done in early recovery. It never worked. Starting a PhD Program in a foreign country, where the women don't know the language; getting married to someone who is newly sober and moving to Africa; taking a job with extensive traveling, which requires training and a lot of overtime; returning to a family that you haven't seen in five years because you're sober and you have to leave your long term treatment facility to take care of them.

It's often more difficult to sponsor someone who's been around for a few years and thinks she knows the AA program, whether she's relapsed or not. Keeping an open mind is essential for recovery and some women think they have all the answers. On the other hand, I've sponsored people who had a lot more time than I, who've been the best sponsees of all. The Set Aside prayer, discussed at length further on, is very useful for someone who's been around awhile.

I use the reality testing principles as a guide in my life and in the life of my sponsee. I encourage my sponsees to do the same.

A very good question to ask sponsees

People don't always give you all the facts. Sometimes they're so obsessed with what they think they have to do or say that they (consciously or unconsciously) hide how things are going. They omit significant areas in their lives for a variety of reasons, none of them healthy.

The best thing to do is to look at the major areas of the sponsees' lives: money, job, family, friends, community service, and significant other (or others), or spending a lot of time finding a significant other. I ask the sponsee to rate these factors on a scale of one to ten. If any item is not at least a seven, you and your sponsee have work to do.

Do this at least twice a month. At the very least, ask your sponsee each time you see her if there is a problem area she doesn't want to talk about.

Even after a long time, it's important to do this, at least once a month. For example, my spending was totally out of control, but I never brought it up, and my sponsor never asked.

WILAA: Silence is golden except when it's yellow.

Knowing what the Big Book says

It's always a good idea to know what the *Big Book* says. I can't tell you how many times I've struggled with what to say and two weeks later found the perfect words in the book.

Here's a funny little story about knowing the *Big Book*. People were talking about a woman who knew everything in the *Big Book*. When sponsees called her she listened to their questions and immediately gave a page number. When I asked her about it, she told me that every page has something that's relevant.

She just picked a number between the first page in the *Big Book* and page 164, gave it to her sponsee, said goodbye, and hung up the phone.

I had a sponsor who had a stock answer when I asked what I should do. 'It's in the *Big Book*.' It was up to me to find out where. In case you wonder why I'm not including citations to specific pages in the *Big Book*-that's why.

Watching people recover, seeing them grab onto the Steps and go from troubled, selfish individuals to kind, thoughtful and helpful members of society is a fantastic gift. I love being a part of it even as I know that I have nothing to do with it.

My boring story: If a person has just come into Alcoholics Anonymous, I usually ask what happened in the weeks before she arrived. If I think it will help, I tell her about my drinking. My story is neither glamorous nor thrilling. I didn't drink, drank some, and then drank every day, and drank a lot. I didn't stop working. I didn't steal, crash a car (because I lived in a city and took cabs), or lose my money, mind, or morals (too much). I just lost myself. The only thing that mattered to me was drinking.

When I'm speaking with a would-be sponsee for the first time I keep my remarks general and don't try to impress her with my wild ways. I'm funny if I think it will make the newcomer less nervous. I'm trying to communicate, which means I have to assess the person and consider what she will hear.

No matter what, I never tell her she an alcoholic. She's got to draw her own conclusions. If she thinks she knows what to do or believes she can handle it herself, I might want to move on.

I had one sponsee who was a suburban housewife with no drama- she just drank a lot of beer. When she stopped, she ended up in a psych ward. She was convinced that she didn't have a low bottom. I think an involuntary commitment to a psych ward qualifies. I told her so and she agreed. She stayed sober.

When you're talking to someone you don't know: If a woman tells me that getting a sponsor is part of a requirements for her to stay out of jail or stay in a treatment facility, I tell her the Twelve Steps work even if she isn't an alcoholic. All she has to do is follow a few simple suggestions and she'll end up with emotional clarity and spiritual growth.

I talk about a risk/benefit analysis. What's the harm of trying the Program? I often suggest that the person stop drinking for a year and see how it goes. If the person can't imagine a life without alcohol, I might point out that's pretty significant.

I also do that after AA meetings when I'm talking to people new to AA. I generally find a rather violent response to the suggestion that they stop drinking for a period of time. The answers are enlightening. Sometimes the person is on an assignment from medical school and isn't an alcoholic. That's why I always ask if the person is an alcoholic before I go into my AA talk.

I might talk to a new sponsee about the relentless, inexorable and painful nature of alcoholism, an illness, a deadly disease, ruthless, agonizing, and often fatal.

I might talk about the pain the alcoholic inflicts upon all those who love and care for her.

I always talk about the need for a power greater than her and the necessity for an honest and honorable life.

Sometimes I lend or give a lady a *Big Book*. I don't rush her. I tell her she should take a look at it and see if she thinks it will work for her. Sometimes I tell her to read the entire book. That's what the *Big Book* tells us to do. To date, only one woman I tried that with actually read the book.

The best thing about giving people some sample assignments is that many of them will decide to get another sponsor. We're both better off.

If I sound flippant, I'm sorry. I take sponsoring women very seriously. It's just that sometimes I need a little humor to lighten the mood. Alcoholism is a fatal disease but it's better not to be too self-righteous.

Lest we forget: we're here to stop drinking

It's nice to talk about the good stuff: The transformative value of AA Sponsorship cannot be denied. Sponsorship has given me everything I didn't know I wanted. When I heard my First Fifth Step I realized how ignorant I was. I knew a lot about the sponsee and wanted her to see herself clearly but not be devastated by what she saw. Words were irrelevant, theories useless, and quitting not an option. I learned more about myself when my sponsee read her Fifth Step to me than in all of my inventories and all my studies.

I saw that I was abrasive, judgmental, contemptuous, confrontational and intrusive. I didn't want to expose a fragile and confused newly sober woman to me. The woman had been abused enough. I didn't like what I saw in me but I didn't know how to change.

I was very careful not to be an abuser and spoke softly. As I struggled with which words to use and what ideas to convey, I forgot about me. For the first time, I wasn't thinking about what other people thought of me, only how I could be helpful. I didn't worry about being right or being smart. I learned how to have compassion and be kind. I learned how to listen, and how to speak so that I could be heard. I experienced the freedom of being with another person and not using her.

I've said that a sponsee and sponsor are partners on a spiritual path. I see her spirit and lose sight of my own. That's when my ego started to disappear, as did my desire for external things to fix me. For the first time in my life, I experienced joy.

Transformations and journeys are great but I don't want to get lost. I'm here to stop drinking. I'm here to help another alcoholic get sober. Everything else is just gravy. I love the side-effects of recovery. They help keep me around but I never forget my primary purpose. If I drink again the transformations go up in smoke.

Many people say 'Yes, alcoholism is a fatal disease, but what has that got to do with me? People die from drug overdoses or in crack houses. You don't die from drinking. I'm not that bad.' A lot of people I knew felt that way until they died.

Who is an alcoholic: Let's talk a little about being an alcoholic. This is useful for someone struggling with the possibility that he's an alcoholic. It might wake him up. A sponsor might also point out that the choir having practice in the room next to the AA meeting is filled with people who never wonder if they are alcoholics. One hint: a non-alcoholic can never understand the craziness that the alcoholics laugh at.

The Alcoholic's Creed

We drink for the feeling of ease and comfort we get from that first drink, and keep trying to get the feeling back, never realizing it can't last.

We drink because we are depressed, but alcohol is a depressant. We drink because we are anxious, but alcohol causes anxiety.

We drink because we keep waking up at night, but alcohol causes interrupted sleep. We drink.

I drank, not realizing that when I didn't take the next drink I felt uncomfortable and uneasy. I needed another drink. The drink set me up to feel exactly opposite from the way I wanted to feel. The longer it took to get the next drink, the less comfortable and more uneasy I felt.

Instead of realizing that alcohol was my master or seeing that it gave me the reverse of what I wanted, I drank more, thinking that this time it would be different.

Why this is so is a mystery. All I know is that it's crazy, and so is the alcoholic. Sometimes the alcoholic begins to realize that drinking isn't a choice but a necessity. The longer I drank, the more necessary it was for me to continue drinking. After a while I had no freedom. I was enslaved by my need to drink but I didn't see it.

So says the *Big Book*. And it's true, whether it's drinking, or eating, or gambling, or anything else. If you look at the Steps, the word alcohol is mentioned only once, in the First Step. After that it's all about characterizing the general problem and the solution, which seems to apply to all addictions. The problem is with my thinking, my feelings, my perceptions, and my responses. The solution is doing the actions as talked about in Chapter Five.

'They can't distinguish the true from the false and think their way of living is the only normal one,' said Dr. Silkworth, a noted physician who treated many alcoholics. He was right.

I never considered my drinking a problem. I never looked at the escalation of my drinking. I ended up working and drinking, drinking and working. My life was all about not drinking. I had changed but didn't realize it. My life was a mess. Alcohol made life bearable until it wasn't. Yes, there was insanity there.

In later years I realized that another form of my insanity was thinking I could go it alone. I didn't understand that self-sufficiency was not a virtue but a deterrent, keeping me escaping from the nightmare of continuous, heavy drinking.

How can this miserable state of mind be changed? I believed that other people were my problem. Well, that might have been so, but the biggest trouble with my life when I was drinking was: my drinking!!!

That was another form of insanity. I was so busy analyzing my problems I couldn't see them. Even when I had a therapist, I was, unconsciously, I think, presenting a distorted view of my life. I was drinking a bottle of Stoli 100 proof every night, plus whatever I drank in bars, which was often a considerable amount. Of course that affected me.

If a therapist asked me how much I drank, I said maybe a glass a night. Sure, I only drank one glass, or more precisely, from one glass. I refilled it quite a few times though.

And I didn't notice. My parents didn't drink much. For the longest time, I had never even finished one cocktail, and that would be when I went out to dinner with friends who drank. I didn't notice when I started drinking a bottle of 100 Proof Vodka daily, plus whatever I drank when I was out for dinner or in bars. I just didn't notice.

In short, I was crazy but not locked up.

The question: If I'm crazy, how can I get myself sane?

I always thought Overeaters' Anonymous was like doing controlled drinking, but it isn't. I guess compulsive eating is no more about food than AA is about alcohol. We all have our craziness, and that insanity keeps us drunk or overweight or hanging out in OTB parlors. Our pathology is ingenious. It enables us to do what we want, feel bad about it, beat ourselves up over it, and then, so distressed, depressed and ashamed, we do it all over again to feel better.

That's truly a hamster on its little wheel.

The process of healing is not instantaneous. Slowly, I was freed from the past. Slowly, I learned how to act in a healthy manner despite my fears, my anger, and my deep rooted, self-destructive ways of coping with life. I'm always suspicious of instantaneous cures. AA offers no Black and Decker solution.

I was on a pink cloud when I came in. It sustained me when the bad times came and life was hard. I had the choice of holding on to hope or discarding it when things went sour. I chose hope. For a vaguely paranoid, non-trusting pessimist, that was a miracle. Even when I got the drinking part, I still thought my ability to handle my own life was my greatest virtue.

I wasn't handling my own life. It was a mess and so was I. I didn't notice. I like to say that I didn't go there. I didn't 'go' anyplace where I might have to make adjustments based upon the reality I had ignored for so long.

CHAPTER SIX: THE LIE OF SELF-RELIANCE

I had trouble with the First and Second Steps. I thought I could manage my life. I thought I could drink safely. I learned that I couldn't. The *Big Book* tells me I have to believe in a power greater than myself and live by spiritual principles. I can't get sober until I do. I have to accept my powerlessness over alcohol and my inability to manage my life.

The people who don't get sober are those who believe that they can handle anything. They worship self- reliance and don't see it for the delusion that it is. Self-sufficiency rears its heard again and again. That means I'm not doing a good Step One. I believe that self-sufficiency returns over and over. That means I'm not doing a good Step Two. I keep forgetting I need a higher power and can't manage my life; I keep forgetting I'm not in charge. Yes, I substitute my wants and my plans, even after many years of sobriety.

For take-charge marines

Imagine you have a cell phone with only one number you can dial. What number? Yours.

You're home alone, late at night and hear a noise in your back yard. You see a shadow coming towards your house.

The land line wires have been cut but no problem. You grab your cell phone and speed dial…..you. Really the police station would have been a better bet.

Imagine your house is on fire and you don't have a land line. No problem. You grab your cell phone and speed dial…you. Wouldn't you want fire trucks and some firemen?

Imagine a family member is at your house and looks a little under the weather. Suddenly he faints or has a seizure or something else awful.

No problem. You grab your cell phone and speed dial…you. Unless you're an EMT with all the emergency equipment, you really would have been better off with an ambulance and some trained personnel.

Self-reliance is good as far as it goes, but you can see that it doesn't go far enough. Do you see how the idea of self-reliance engenders fear? You're stuck with you and you're not enough.

When I see people who have a compelling urge to rely on themselves, I am usually at an AA meeting or on a psych ward.

Ironically, the less control I have over my life, and the less freedom I actually have, the more I refuse to get help or listen to others.

It's about the need for control, but being self-reliant doesn't mean being in control and it doesn't mean I'm free. I happen to know I'm not a loser if I can't do everything better than everyone else on earth. A lot of people don't. (No kidding.)

It's all about the First and Second Steps. It's too bad that the *Big Book* doesn't give specific instructions on either Step. As a sponsor you have to help your sponsee understand that recovery is admitting that if you're an alcoholic you can't get sober on your own.

One definition of insanity is the inability to know what's real. You get in trouble when you insist upon acting on perceptions and beliefs that are inconsistent with reality.

In AA, you'll find a lot of clueless people who really believe they know what to do and have the ability to do it. Usually, the people are homeless, jobless, or living in their parents' basement. They've just left their seventh rehab, gotten four DUI's, been in jail for extended periods of time for episodes of drinking, and/or involuntarily committed to a few psych wards. They come into AA and know what to do better than anyone else. Seems crazy to me.

WILLA: *It's a good thing to know what you don't know.*

Chronic relapsers might believe they have no knowledge and power to stay sober without outside help. That's a good beginning. It's good to know that you have no power but it isn't enough. Lindsay needed the directions found in the Steps. She needed a sponsor who helped her. She needed a fellowship of the spirit composed of people who shared a common bond.

There are alcoholics who accept the fact that they have neither knowledge nor power to stay sober on their own BUT believe that in regards to everything but their alcoholism they do. This is pretty much the same kind of insanity. Alcoholics with many years of sobriety often speak of the way that self-reliance crept back into their lives.

Inadequate coping mechanisms

Many abused or neglected children felt that they had to go it alone. Perhaps the obsessive need for control or power can be described as an inadequate coping mechanism. It might have been useful as a child but it doesn't work as an adult. As alcoholics, we have a lot of these 'coping' strategies.

Fear (or terror) overcomes the need for health and happiness. Better to think you're the most powerful person in the universe, even if all evidence is to the contrary. How terrible to have the belief (illusion, delusion) that you are all powerful. It must be very frustrating when things don't go the way you planned.

I remember 'Ten Year Steve' talking about his time as a patient at Manhattan State Hospital, looking out the window, and watching traffic jams with people trying to get to work.

'Suckers, I called them. I waved to them and said, 'Hey, sucker,' Steve told me. 'I'm in paper slippers and doing the Thorazine shuffle. And I'm laughing at them. I knew more than everybody-not.' He knew he was better than all those saps. Of course he couldn't distinguish the true from the false. After all, he was in a mental institution.

I've found it's better to acknowledge my limitations and not try to conquer them. Sadly, some people honestly feel they are all powerful and have no restraints. You might like to be a king or President of the United States, with all its attendant pressures, but the truth is none of us is a Master of the Universe.

The (realistic) choice is not between being powerful and unhappy and powerless but happy.

It's a choice between (a) holding on to illusions and being miserable and (b) accepting reality and having a chance at happiness.

I can choose chaos and confusion or I can choose love and peace

When I practiced the Program of Alcoholics Anonymous, my fears were removed, my chains were shattered and my ego shrunk. I now mostly live in the moment. I'm not driven blindly by my instincts and make, mostly, rational, healthy decisions.

All it took was believing I needed help and that help was available. All it took was putting more numbers on my cell phone.

The process of Alcoholics Anonymous

The Steps are numbered and in order but the process of AA is not linear. It cannot be taught but it can be learned. The Program is learned by practicing spiritual principles. I want to talk about the process of AA.

I stopped asking why and started asking how

I surrendered. When and how I surrendered started before I took my First Step and continued until this day; it will continue for the rest of my life. Some people say you surrender once and that's it. My experience is that it's a process which begins with the First Step and continues long after my first go- round with the Twelve Steps.

People like to understand things. AA isn't about understanding but doing. Our experiences enhance our beliefs.

Aristotle, one of the greatest philosophers of all times, believed that action was the basis of moral and psychological change. AA experience has demonstrated this is true over and over again.

Neuroscientists have made great strides in the last thirty or so years. We now know the brain is very elastic. New neuronal pathways can be created by different activities and behavior. Aristotle couldn't have known about that. Bill Wilson and Dr. Bob Smith didn't know either. AA is based on it.

Go figure.

WILAA: The process of AA takes time. That doesn't mean we should dilly dally with our step work. I do it like the founders of AA did, and then go back, and go back, and go back. We trudge the road of happy destiny, although sometimes we do skip lightly down the yellow brick road.

For me it's often been two steps forward and one step back. I had too many moving parts but they were all moving in different directions.

That's another reason simplicity is so important. AA doesn't impose order but it teaches us to be orderly.

The single most important concept is this: 'We cannot think our way into good thinking but we can act our way in good living.'

Aristotle made this principle the foundation of his theories of ethics, psychology and human behavior.

'How do you become good?' he asked. The answer: 'By being good.'

'How do you know what's good?' he asked. The answer is 'Look at a good man.' That's pretty much a summary of the Twelve Steps.

What does it take to see?

Before we can learn, we must see. It takes years to be able to see who we are and how we act; it takes an instant to see how desperate our situation is. Sadly it may take years of pain before we arrive at the instant of seeing, or, of our spiritual awakening. I call that instant, 'grace.

I remember a very intelligent PhD asking what he was supposed to do until that moment of grace came. He was complicating something simple. He was in AA because he had an inkling of his problem. He didn't don't need a brass band or a burning bush.

I remember his name. I remember how he looked. I loved his humor and his insights. I missed him when he stopped coming to meetings. He never nurtured the hint of grace he had received which got him into AA. He waited for ultimate enlightenment.

That works for spiritual beings but not so well for those with a fatal disease. They tend to die before they're spiritually awakened.

The 'we' of the first Step gave me the faith to move forward. When I felt my situation was hopeless, I drank. That others have been able to be healed enabled me to hope to be healed as well. In Step One, I trusted that the path that others just like me have followed would relieve me of my misery and desperation.

Every AA meeting presents undeniable proof that AA works. People walk into AA with dead eyes- nobody home. Often, within weeks, they are no longer zombies enslaved by alcohol and by their own psyches, brains, and beliefs. Look into their eyes: warm, compassionate and caring. That's proof to satisfy the most skeptical.

At first I need only say that 'I'm in' and willing to do the rest of the Steps. As time passes, I again find myself beset by the 'bedevilments' (*Big Book*) which poison every aspect of my life. I know I need something, but don't really know what.

Knowing that my solutions always failed me, I turn towards the solution of those who have preceded me. I need a new set of values, and I need to live by them. If you had asked me, I would have told you I had great values. I talked great values but you couldn't find them in my life.

But it is never enough: Aware of how far I've traveled, and how far I have to go, I ask for help for the rest of my journey and commit to this new way of life.

CHAPTER SEVEN: THE NECESSITY OF FORGIVENESS IS WOVEN INTO EVERY ASPECT OF THE TWELVE STEPS

Forgiveness is first mentioned explicitly in the Fourth Step but think about the first Three Steps. The first members of AA became our teachers and our hope. Their experiences enabled them to help others and forgive themselves. Step Two presents the possibility of great growth and does not condemn the alcoholics who appear in the rooms of AA; rather we are all part of a process of forgiveness, from God and from others. Step Three sends us on our spiritual journey, affording us the opportunity to be, one more time, forgiven, and move on to forgive others.

The short form of the Fourth Step Prayer is: 'Lord, save me from anger. This is a sick person. I pray you help me forgive him.'

The last thing I wanted to do was forgive anyone. The people who hurt me were wrong. They deserved to be punished. After thinking about it, I was willing to give forgiveness a chance as long as I didn't have to say that the destructive behavior of these people was acceptable or that they were good folk.

Forgiveness is dynamic and expands exponentially. As I forgave others, I learned to forgive myself. As I forgave myself, I stopped hating and began to forgive others. As I rectified the wrongs I'd committed, learned to forgive those who had hurt me, and concentrated on the wrongs I had done, I became free to glory in my life and myself.

Forgiveness grants me entry into the world of the spirit. It may signify a turning to, or a returning to, a religion of earlier days. It may mean a Judeo-Christian God. It may mean a thousand other deities. It may mean none.

I dwell in a world where my ego is checked, my instincts are functioning properly, and I feel vaguely at peace

I've had many spiritual awakenings over the years. As I continued practicing the principles of the Steps, as directed in the *Big Book* in Steps Ten and Eleven, and carrying the message of recovery, I received many wonderful consequences, the best of which was not drinking for a long time.

I try to be truthful but not brutally honest. I try to be tolerant and not come across as judgmental. A sponsor is not a therapist and deals differently with the emotions. The Steps give me an avenue to emotional, psychological and spiritual growth, all of which are important for me. If I haven't achieved such growth through the Steps, there is no way I would be able to help anybody.

I don't join the AA militia. My job is to make sure my behavior is fine, not anyone else's. That's more than enough work for me. I don't need more, and that's true even if I am someone's sponsor.

Service positions

Service is very important for me and for my sobriety. I believe all members of AA should participate in their fellow alcoholics' sobriety.

St. Elizabeth's is a large mental hospital in Washington DC. I arranged for a few of us to take a meeting there every Wednesday morning. One gentleman agreed to do this every week for two years, bringing someone with him to lead the meeting each week.

I went with him one week when they were on lockdown. The patients were sitting in an enclosed porch but could see my friend. They called out to him, loudly. It was like *Cheers*, where everybody knows your name.

Lindsay, the peace lily lady, took over after I told her it was time for one of the tough service jobs. I went with her one day. The orderlies and nurses stepped away. They had given low doses of medication to the patients, who were uncharacteristically unruly.

I thought my sponsee was terrified. I felt terrible. I had pushed her to go to St. E's. After we left I told her she didn't have to do it anymore.

She told me, very indignantly, that she would continue going, which she did for the next two years. Later she said she dreaded going each week but was glad once she got there. 'Holding hands at the end of the meeting was the closest I've come to feeling God's presence.'

I later met two ex-patients of St. E's. They both said that they treasured the meetings when outsiders would come to the hospital, each and every week, over a long period of long time. It made them feel they were worth something.

I met one of the men at a speaker meeting. He'd been in the institution for six years. He had four friends who didn't want to leave. They had all lived on the streets and were frightened of going back. When they were discharged, his friends went back to the streets and were dead within a few years.

He started shining shoes. He said it was the only job a schizophrenic high school dropout could find. He wanted to contribute to his son's support and not be dependent on social services. He got his GED and later a BA. He is still sober and now makes critically acclaimed documentaries about the plight of the mentally ill.

The other man is a friend of mine. He told me that he often wanted to say something at the meetings but he'd been on so much medication he couldn't speak.

'I remembered what they said. It helped me stay sober. It's one of the reasons why I do so much service now.' He took the prison and street route to get to AA. He was transformed by Alcoholics Anonymous. He is a humble and spiritual person and another joy in my life.

It's not about inspiring the other person or having someone thank you.

You go. That's your job. You hope it helps somebody but that's not your concern. Anything more is ego. After six years there was trouble finding someone to take over the St. Elizabeth meeting. One man did it for a few weeks but found it unsettling because there was no enthusiasm and no feedback. He didn't return.

I had moved away but heard about what was happening. I think someone is doing it now. I'm not sure. My job was to get it going. The group that took it over had the job of keeping it going.

Not everyone in AA lived on the streets. I have one friend, a very talented artist, getting his second PhD. He is a brilliant man and a compassionate human being. He devotes many hours to helping other alcoholics. Another friend, a very successful, very charming attorney, had what is called a 'high bottom,' but it was low enough for him to come to AA and stay here. He, too, devotes many hours to being of service.

My friends are kind and humble. We talk about how hard it is to be of service and how watered down AA is but we all keep going. If I list the gifts of the Program, I have to include the many beautiful people who share my values, my goals and my recovery.

One thought: People with very low bottoms often look with disdain on those of us who managed to maintain a semblance of normalcy while we drank. Sometimes they think we might not be alcoholics. They often believe that only their stories are relevant or necessary to hear.

I think they are wrong. It's possible to be powerless over alcohol and have drinking ruin every aspect of your life, even though you haven't lived on the street, lost everything you cared about, or were a mental and physical wreck. The stories of those who 'coped,' might not be as dramatic, but they are equally necessary and can be equally inspiring.

When I came into my rehab, my blood pressure was 180-120, and my cholesterol was over 500. I was a stroke waiting to happen. I thought I was fine. If I had kept drinking, I would have died long before I ended up on the streets. God worked in my life. I received the grace to get and stay sober.

I won't feel inferior because my story doesn't include prisons, crimes psych wards and high speed car chases. I can talk about the incomprehensible demoralization that got me into AA, and that talk can be what other people need to stay sober.

CHAPTER EIGHT: MY JOURNEY THROUGH THE STEPS AND WHAT I LEARNED

When I got sober I thought taking alcoholics through the steps meant explaining (teaching) the steps. As I got healthier, emotionally, physically and spiritually, I was better able to share my experiences. As I shared my experiences, I healed even more.

The process of AA is dynamic. Each moment of well-being leads to a greater facility of sharing. I am learning to see, and in seeing, am growing in every way. Some people use the Steps as tools for solving their problems. This really isn't the way it is.

A little more about self-sufficiency, and there's always a little more to say about that

I need sponsors and later I need sponsees. I learn from others and I share what I've learned with others. Going it alone is a recipe for failure.

One of my dearest friends in the Program of Alcoholics Anonymous describes the time when he realized that he had no power. He was seventeen years sober. He had just brought his eight year old son to the hospital, suffering from very high fevers and confusion. The doctor was performing tests and looked very worried.

My friend walked into the hospital Chapel, bereft, afraid, and feeling totally impotent. This very intelligent, very successful, happily married husband and father knew there was nothing he could say or do that would make a different. He got down on his knees and prayed, saying only, "Father, I am in your hands. My son is in your hands. Thank you."

He knew, for the first time, that he had been self-reliant for the first seventeen years and didn't even know it. He says that his spiritual journey began in that Chapel and has continued to the present day.

WILAA: We may think we have stopped believing in the need for self-sufficiency but it returns to haunt us. There is constant tension between the necessity of believing in a power greater than myself and my compulsion to take over and do things right.

I think of alcoholics as imperfect beings with the possibly added handicap of a brain damaged by alcohol. I'm better off not thinking. I just trudge along.

The difference between 'knowing' and knowing: You may know in your heart or you may understand cognitively but not really believe that it applies to you. It doesn't matter what you know, however. It is important what you do. It's also important to know what you don't know.

These concepts have been around for a long time. What's new is this method of action. I told you what I did. I was in AA and I wanted to make the most of it. If I wasn't an alcoholic I hadn't lost anything, just a lot of nights in smoky bars that smelled of urine, sweat, and sometimes cheap perfume. I could always go back and drink triples until I caught up.

As a sponsor all I can tell anyone is that I put recovery first. I found out what the Program was and learned how to practice it. I don't think any of my early sponsors went into much about God, or at least I didn't hear it. Since I saved all my written assignments, I do see that there was nothing about God, or self-sufficiency, but I stayed sober.

I see woman after woman in the treatment centers go to meetings but don't listen, get a sponsor and don't do the Steps, and make no attempt to be honest or honorable They think they're in AA but I think they're around it.

I need principles that direct me to act in healthy ways. Simple things I can remember. Some people think that words like honesty, willingness, faith are principles of action. They're not. They're words that describe characteristics. Those little cards that tell you what the principles of the Steps are have it wrong. It's like the Internet. Don't believe everything you read.

The idea of studying, working or doing the Steps is so that I can learn how to practice them. I remember that practicing the Steps, which are spiritual in nature, will remove the obsession to drink and make me happily and usefully whole.

That's why I'm did what I did and do what I do. I do this because a lot of people did precisely this and got and stayed sober.

I wanted to get to the Fourth Step. Then I'd understand everything. Then I'd be happy. I did a few Fourth Steps and I wasn't happy. I wasn't drinking but I wasn't happy.

Eventually I did an honest Fourth Step. I was one more alcoholic on the path of recovery. I was no longer alone. People understood me, sometimes better than I did myself.

So for all you non-alcoholics who were thrust into AA by the legal system or your families or your work situation, just relax and enjoy the ride. You must have been doing something wrong or you wouldn't be here. You didn't get sent here because you had a few too many milk shakes. Still, you may not be an alcoholic. You will hear a lot that will help you improve your lot in life, even if you're not a drunk.

Alcoholic, or not, the lie of self-sufficiency can ruin your life

AA is a proven way of learning how to live a full and rewarding life without taking a drink. Let's face it, drunk or sober, alcoholic or teetotaler, it isn't easy leading a full and rewarding life.

AA doesn't have the cream of society. Convicted felons, sociopaths and other types of people with personality disorders abound. Sure there are people who have enjoyed economic or professional success, but I have yet to meet anyone who said 'Life was really great so I decided to come to AA.' Doesn't happen. Who would come here if they didn't have to?

Sure, some of the people might be given to hyperbole, but on the whole, the stories of people's transformations abound. If you stay in the rooms of AA long enough, you will see how people change. If you stay long enough, you will know how you have changed.

Learning to accept help is key. Learning to be useful to others is essential.

Recovering alcoholics perform the actions as directed in the *Big Book*. We do this in a disciplined and orderly way. We are restructuring our brains. We are reforming our souls. We are energizing our spirits. Our problems may be solved, but not through our unaided will.

The problem with alcohol is solved. The difficulties I have will not stop because I practice the principles of the Twelve Steps. I will be able to deal with them differently. As love and tolerance becomes my spirit's song, I see my surroundings differently. I interpret events in a more realistic way.

I behave differently and others treat me differently as well. Sometimes I think I've learned very little. Other times I know I've learned very little but the 'I' has been transformed so that I am a new and better person and better able to deal with others and treat others well.

The transformation occurs. It isn't cognitive. It isn't theoretical. It is. We are blessed and we are graced. Need we 'understand' it as well? I think not.

Spiritual fitness

I have a friend who is the only person I know who sponsors pederasts. They need sponsors too. He's a very kind New Yorker and actually lived a block away from me when we were both drinking. We went to the same clubs and restaurants although we didn't know each other.

He's one of the most intelligent man I know and incredibly funny.

I can't sponsor child abusers. I'm not that spiritually evolved. Maybe someday but not now. I am too judgmental and care too much. That is ego.

My friend can sponsor these 'reprehensible' men. He can, but tells them he'll turn them in if he sees them at a park or a playground.

When I asked him some questions about this book, he was very helpful. Then he laughed. He had no need to be a hero.

He told me to call him Bozo. 'We're all Bozos on the bus,' he said. That was his suggestion for the title of this book.

Some ladies I'd like to talk about. I can't call them my successes, but I do call them my friends.

I'd like to talk about a lady who asked me to be her temporary sponsor while she was looking for someone who would be more 'appropriate' for her. I thought I would be a very good sponsor for her. It's seven years later, so I guess it's working out okay.

We didn't have similar backgrounds. I thought we had a lot in common, even though she is far more organized than I and better able to negotiate the corporate world. Count me negative on that.

Anyway, at first this woman insisted that she had no intention of putting AA first. She wanted to stay sober but had a lot of other plans as well. That's what she said, but it wasn't what she did.

She is very creative, and has a rich and very full life. She's just retired and can't believe how busy she is. She still goes to a lot of meetings and has two very meaningful positions, one taking a meeting to a local jail bimonthly, the other working on a group that does policy, planning and groups for children in the area schools, both of which she's done for a number of years.

She sponsors a number of women and continues reading, attending workshops and learning more about the Program of AA. Because she is so intelligent and organized, she keeps finding ways to facilitate the growth and development of AA in jails and prisons. She keeps looking for, and finding, new ways to get closer to the God of her understanding.

What can I say? Staying sober (and helping another alcoholic) was always of paramount importance. She voted with her feet and casts a very powerful vote. She is also leaving a very potent shadow on the AA landscape

I'm glad I didn't give her the old lecture about what her primary purpose had to be. Remember, I'm not here to teach or preach. I told her what I did and made a few suggestions about what was open to her and she ran with it. She is one of my sponsees and a very commendable human being who makes AA a better place.

Another lady I'd like to talk about is someone who drank for only three years and got in a lot of trouble. When she was fifteen her parents told her they were taking her to Disney World. They boarded a plane and took a taxi, which drove down a long driveway.

She and her parents got out of the cab, she with her little suitcase. This was definitely not Disney World. Her parents kissed her goodbye, got in the cab and drove away from the rehab, where she stayed for a pretty long time.

Thirty odd years later she is still in AA and still sober. Married, with two adorable children and one adoring husband, she has a full time career, goes to AA meetings, sponsors a number of women and is also a member of the group that works with children in the area, as well as being very active in her Church.

She and her husband, both very intelligent human beings, are good, giving and kind, as are the two other ladies, all three beloved, respected and sought after as sponsors and friends.

She is a person who was given the gift of seeing the future. What she had experienced in her few short years of drinking was pretty bad, Somehow God had graced her with sobriety and she grabbed on with both hands.

Why did she remain in AA when so many others didn't? I guess God came to her and she fell in love.

The last young woman stopped drinking and went into a full blown manic, psychotic, episode. She ended up in a psych ward where she now takes an AA meeting every week.

The psychiatrist told her that if she didn't treat her mental health issues she would be back on the psych ward. He also told her that if she didn't go to AA she would be back as well. She also listened, and believed what the physician told her. She does come back to that psych ward, weekly, when she brings the AA meeting into the facility, but she never drank again.

When she was newly sober she came to an AA meeting and wrote down a few telephone numbers. I was not her choice of sponsor. She called me by mistake. The woman she wanted to sponsor her was a fantastic human being but wouldn't have been the right sponsor for her.

I met her at a local restaurant and she asked me to sponsor her. I've been sponsoring that woman for ten years and she, too, is a shining light in the AA world.

Sometimes people's backgrounds are just too different. Sometimes women coming into AA come from a background of privilege, which can get in the way of the sponsor relationship. The sponsor is, sadly, too jealous. Sometimes the women have backgrounds of such degradation that a sponsor cannot overcome her judgmental attitude. In many cases, the history, which shouldn't matter, does.

If you are bipolar or have relatives who are, you're better able to understand why someone is just acting up, despite taking her medicine. If you have been around people of wealth or fame, you can understand that money or prestige doesn't guarantee serenity or peace.

If you're spiritually fit, personal history is just another way to understand someone. If you're not, it can definitely get in the way. That's only theoretical until a sponsor allows personal feelings to interfere with taking someone through the Steps.

So, here are three women I've sponsored, first nighters, those who came in and never relapsed, those who stayed and flourished, in their own way and their own time, all of whom have far exceeded my limited efforts. I have learned much from them. I hope they learned something from me.

One last thing. I don't think any of these women know how beloved they are in AA, and how respected or admired. Maybe that's part of their charm. Maybe it's their humility. Whatever it is, I am very grateful that they are in my life.

CHAPTER NINE: WHEN AM I READY TO SPONSOR SOMEONE?

I'm not sure I ever am. I often think I owe an amends to everyone I ever sponsored. Sometimes I think I was a better sponsor in my early days of sobriety. I can only sponsor as well as I can sponsor.

I make sure that I am constantly practicing the Steps and doing my best to be better at it. That's why I have a sponsor. That's why I keep on doing a lot of inventory work and do my reality checks. It's why I don't sponsor too many people now. I just don't have the energy for it, and that means I don't have the patience for it.

Why I needed time in Alcoholics Anonymous to be a good sponsor

Over the years I became more self-aware and better able to control my need to act when my actions were unnecessary. Many of my character defects had become known to me. By Step Six I understood my values had to change. In Step Seven, I began moving forward to a more spiritual life. Here is where I commenced a new way of living.

Even so, knowledge was not, and has never been, enough.

The parts of my brain that control my actions are not areas of rational thought. I voted for instant gratification and being respected and loved by others even if I didn't respect or love them.

I wasn't looking to see what I could do for others, but only what they could do for me. If you ask me now if what I'm doing is God's will, I couldn't give you an honest answer. I know, though, that when I am searching for pleasures in the material world (sex, security or prestige), I am in a constant state of turmoil. I'm always looking for the next fix. I am incomplete and become more fragmented as I pursue that which cannot satisfy me.

The three years when I was sponsoring chronic relapsers

I learned that I had nothing to say and nothing to do that would help them. I couldn't and can't get anyone else sober. I hope that I practiced love and tolerance most of the time. That was the best I could do. I felt they needed to take a journey of self-examination. They weren't interested. I extricated myself from the sponsorship relationships because I was obsessing over the women.

I wanted to be helpful but I wasn't doing any good. I finally saw the ways I was trying to control the situation, the ways in which I was playing God, against all logic and reason. Pretty soon I gave up the delusion that I could help.

I recognized the times I was behaving in irrational or fearful ways. My efforts at control were sometimes the result of fear, but self-seeking, dishonesty and anger played their part. All I could do was run. I was just worn out.

My hope is that the women are sober and doing well. Maybe someday I will be able to sponsor women who have trouble hearing anything or seeing the truth, women who do not want to change despite the poverty of their lives and the pain they constantly experience. Maybe not. Maybe so. Right now I just I need a break.

Ego deflation is a peace gaining activity: I have less to prove and less to do. I am thinking of completing a PhD program in philosophy/theology started long ago. It would be just for me but I would enjoy it. It's difficult to do that when you're sponsoring nineteen women who are busy fighting you every step of the way but enjoy calling you to talk about it.

I've been in the trenches for almost twenty one years now. I'm sponsoring six people, taking a meeting to a psych ward, running a monthly Step-study group, and going to at least three meetings a week, plus writing this book and, finally, beginning the blog about AA I've been planning for a while. This should be enough for a 74 year old woman with one kidney who is also suffering from myasthenia gravis.

I'm a woman who has a loving family with two children and their wonderful spouses and six grandchildren who are the most beautiful, best grandchildren in the world. (I may sound like a grandmother here, but indulge me.) I'm a woman who also has made many, many friends, both in and out of AA, whom I like to see now and then. I remain a compulsive reader, as I have been all my life and do like to get to a few movies and some lunches or dinners around town.

So why do I feel guilty about not doing more in AA?

Well if my primary purpose is staying sober and helping another alcoholic achieve sobriety I have to make sure I'm not fooling myself.

I've been writing a book called *The Book of Infinite Joy* for years now. It's time to polish it up and get it published. I just don't have enough time or energy to do everything I want to do. Fighting those ladies who knew so much more than I about everything in life including how to stay sober became tedious and tiring.

I was so busy trying to change what I could not change, that I had no time or energy to change what I should have been changing.

I'm no Mother Teresa nor do I aspire to be. I'm just an old woman who has been given many opportunities. At times I have bemoaned my fate and wish I could still be running, lifting weights, playing golf, tennis and racket ball, sponsoring more people and going to more meetings but myasthenia has stripped strength, energy and coordination from me.

That, too, is life.

If I didn't have AA, I would have had a short life at some smelly bars, bemoaning my fate and bitterly complaining about what life had done to me. After all, alcohol and myasthenia gravis is a deadly mix. I don't forget where I would have been without Alcoholics Anonymous: suffering, resentful, angry, isolated, alone and then dead.

WILAA: My life must be in balance, sure, but more important, in harmony. Doing some things that give me pleasure, and that might be useful to others help me lead a harmonious life: I've learned how to practice the principles of AA in all of my affairs, and not make AA all of my affairs. I am, indeed, entitled to have a life.

My sponsor has encouraged me to spend a little less time on AA and a little more time on me. That's not because I'm so wonderful but because I, too, deserve some fun. If studying philosophy or learning digital art is my idea of fun, so be it. It's a lot better than drinking my life away, one shot of stoli at a time.

The problem is that if my primary purpose is to stay sober and help other alcoholics achieve sobriety, I can delude myself with theories and ideas.

Many people quote the *Big Book* at meetings. Some of them understand it. They become the local gurus. Everyone wants them for their sponsor. They start believing that they are a better sponsor than everyone else. That's very dangerous. There aren't grades in humility but arrogance deserves an F.

Sponsorship is more than conveying information

It includes how the Sponsor behaves. Miss-Know-It-All gets no extra points because she can quote the *Big Book*. Love and tolerance should be her code. She should allow other sponsors the opportunity to learn how to sponsor, on their own and in their own way.

I have to take my own advice. Love and tolerance is my goal, even if it isn't hers.

I have to remind myself constantly that nothing in recovery is about teaching or preaching. If I find myself doing either, I step back and look at myself. I am not being loving, kind, or tolerant. I think I know best and am impatient with those who don't agree with me. Better I should try to understand what they're saying. That way I can learn something.

My assessing another will not go unnoticed. Not preaching or teaching can be very restrictive but ultimately is the best form of rescue from the ego.

It's also the best way to carry the message. People hear more of what I don't say than of what I do.

Don't forget the idea is to carry the message, not the mess. Some folk learn to detach with love in Alanon. It's pretty much the same thing in AA. The Third Step gives us a lot of help. We're not God but (sometimes) his agent. That deflates the ego, which is a very, very good thing.

CHAPTER TEN: THE URGENCY OF NOW

There is only one time to change and it is this very moment. There's only one time to get sober, and it is this moment. That's the urgency of now.

The urgency of now means living in the moment, in the here and now. I don't want to bring the past into my present, nor daydreams of the future. The Tenth Step is great at keeping me anchored.

'The urgency of now means I must renounce my fear and move towards love and kindness. When I help others with no reward, I'm transformed. The only time to begin is immediately, and the only place is here.

There's only one time to quit drinking, and that's right now as well.

WILAA: Part of my inventory is checking to see if I had spread chaos or joy, confusion or harmony.

Bill Wilson and Dr. Bob Smith, the co-founders of Alcoholics Anonymous, devoted hours to discussing possible solutions for incurable alcoholics. The *Big Book* of Alcoholics Anonymous, drew upon many sources. A lot has been written about the theories and beliefs incorporated in this Book.

Practicing the presence of God

One very important concept came from Brother Lawrence's writings. He was a seventeenth century French Monk who spoke a great deal about 'practicing the presence of God'. Each of the twelve Steps can help me practice 'the presence of God.' See also Emmett Fox, *Sermon on the Mount*.

I can sit around hoping that I'll change. Why haven't I seized the moment? I think I'm too afraid. Step Ten is where I start to get insight into myself and the world. It is where I begin to get the strength to quiet my fears. It comes from habitual behavior that becomes second nature to me.

I don't fight my demons. They'll always win but habitual behavior may restructure my brain, my heart, and my soul. Good action becomes second nature to me. I am no longer fettered by the bondage of self. Fear is not my master or even a fellow traveler. I know what I have to do and, unthinkingly, am able to do it.

I'm developing a vital sixth sense. I still must go further, which means more action. I am trying to practice the presence of God and experience more intimacy with Him. This doesn't have to be a return to a

Judeo-Christian God. An atheist can easily substitute her Higher Power for God. I've got Good Old Fred.

Through AA and the practice of the Steps, I have new feelings of community and peace with others and the universe. I am no longer isolated and alone. I am part of the beauty of life.

I have known many atheists who feel comfortable with the concept of practicing the presence of something better and more powerful than themselves. It works for them.

I am amazed that so many people take courses for work, go to therapists for emotional problems and to workshops and sponsors for issues with the Steps. I don't know many people who get outside help from qualified mentors on spiritual matters. Some read a variety of self-help books or books on spirituality. Some take a course here or there at a university.

But outside help, guidance and direction? Not so many. You know getting close to God is more complex than anything else I can think of. I think people who belong to organized religions have it much easier. They have found their 'outside help.'

I work diligently with sponsees so they can find their outside help. It generally isn't me.

Sometimes people are hesitant to try something different. They might need a little push. I've been to Quaker Meetings, Buddhist sitting meditations, and even a Baptist Church service. I go with a sponsee the first time and then she is able to go on her own.

So many sponsees try to do prayer and meditation in their own way, often without paying attention. That's why they need guidance from someone else. One of the things that convinced me of this was when I handed out guided meditation tapes to a number of sponsees.

The first spoken words on each and every tape were 'Don't use these tapes while driving.' Guess how many of the women told me how great the tapes were and how they listened while they drove to work. I wondered if they had even listened to the tapes. (Sadly, sponsees have been known to lie.)

CHAPTER ELEVEN: TALKING ABOUT THE TWELFTH STEP IS ANOTHER WAY OF TALKING ABOUT BEING A SPONSOR:

(It has taken me a long time to heal.) There are three part of the Twelfth Step: having a Spiritual awakening, carrying the message, and practicing the principles in all my affairs.

Part one of the Twelfth Step: 'Having had a spiritual awakening as the result of these Steps.

My first spiritual awakening occurred in the first months of sobriety. I suddenly realized that drinking vodka was like drinking lye. Alcohol wasn't my friend.

My greatest awakening was seeing the world differently. I came into AA angry, paranoid, judgmental and afraid, isolated and alone, dwelling in a hostile universe with brutal people who wanted only to see me in pain.

As I recovered, things changed drastically. I learned love and tolerance and was able to feel the love others had for me. I was part of a large community with shared interests and shared values. Slowly, very slowly, I began to feel the presence of God.

I had a spiritual awakening but not a complete transformation. I saw the darkness in the deepest part of my soul. I learned to contribute order rather than chaos, goodness rather than hatred. I was not a victim any more. I learned to forgive and be forgiven. My inhumanity was retreating.

I saw myself as a child of God, kind for the sake of kindness. I saw myself as worthy, not because of what I did or had accomplished, but because I was worthy. I entered the World of the Spirit in Step Eight when I forgave those who had hurt me and made reparations to those I had harmed.

I began to forgive myself and love myself. I saw that what I called my darkness was the side of me that hadn't accepted God. I began to see that I was not a villain or a vile human being, just a frightened one, and that my view of 'my darkness' was as erroneous as my view of the world.

Part two 'Carrying the message'

WILAA: It's hard to carry 'the' message if you haven't done the Steps.

That's one reason why it's good to do the first run through of the Steps right after you get sober.

There's a difference between carrying the message and being a sponsor. Every sponsor hopefully carries the message but every messenger is not a sponsor. We carry the message often and in many ways, but it's generally not part of ongoing, one-on-one relationship.

I've think I've been more helpful to people I meet in AA who call me occasionally wanting to know something about how to do the Steps than those I've sponsored. I'm very good at seeing what's really going on very quickly. I'm even better at finding solutions in the Steps.

More on when someone is ready to be a sponsor

It isn't a question of time but (1) whether the person has gone through the Steps and (2) whether the sponsor thinks it's a good idea. Dr. Bob went on his first Twelve Step call when he was sixteen days sober. To repeat, the *Big Book* isn't about working on yourself until you're ready to work on others. Doing Twelve Step work is the best preparation for doing Twelfth Step work.

It's a good idea to be somewhat recovered emotionally before you sponsor someone. It's best not to inflict your character defects on someone else.

Somebody said that you can't do Twelve Step work wrong. Sure you can. I see it all the time

I've heard a sponsor at an AA meeting talk about her sponsee, who was in a psych ward after a serious suicide attempt. That's wrong. I've seen sexual predators 'sponsor' people and end up in bed with them. I've seen sponsors take money, rides and more from sponsees. That's wrong too. Sponsors sometimes use their sponsees as lay therapists, to hear about their pain. That's because no one else will listen any more.

Character defects get in the way of the sponsor-sponsee relationship. In Buber's terminology, it's when someone uses another person rather than meets them.

When I say that there's only one way to do the Steps, I'm teaching and I'm wrong. When I give advice about all areas of sponsees' lives, I'm sponsoring wrong. If I'm acting as a surrogate mother, an attorney, financial advisor or Dear Abby, I'm wrong. If I give advice about medication, I'm triply wrong.

Rather than give advice, I ask the sponsee if her proposed action brings her closer to a drink and closer to ruining her life. Sometimes I turn it around and ask her what she would think if I decided to follow her actions.

The only thing I say when someone persists in following their own, self-destructive course is that she knew the consequences of her actions. Enough of us have told her about that. She's waived the right to talk about the problems that followed.

She also can't ask me what will fix the mess she's in.

When I was a divorce lawyer, back in the day, I would meet a client and explain that he/she should prepare financially for the future. Many times I would advise her (let's keep it simple) to make sure she has access to enough funds so that she would be able to function if the couple separated. I'm not telling her to take all the money and run, just to prepare herself for what might be a hard time.

Later, when the husband served divorce papers on the wife (or vice versa) the person would come to me for help. The wealthier party closed all bank accounts, shut down all credit cards, maybe even changed the locks on the door or didn't pay the monthly payments on the car.

The other person had no money to eat, no money for gas in her car or to pay bills. She had no money to pay attorney's fees.

All I could say was I gave you good advice then. I don't have any advice for you now.

People often want others to pay for their own mistakes. If they have no money to pay their lawyer, why can't the lawyer represent them anyway? They'll pay it back later. I'd seen that happen countless times.

That's how it is with sponsees.

You don't have to stop sponsoring them, but you don't have to hear them whining about how hard things are either.

Part three: Practicing these principles in all of our affairs

I believe that living the principles in my life as well as in AA is an important way I carry the message. In that regard I am a visual aid. It's about not drinking. It's about living well. As I look at my life over these past years, I can see how my practice of the principles of AA has affected those around me.

As an athlete, I practiced a great deal. I did this so that it became second nature. I did it so that I did it well. That's what Step practice is.

I try to carry the spirit of AA in my daily life: love, tolerance and restraint of tongue, pen and email. I try not to gossip or show my displeasure at something someone else had done. I listen rather than speak. That way I can connect with others.

This is about accepting the events of my life. I change what I can and accept what I can't. My prayers are about acceptance. I don't ask that my myasthenia be cured. I pray that I can deal with the disease calmly.

AA doesn't say that life is an illusion or that my desires be denigrated. Joy derived from a life lived well is one of the fundamentals of the Program. We reach a joyful state by placing goals, objects, and desires in their right order. I learn what is truly valuable.

The longer I'm in the Program of Alcoholics Anonymous, the more I see how little I understood.

I have a sense of sisterhood. The universe is not hostile or emotionally neutral. I am dwelling in a good place. I am content.

For me, this is about practicing the presence of God. I am, mostly, balanced in mind, body and spirit. Recovery remains the most important aspect of my life but my practice of the Twelve Steps has changed. I don't sponsor as many women because I'm old and no longer have the energy to do a good job.

I have a number of serious ailments but I can face death with equanimity. I've maintained my spiritual practices in the ICU after surgery and everywhere else in my life. I am never too busy to do my daily routine.

I have no regrets about the choices I've made.

In Step Three, the Serenity Prayer is in the first person singular. In Step Twelve it is in the first person plural. I believe that signifies our joining the human race.

We each have our own higher power

I have a friend who's an atheist. She says she doesn't practice the presence of God. She tries to be present in the moment and participate fully in her life. She practices the spiritual principles of the Program. She is a beautiful human

being. As she says, above all she tries, always, to: Be kind, be kind, be kind.

Principles of the Twelfth Step, which I, particularly as a sponsor, attempt to practice always

> **Do the Steps assiduously and make sure I have had a spiritual awakening. Think about what it is carefully. It is my message.**
> **Carry that message when and where it can be helpful.**
> **Practice the principles of all Twelve Steps in my daily life. I become part of my message. Make sure I know what the principles are and my daily inventories to check that I'm practicing them.**

The serenity, courage and wisdom that I need in order to behave rightly doesn't come easily. It requires time, energy and work-basically the work of learning what the principles of the Step are and then practicing them in my daily life.

Pretty awesome. The answers to all of my questions are in the *Big Book* and *The Twelve and Twelve*. I just have to know where to look. The answers to all my problems are there too.

CHAPTER TWELVE: THE SPIRITUAL INVENTORY

When I feel that my relationship with God is lacking, it's time to do a Spiritual Inventory. I begin by doing a **Third Step reality check**:

- **What do I think about? What do I talk about?**
- **What do I want in life and what am I doing to get it?**
- **How much is about my ' little plans and designs?' How much about my relationship with God?**
- **If I had a choice (1) between a million dollars (or whatever amount I think would make a difference), a new man, a new job, a new something, and (2) getting closer to God, which would I choose?**

Rating: rate myself on a scale of 1-10 as to how important practicing the Steps is for me. What ratings do I think the significant people in my life would give me?

I might say 'How can I best serve Thee? Thy will, not mine, be done.' How good am I at carrying the vision of God's will into all my activities? Do I mean it? Do I do it?

Of course I do this with a sponsor.

I have learned not to be discouraged when I see how much help I need. Carrying the vision is one of the most ignored concepts in the *Big Book*. By the way, how do I conceive carrying the vision of God's will at this time?

Whenever I feel disturbed I do this inventory. I write down the answers. I've saved them. I see that I am on a good path, although I find backsliding.

Finally: If God were truly in my life: What would my life be like? What would I be like?

I trace a path through the Steps which lead to a spiritual awakening and the presence of God in my life and in me. Practicing the Steps in a disciplined, thorough and meticulous way transforms my life and me.

I have repeatedly asked myself why I don't practice the Steps (the Program of AA) with all my heart and soul. I write down the answer to that and find that, like the rest of the answers, my explanations have changed. Mostly, fortunately, my actions have changed, and have proceeded in a positive, healthy way.

CHAPTER THIRTEEN: SOME QUESTIONS I'VE BEEN ASKED ABOUT BEING A SPONSOR

I answer based on my experience. This is what worked for me. A Tenth Step inventory is always appropriate when you're unsure of yourself and need help. I would ask the people asking the question if they'd done one, and if not, why not.

When a sponsee asks: 'What do I do? No one asks me to sponsor them.'

What do I do? No one asks my sponsee to be a sponsor.'

(When someone else asks I always say 'Speak to your sponsor and ask if she has any suggestions.' If the person says she has, or that her sponsor told her to talk to me, I proceed as though I were talking to a sponsee.)

Stress the need to go to beginners meetings or meetings where there are a lot of newcomers. When you share, talk about the Program and how it helped you. Add a little bit about God.

Talk to newcomers after the meetings. Be friendly and don't give them the third degree. Ask if they have any questions.

Don't give your phone number unless someone asks you for it. Make sure to be discreet here. Cells phone numbers are better than landlines.

Note: I don't believe that anyone should dress in their finest clothing, but being neat, clean and well- groomed works well. Too much jewelry is always a mistake. On the other hand, if you are a free spirit, you shouldn't change your style, likewise if you're a wanna-be soldier.

This is a Program that demands rigorous honesty. Pretending to be someone else is making a mistake. Just be a neat free spirit or a neat soldier.

That applies more to women than men however. A lot of women care how the sponsor looks. Women are often more sensitive than men to expression, dress and attitude. Although most of this book is gender neutral, being well groomed is generally not as important for men when they pick a sponsor.

When helping someone see you might ask:

Why do you think no one has asked you to be their sponsor?

Ask yourself why you want to be a sponsor. Is it about carrying the message or being able to say you have sponsees?

Is it about your emotional and spiritual growth and not the other persons?

Check your message. Does it have depth and weight? The message is the most important thing. You see how easy that is?

Sometimes I take a less intellectual approach. Before I begin I say a little prayer asking that blame and shame be removed from my remarks. I remind myself not to preach or teach. Then I ask a number of questions, which is like having them do an oral inventory.

How do you plan which meetings to go to?

Do you stay at the same ones because you feel comfortable or go to a lot of different meetings because you don't?

Why do you share at meetings?

Do you find that you talk for five minutes or more? Do you see that you're talking about problems or people or movies, rather than the Program of AA? Why do you do that? Give some specific examples.

Are there a lot of people there that are great sponsors with more time and more charisma?

Are you critiquing the other people who shared or other people in general? Why do you do that? Do you always speak to newcomers before and after the meeting? If you don't, why not?

Are you open and friendly, but not overtly needy?

Do you make sure you're reasonably neat before you leave your home? (Your sponsor may have mentioned this to you before, or you may have mentioned it to your sponsee before.)

One last remark: the way you dress. If you're homeless and can't stay clean, ask yourself if you have a few things to attend to before becoming a spiritual guide. Homelessness is not only a place to live but also a state of mind.

I don't think anyone should offer to be a sponsor. It's better to wait until you're asked. It's a little arrogant to go up to someone and tell them you'll be their spiritual advisor. If you don't know why, please ask your sponsor.

Basics of Sponsorship: When do we start working the Steps?

Why do people think today's newcomers are so much weaker than those in early days? Bill or Dr. Bob would get a prospect on his knees and do the first three Steps in the few minutes before the fellow's first AA meeting.

First I talk with the sponsee. I ask if this is her first visit to AA. If she's been around, I ask her what Step work she's done before. In any event, I am interested in learning about her, if she's married, if she has children, where she's working, and what she does for fun.

I begin the Steps at our first meeting as sponsor and sponsee. I give a very short verbal summary of the Steps. I have a one page condensed version of the Steps and ask the sponsee to read it at home. I talk about the inability of an alcoholic to stop drinking on her own and tell her that alcoholism is relentless, painful and fatal. If she doesn't think she's an alcoholic or that she can stop on her own I ask her to convince me that she's not an alcoholic, maybe writing something down for us to talk about the following week.

I may ask her to convince me that she is an alcoholic. Whatever seems the best way to go is where I go. I ask her to promise to do ten things before she takes a drink. I also ask her to write 100 or less good things about herself.

I tell her I plan to get through all twelve Steps within three months, and then go back and go over them more thoroughly. Sometimes I tell her that we go through the Traditions as well. It all depends on the sponsee. If she seems overwhelmed by all this information I tell her that the sheet I give her will help. I reassure her that things will get easier.

I might explain that she does the Steps to get sober but also so that she has the knowledge and experience to help others do the Steps as well.

When is it time to say good-bye?

When I meet with a prospective sponsee I lay out very clearly what I'm willing to do and what I expect a sponsee to do.

I ask her to get a notebook and write down what she agrees to do and what she won't do.

I give her an assignment for the following week, and we find a definite time, day and hour and place, where we will meet, hopefully on a weekly basis. That will be her time, although occasionally either she or I won't be able to make it. We give as much notice as we can.

I explain that I don't put any more energy into the relationship than she does. I want her to care more about her sobriety than I do. Otherwise we can't go forward.

I stress the need to believe in a power greater than herself and lead a principled life. If the life my sponsee leads is too slimy and her only higher power is herself, I worry. If there is no progress, I give it at most three months or so, and then surrender.

I tell her that she is to get sober in her time and not mine, but if we are too far apart, she needs a different sponsor. If she agrees to do the work but then doesn't do any or doesn't meet at the specified time or go to meetings, I will talk to her about it. By some reasonable time, I will say good-bye.

You see there's a difference between she can't and she won't and it's not always easy to distinguish which is which. After a while it's a matter of she doesn't. No matter how much I like the woman, I have to let her go. I'm not enough of a motivator for her.

The *Big Book* tells us not to waste time on the person who doesn't want to be sober. I take that to mean not to waste time on someone who doesn't want to practice the Program, even though she says she want me to sponsor her. Every time I've tried it, it's ended badly.

People's lackadaisical attitudes have worn me down. Most people slack off after a period of time, so someone who starts by doing almost nothing has nowhere to go.

For the last few years I haven't 'fired' anyone. If they are in a complaining period, I ask them to complete a series of questions about the matter (an inventory) and tell them to call me when it's done. They do it, get another sponsor, or just drift off.

I sponsored one woman once, who was assiduous about meeting with me, going to AA meetings, taking easy service positions and doing some step work. There came a point in time when she was complaining about her mother, her significant other and her best friend. She had done a Fourth Step which included all three but had not forgiven them. The complaining went on for months.

I asked her to write a mini-inventory on the three people. She didn't find it necessary. When I asked my sponsor what I should do, she told me that I was controlling. I was trying to get the woman sober in my time, not hers.

I said that I didn't care whether I continued sponsoring her or not. I just wanted to know what the right thing to do was. I didn't know. Should I continue and let her run the sponsorship, or should I give up? It was fine with me either way. I just wanted to know which was more beneficial for the sponsee. My sponsor didn't know either.

My solution: I told the woman that I was fine with her not doing the inventory but not fine with hearing her complain about the people. I would sponsor her but I wouldn't talk about her anger towards, and resentment of, them. She had tools to deal with them. If she didn't want to use them, I didn't want to talk about it any longer. I didn't fire her. She fired me the next day, by voice mail.

If the person refuses to do daily Tenth Steps and I refuse to discuss her feelings or the consequences of her actions a few times, she generally fires me. Usually we're both relieved. I do say that some people don't do the Step but have the habit of self-scrutiny and disciplined spiritual practices. In that case, we continue on.

At this point in my sobriety I am sponsoring six people. Four of them have done the Steps but don't want to do Step Ten; two of them don't want to do Step Eleven. My sponsor believes that they are all not drinking and doing very well. Again, it is suggested that the problem is with me.

It's very difficult to talk about things that could have easily been solved by repeated forays into formal Steps Ten and Eleven. I also wonder how anyone would feel comfortable sponsoring someone when the sponsor isn't doing Steps Ten and Eleven. I know that I ask less of my sponsees than I ask of myself but I also know that the time is coming when I will no longer be able to sponsor them, a time that is coming soon.

My problem is that I know many people in AA who never do a formal Step Ten or Step Eleven, but do admit when they're wrong and do pray and meditate. I worry that I am being too mechanical and that my way is not the only way to be sober. I also fear that since I am not terribly spiritual, I'm not a good example of following the *Big Book* and not enough of a motivator.

This is all too much thinking. As I write this I have made a decision. I have decided that I will ask the sponsees to do a formal Step Ten and Eleven as written in the *Big Book* for a month. At that time, they can decide to reject that manner of sobriety, but not until they have tried it.

I've started a monthly Step Study group. When we finish Step Three, I shall ask them to do that month of continued inventory and prayer and meditation, exactly as it is in the *Big Book*.

At the time the *Big Book* was written, few people had gotten sober through AA. There weren't enough recovered alkies to make Twelve Step calls. The New York office was sending people out who had a week or two of sobriety. That was the best they could do.

It's quite different today. People spend years studying the Steps and talking about them. This is a different world. We have the luxury of working with someone for a few weeks or months or even years, and seeing how it goes. I don't want to be an enabler but I do want to be sensitive to someone's deep-seated fears and anxieties. I give a newcomer a chance and then give up. I've held on for more than a year with some women and weeks with another.

I've become very basic. I can't read minds. If a person can't honor her promise to do the step work or practice the principles of the Program in a meaningful way, I wait a while and then surrender. I have enough trouble fighting my own demons. I don't have to fight hers.

I'm not telling her what to do or punishing her for doing something I've urged her not to. At the same time I don't have to relive her problems when there are solutions for them.

It's that old Florida-Alaska dyscrasia. If you tell me you want to go to Florida but end up on a plane that lands in Alaska, well, that can be a mistake. The third time you're in Alaska rather than Florida I'd have to say you wanted to go to Alaska. You didn't want to go to Florida. I know that. You know that, except maybe you don't. The person who keeps on buying that ticket doesn't always know what she's doing. A little crazy?

Maybe this is simple-minded, but it follows a good principle: look at a person's feet to know where they want to go. I can't read your mind but I can observe your behavior. It's not what you say you want. It's not what you say you feel. It's what you do.

I always make one last try and again ask the person to write down what she's willing to do to stay sober and what she isn't willing to do. Mostly, the women I ask tend not to write down anything, which tells me what I want to know.

When a sponsee relapses

If she hasn't gone to meetings, done no Step work, and followed no suggestions (like moving out of the crack house where she's living with her boyfriend) I may say that I can't sponsor her. On the other hand, some women just need more time to get straight. I do draw the line at three relapses in a brief period of time. I ask her if she's willing to go to a detox or a treatment facility. If she refuses, that's it for me.

If she's tried to do the work

I talk to her for a few minutes about the First Step and then return to whatever Step we were working on. I'm pretty good at being kind here. None of my sponsees has ever felt condemned. That's because I don't take it personally. I don't feel good about her relapse but I know I can't keep anyone sober and I can't get them drunk. I do ask if she had done the ten things she promised to do before she took a drink.

It's not time to say goodbye

When a sponsee doesn't follow my suggestions about the Program I talk to her and ask what the problem is. She may have specific reasons why she cannot take a suggested commitment (work does not afford her the time; she might be breaking her anonymity if she goes to a jail, or some other matter where it would not be appropriate for her to go forward). I suggest other things she can do. Also, all people cannot do all things.

About her life: This is very rare because I seldom give advice about behavior. I don't believe it is my place to object if the suggestions are not followed. I do feel that sponsees lose their right to complain about the results of their actions. I don't stop sponsoring them but I don't want to hear about how bad things got.

Examples

Staying with a physically abusive boyfriend or husband.

Not following suggestions about how to get along at work when you're on the brink of being fired. Not finding a good day care for your kids.

Spending a lot of time on-line and then complaining you have no time to go to meetings or do Step work.

Of course, when I keep on talking about the Steps instead of problems, the women mostly get another sponsor.

What do I do if someone other than a sponsee isn't sure if she should keep the same sponsor, or if she needs help with a step?

This one is very difficult for me. I often want to say that the woman's sponsor is doing it wrong. I want to help her with the Steps. What I do is say nothing except that she has to talk with her sponsor.

Very occasionally someone asks me if she should stay with her sponsor because the woman hasn't behaved well. In a few cases I know the sponsor and feel I should say something. There are a lot of crazy people in AA and a newcomer doesn't have to stick with any of them. The same goes for vicious women who are playing head games. I generally don't tell anyone what to do but I will ask a few questions, like where is someone with the Steps, service and God. Her answers will tell her what to do.

I might talk about the history of AA and how they did the Steps in the old days, or the need to get the Steps done before the first year. I also say that Dr. Bob started doing service when he was sixteen days sober.

I can ask the woman how she feels about her sponsor and if this reminds her of anyone. People usually said it's just like being with Mom or Dad. I ask if she has a therapist. Very reluctantly I might say something. Sometimes I think I have to.

WILAA: Silence is golden except when it's yellow.

CHAPTER FOURTEEN: HOW DO I NOT GET INVOLVED IN THE SPONSEE'S LIFE? WHY +

When I get up in the morning I make sure I do a complete Eleventh Step. Right before I meet with someone whose problems I can't seem to resist. I pray that I will stick to solutions and not problems. I still can get caught up in my sponsee's problem. I want my sponsee to be happy. I like having specific answers that will make them feel better.

I've started praying that I act with courage and kindness, become aware of my motives and ask that my ego be quieted. I want to furnish a solution which invariably is about some part of a Step, or Steps.

Above all, I don't want to make things worse. I have to remember, always, it's not about me. If I do get overly involved, I do a Tenth Step. If I'm sponsoring a newcomer, it may not be possible to direct her attention to the Steps. I do have to try.

When all is said and done, it's not about the answers the women are seeking or the questions they ask. One more time, it's about the Steps. Whether it's a divorce or a bankruptcy or getting a better job, a sponsor's job is to help the sponsee become calm, centered, and spiritually fit. The sponsee has to make the decisions. She's got to live her life. I remind myself, always, that my job is to guide her through the Steps.

That way I don't have to worry whether she thinks I am cold or indifferent to her pain. I don't want her to feel that way. By stressing the Steps when we start, she understands what my role is, and it's not to be an emotional Band-Aid.

I haven't found many women who are interested in +following all of the directions in the *Big Book*. Maybe it's because I'm not spiritual enough. I'm a very superficial person. I try not to teach, or preach or give advice even when I'm sure what the right answer is. I try to practice the Program of Alcoholics Anonymous (and my rules).

A big part of my problem is that I grow to love my sponsees and want their pain relieved. I listen to their problems because they need to talk about them. When I take the discussion back to the Steps, I feel like I'm not being kind. It's difficult to sponsor someone for seven or ten years when they do sporadic prayer and meditation, and ignore the Tenth Step, except when they are extremely upset. At that time they usually just do the mini-inventory and ignore the rest. It's especially tough when they're in great emotional turmoil. On the other hand, it's discouraging to feel like a broken record.

After a while some of the women I sponsor drift off, calling sporadically, usually with specific questions on how to sponsor their sponsees. I used to have a big talk with them about getting more involved in the practices of AA, which usually ended with their firing me. Lately, I've said that in every sponsee's life there will be a time when the sponsor asks the question: What are you willing to do to stay sober and what are you not willing to do? I've asked them to think about it and write it out. I did it short and sweet. The discussion was mild, with no advice giving. Usually the sponsee disappeared from my life.

If the sponsee comes back with 'willing to do whatever it took to stay sober,' I mildly observe that her spiritual practices have fallen off, or she doesn't have service positions, or worse, that she seems stuck. She may have experienced personal growth, I say, but I don't think she's ever gone over the Steps again. She seems to be repeating stuff we talked about five years before.

I know we talk about maintaining our spiritual condition but we also talk about improving our conscious contact with God. If someone goes to Church and prays but doesn't increase her knowledge of the Steps or her knowledge about the Program I won't say she isn't improving her spiritual condition. If she still has the same personal problems and is stuck in the Steps as she learned them five years ago, I would say her spiritual condition needs improvement.

It's not for me to comment on her relationship with the Church. I am not qualified to do so. If she wishes to seek solace from the Church, why is she calling me? There's a lot of drive-by AA and I've reached the age where I don't want to be a party to it.

I find it's very difficult to have women in a lot of pain call me or meet with me. When I didn't care about anybody, it was easy. I could listen to what someone said, be comforting, and walk away and order a milkshake. It's not like that now. I share a woman's pain and it hurts.

When I'm talking with someone who has bad things happening in her life I look to see whether it's avoidable or unavoidable pain. If a sponsee didn't listen to her friends, her family, her therapist, and me, and married some guy she met six months before at an AA picnic, it's hard for me to feel sympathetic.

I've participated in someone else's discomfort. It hurt. Even worse, nothing I could say would make any difference. I knew the sponsee would continue doing things her way, which will result in more (avoidable) bad things happening to her.

A lot that seems unavoidable isn't: When unfortunate circumstances arise out of personal decisions, I speak with the sponsee and explain that she could have prevented some of the bad things in other life, and not others.

I ask her to think if the situation she's in came about because she didn't listen to anybody and just did what she wanted to do. Marrying a man she just met, who has seven months of sobriety, just got out of jail, has no job, lives with his parents, and visits his young children on weekends, is not a sign of good judgment.

If a woman does everything for her mother and step-father, even though there are siblings in the area who are very capable individuals, and insists that she's the only one who can do it right, I agree with her. There is nothing she will hear. I tell her that I'm not equipped to handle the consequences of self- reliance and ask her to get another sponsor. This is true of many of the obligations that someone thinks she has but not always.

I don't know what to tell a person who has been sober for a long time and is sacrificing her life for her parents because there is no one else to care for them, or her emotionally disturbed child, or whatever other situation applies. That's a time for the sponsee to do an inventory, time for us to talk about the problem and maybe a discussion of time management, alternative solutions and motives.

Usually love is about addition. I justifiably expect love to enhance my life. When it's all sacrifice it's time to look more closely at why I'm doing it. Again, this can't be solved with a short and neat solution. A good amend allows the sponsee to live in the present and not keep making up for mistakes she made in the past.

When I was new to sobriety and sponsorship, I dove in with alacrity. I could solve anything. As self-awareness grew, I saw that I couldn't solve my own problems, even when I had all the facts! With time, I learned to use the Program before I put on my white hat and got on my horse.

I always examine my spiritual practices, my message, my character defects, and my motives when I'm in a problematic situation. If I'm wrong, I promptly admit it. If I've spent my time on her problems and not her solutions, I backtrack and have another conversation with her about her problem but stick to solutions. If she can't or won't, I tell her it's time for us both to move on. Someone with more patience might be better for her.

I want to talk a composite of a sponsee, one who has been in a committed intimate relationship for a period of time. She is intelligent, attractive and in a lot of pain. At one time she was anxious to do the entire Program. Somewhere around the Tenth Step that stopped. Her marriage (or relationship) is not going the way she wants. She's been thinking about leaving.

Things happened in her life. There were things she did that she didn't talk about, before and after she got sober, to her other sponsor and to me. She didn't go forward with the Steps, except to continue doing them the way she had before.

I have to be careful about not interjecting myself into the problem. . I've been divorced and know how hard it is for her and her children. It's not easy not to give advice. When you empathize with a sponsee, it's difficult not to get involved in her emotional distress.

So I think about what I should do. I have to tell her +that she has been doing things her way and that it didn't work. I would assume she has been doing the same with her husband. I'm not surprised he's not happy about it. I don't take her not being a team player personally. I'm sure he does.

They aren't a partnership. They don't (either of them) cherish their union more than they cherish their need for self-reliance. They are two fine human beings who are mired in their character defects and won't use the Steps to escape. The First Tradition is very helpful here too.

I've sponsored many women in relationships. They are all different but share some similarities. I realize that I'm not in their homes. Is the partner's behavior unacceptable? I don't know. If my sponsee can't accept his behavior, that doesn't mean it's unacceptable. I believe she has to do the Steps to see the whole picture. Even if he doesn't change, she may be able to save her marriage and at no cost to her integrity.

How can I make a woman understand that acceptance is the answer to the problems in her marriage? Sometimes you have to accept your mate for what he or she is. Sometimes you have to accept that the mate is cruel, manipulative and uncaring. That means leaving.

If someone has done all the Steps, had a spiritual awakening and been sober a considerable amount of time, she is theoretically able to determine if her behavior contributes little, some, or a lot to the general dysfunction.

What I generally suggest is that she forget about her relationship problems+ +and do one month of prayer, meditation, service and inventory. Actually I've told her that at least one time before. At one point we read the Traditions and applied them to her marriage. That helped a little. Love and tolerance is the answer to the problems in her marriage. Doing the Steps will help her accept her husband as he is and help her see all the good that is in him. It will also show her what her part in the marital difficulties is.

Then, and only then, will she be able to make a reasoned and informed decision.

At the end of that month she will be better able to make that decision. She may not even have to. Very few people believe that the problem is themselves or that the answer is in the *Big Book*. That's one of my spiritual awakenings

The only cost is to her ego and her need for freedom and control, which we already know is illusory. It's all a matter of what's important. I would like her to understand that before she takes any action.

I have to let go of my feelings and not get into her problems. I want her to get into AA's solutions. That's really what we have to do, each and every sponsor. I've done several Tenth Steps on getting too involved in the sponsee's difficulty. Of course I'm selfish, dishonest and afraid. I become resentful because she doesn't follow my suggestions. I forget about the DPDT rule. I learn not to get involved in the problem and move to the solution.

I see that I confuse carrying the vision of God's will into all my affairs with carrying my vision of what should be done in any particular case. I remind myself, again, and again, I am a messenger. I have to read the lines as written. It's not all about me. In fact, it isn't about me at all.

I sponsored a newcomer once, whose husband was a heavy drinker. He did not physically abuse her but did act bizarrely at times. She told me her best friend had told her to throw him out.

I didn't tell her to do so. I had no idea what the right thing to do was. Besides, it would be teaching and preaching, and I don't like doing that.

I again told her that she would be best off if she worked the Steps, went to meetings, and did some service work. Prayer and meditation would give her some answers. The right answer would come to her, I said.

Before the answer came, her husband came into AA. That was more than ten years ago and they're still married.

I had believed her friend was right but fortunately I knew my job description and didn't tell her my opinion. One more time, it wasn't about me.

Acceptance has many forms. I have a terrible neurologic disease. I've learned to accept my disabilities. I don't whine about it, too much, and I don't blame fate for my situation. I live with being tired, and in pain, with my teeth crumbling in my mouth, and my brain slow. I live with it and make the best of it.

Maybe if I could be divorced from myasthenia I would feel differently. Acceptance is easier when there's no choice.

CHAPTER FIFTEEN: DO I EVER REFUSE A REQUEST FROM SOMEONE IN AA?

First, I limit that to requests for AA activities. There was a time in my life when five new women ask me to sponsor them in a one week period and I was already sponsoring ten. I couldn't agree because I couldn't do it without sacrificing the rest of my life. Even I did, it wouldn't be fair to the new women.

I've seen married men with children spend most of their time going to meetings and working with sponsees. I don't think that's what we're meant to do, particularly in the area in which I live. There are other men who are very good sponsors and could take over. We really should fulfill our obligations.

We all have responsibilities, family or occupational as well as to an orchestra or team or whatever. Of course we can't use that as an excuse for doing nothing but we are supposed to practice the principles of AA in all our affairs and not make our affairs only AA. I have sponsees who are single parents. It's very difficult for them to balance job, children and AA. I urge them to look for harmony, not balance.

Balance is about numbers and having things in order. Harmony is spiritual and not quantifiable.

Who I don't sponsor

Anyone who is newly sober and been put on more than three meds for treating psychological conditions; people who aren't interested in stopping drinking; and the 'unsponsorable'. I used to sponsor them but I'm too old and too tired. I leave them to the young.

I also don't sponsor individuals taking drugs which suppress alcoholic or drug compulsions or obsessions. My experience is that they have a very hard time getting sober once they're off the meds. The time when you first get sober is when you're most desperate and most willing to get involved in the Program. I think the pills prevent you from hitting bottom.

Usually the addiction specialists (physicians) proscribe a sleep aid, a mood elevator and a mood stabilizer, as well as at least one anti-depressant and maybe some vitamins. I've found it difficult to communicate with the women because they often are very foggy. I'm not criticizing the medical treatment. I am not qualified to do so. I just can't sponsor people who don't know what they're saying and don't remember what they said because of the pill cocktail.

I've observed that the substance abuse specialists say the problem with the efficacy of the meds is 'non-compliance.' That means that even though the compulsion is gone the alcoholic still wants to use. When all else fails, blame the patient. Often the doctors give longer lasting dosages by injection. I wonder about the long term effects of taking medication that radically changes brain chemistry. I don't believe there are any convincing studies about that.

I don't sponsor people who are primarily drug addicts or people I judge harshly. I'm talking child abusers here. I am basically an alcoholic with no allegiance to other drugs, one of a dying breed. I would do a disservice to an addict because we have very different experiences. I have sponsored drug addicts in the past and it worked out very well. NA has changed in my area though and I don't think my sponsoring an addict would work as well now. For some reason, some NA groups have become anti-AA and anti-alcoholics. Even if I do sponsor an addict, I insist she go to at least one NA or CA meeting a week. This is based on what my friends who are addicts have done.

I also don't sponsor someone who has very different life experiences, values and goals. I've found that all I am is judgmental. That's when I'm not fooled by them. I've found that I don't have to have the exact same experiences, values or goals but they must be remotely similar. Otherwise I am just in over my head.

I don't sponsor people who refuse to go to a detox or treatment facility after I suggest it. They continue drinking and I don't think I can help them. I refuse people who won't stop taking medications if they have no prescriptions for the medicine. Getting a lot of script from several different doctors is also a no-no for me. Besides, it's illegal.

I'm not saying everyone must do it this way. I've arrived at my list of people I can't sponsor after some bitter experience. Certain things don't work for me. They may work very well for you.

CHAPTER SIXTEEN: GOD AND RELIGION

The *Big Book* tells us to burn in the consciousness of every alcoholic that he must trust in God and clean house. Not too many sponsors start off that way. Some do talk about the need for a Higher Power and a very few about the fatal nature of the malady. I think sponsorship has changed drastically, and for the worse.

The First Step used to be 'Shut up and get in the car.' Now it's 'Let me love you until you can love yourself.' There's not a lot of burning and nothing about the Steps or service. That's not what the *Big Book* tells us to do. I've heard many people at meetings say that they would have left AA if they heard so much about God or if they had been told they had to do the Steps. Well, good for them. That kind of talk is all about ego. It is part of the watering down of AA. It's some message for the newcomer to hear.

I heard a story about Bill and his buddies debating on how much God they should put in the *Big Book*. Lois, coming home from work, walked into the house and heard the discussion. She was not pleased by it, as evidenced by the loud sound of a door slamming as she went into the kitchen.

Bill went after her.

'You're forgetting what got you sober and kept you sober,' Lois said.

Bill walked back to his boys (that's how they spoke in those days) and said 'God stays in the book.'

When I talk to the atheist I tell her that the opposite of spiritual is materialistic. It has nothing to do with God at all. Spiritual principles don't have to include God either. The brilliance of AA stresses only the need to believe in something more powerful than you and lead a principled life.

I talk to the sponsee and tell her that she can find a higher power or borrowed someone else's. I would prefer that it's more powerful than she and can get her sober. We talk about substituting the words 'Higher Power' for God. This works in about ninety eight per cent of the time.

Take a look at Bill's story. He recoiled from Ebby saying 'I got religion.' He wasn't happy about it but he was interested in the power that Ebby had, a power that he hadn't had before. When I got sober I thought that if it was good enough for Bill Wilson, it was good enough for me.

I've quit the debating society. I was good at philosophizing. I even went to graduate school to study it. Looking back over my life I wonder what I was thinking. (That's a pun, folks.)

I do tell the atheist about the old standby: 'If you don't believe in God stick around. You'll be contacted.'

I've never understood people not believing something was more powerful than they. I know there are many powers greater than myself, ranging from the IRS, the police, and the US Army to gravity, ocean tides, tornadoes, and cancer. I could probably name a hundred more in the next three minutes.

The three places I've found large numbers of people who believe that nothing is more powerful than they: AA meetings, psych wards, and Capitol Hill

If someone says she can do it alone, I ask her to stay sober for a year. If she says she could do it, but might not want to, why then I invite her to come back in a year to resume the conversation. Most of these naysayers do drink again. Three women actually came back and asked me to work the Steps with them.

The rest still had reservations. Now reservations are good for air travel and restaurants. They don't do well in AA and the women didn't either.

God is either everything or nothing

In one sense it doesn't matter if God exists or doesn't exist. If you don't believe in a power that can help you stop drinking because you know it all, you won't stop drinking and you have a good chance of a not very happy ending. If you believe in a specific God, with specific powers, then it certainly does matter if God does exist. Otherwise not. In any event, you must find a power that will give you the power you need to stop drinking and stay sober.

If a woman goes to Church regularly and thinks I'm not very spiritual, I agree. I explain that AA is compatible with most religions and very pious people have no difficulty in AA. I outline the need for self-appraisal and ask if she's done any of that, in her religious practices, or therapy sessions, or just when she's trying to figure out why her life is so miserable.

I frankly would prefer not to continue. Actually, I've sponsored a few very spiritual women. They had no trouble with me or my beliefs. I learned a lot from them. I have sponsored some of the judgmental women, though, and it never worked out.

When I was first sober I would ask myself what I was doing 'here.' Why was I with 'these people'? I was a white middle class woman who drank too much. I didn't belong in AA.

I was about two months sober and finally permitted to leave my sober living community without an escort. I felt I didn't belong in the low bottom meetings I'd been attending. I went to an early morning spiffy, upscale meeting in Marina Del Ray. One of the women, a professional musician, was sharing and she said, either 'between you and I,' or 'irregardless.'

I mentally sneered and told myself all the meetings, upscale or low scale, were the same.

And then it came to me. I was the common denominator at the meetings. The problem wasn't the other people. It was me. I would never be happy if I spent my time finding fault with everyone else. That was a spiritual awakening. It was the beginning of my feeling at home at all meetings. I felt that something outside of myself was guiding me. I have had a number of eerie experiences which convinced me that God exists. Take a look at my experience on a golf course, which is a little further on in this book.

I don't understand how people can believe that they're the most powerful person in the universe, or the smartest or the most all-knowing. In their heart of hearts they truly deny that there is a power greater than themselves.

You can look at this as being about a lack of honesty. The people who can't see that there are many forces that are superior to them are just being dishonest, intentionally or otherwise. They're the ones who can't stay sober. The ones who feel inferior to everyone else are equally dishonest. It's no more humble to think you're the worst, when you're not, than to think you're the best.

Some of the language in the *Big Book* sounds like the Bible. Bill might have gotten carried away. On the whole, it's pretty easy to substitute your Higher Power for the traditional Judeo-Christian one. When you are praying it can be to whatever your higher power is. *After all, the significance of praying is not that God answers your prayers but that you're talking to Him.*

A big time spiritual awakening: I was an atheist when I came into AA. I couldn't stop drinking. I worked and I drank. I drank and I worked. That was my life.

One day, I was at my favorite bar. My favorite waiter gave me a triple Stoli on the rocks. I said 'No thank you. I don't want any.' I didn't even think about it.

No drama. No chaos. No *Big Book*, meetings, or fellowship. I was at a bar where I always drank like a pig. I didn't have a drink. I haven't had a drink since, except for the one drink the counselor told me to have before I went into rehab.

It was many years before I understood what that meant. I don't know if it was a miracle, which is the '…interference with Nature by a supernatural power.' (*Miracles*, by C.S. Lewis.) I don't think it matters.

I keep it simple. Everything follows from the fact that I can't stop drinking. I haven't had a drink in a lot of years. Whatever that power is that enabled me to stop is my Higher Power. Is it a supernatural power? Beats me.

I have a lot more sympathy for the believer and the atheist. I don't get the agnostic. God is or He isn't. I think the agnostic is engaged in some mental masturbation. It doesn't matter if God exists or doesn't exist. Either way you find a power that will give you what you need.

I think there are seven proofs of the existence of God and five refutations of His existence. No matter. Philosophers can't prove the existence of the external world, other minds and or themselves. I kid you not.

I could get caught up in that and never leave the house. I could also use common sense.

I see people. I see the world outside of me and I believe people think and aren't robots. That's how I answer philosophical quandaries. I don't live as though everything is a mystery. The philosophers who espoused some of these theories still talked and walked carefully around speeding automobiles, wild animals and threatening looking people. I don't think that's very consistent.

What I know is that I meet people and converse with them in a meaningful way. My proof that God exists is just like that. I have met God and God is very good.

CHAPTER SEVENTEEN: THE VISION THAT SAVED MY LIFE: I HAVE MET GOD AND HE IS GOOD.

The early morning sun shone over the country club, illuminating glistening fairways and dew covered greens. I was the first one off the tee, having tipped the starter generously. This was my new life, plenty of money, plenty of time, and a good golf swing.

The golf cart moved along smartly as I jumped out, took a practice swing and then slammed the ball down the fairway. If the ball sliced or hooked, no problem. I moved on. I was playing golf, not looking for golf balls. They were the used balls I bought at a roadside stand so no biggie.

I got to the seventh hole, pleased with my progress. I had hit a lot of good shots and didn't count the bad ones. My only concern was my putting. I couldn't sink a three foot putt. I had never been a good putter but was sure practice would put that right.

This was ridiculous. My score would have been in the hundreds because of all the putts. My second shot unfortunately hit the green, about forty feet from the hole. I considered moving it backwards onto the apron so that I could chip it close. I wasn't playing by any rules here.

I looked up. I saw the figure of a boy standing across from me, bathed in sunlight. I could feel goodness and peace emanating from him, a glorious joy. I looked closer and it was Doug, the beautiful, bright, lovely young man who had been my son's best friend. Doug had the best parents in the world, the best family, kind, loving and accepting, able to teach the values that all men aspired to but few cared to practice.

I looked again and Doug was standing there, totally at peace, incredibly happy and impossibly present. A non-Hodgkin's lymphoma had felled him a few years before but he was now whole and himself and ecstatic.

"Why are you here?" I asked him. "I can tell it is very good where you are. Why would you come back?"

He smiled. It was if a thousand angels lit the sky. I knew he was there. I could see him. I could walk across the green and touch him. This was insanity.

"If this is you, Doug, please give me a sign. You know this is very difficult for me to believe," I said, my atheistic, benighted soul defiant in the face of fact.

Doug just smiled. I was suddenly jubilant. "No," I said. "Please give me a sign.

Doug laughed, a blissful song of delight as sunshine lit the world, the entire world, and the world and all the people in it were good and filled with joy.

"Okay, I'm going to putt now," I said, and flicked the club at the ball without aiming. The ball went unerringly over the bumps of the green, a little left, a little right, and softly rolled into the cup.

I was a believer.

"But why are you here, Doug? Why are you here?"

I knew he had something to tell me but I didn't know what it was. It had to be very important because he had left a place of utter joy to come back to earth. It had to be very, very important.

Despite the wonder of the moment, fear filled my heart. I half ran to the golf cart. I threw the putter in my bag, leaving the golf ball on the green. I sped back to the starter, smiled, and got out of the cart. He would get my clubs cleaned and back in the locker.

I rushed home in a panic. I thought maybe something terrible had happened to my family. I called them all. Everyone was fine.

Doug had a message for me but what was it? I didn't know what it was. I made an appointment with a local internist, thinking the message might have been for me.

It took a while, maybe a year, before I was finally diagnosed and then several years more of pain and treatment including three lifesaving surgeries before I was out of danger. I am sure now that that wasn't Doug's message.

I'm glad he could go back to his new joyful existence. Only he, so good in life, would leave paradise to help someone on earth. He had been so beautiful, so kind and loving when alive. Now I knew he, truly, was in a better place, the best place of all.

I did not believe in God or heaven or an afterlife when I saw Doug but I saw him. He was joyful. I wanted to call his parents and tried a few times. I was afraid they would think I was crazy and that it would be hurtful to talk to them.

I was sane, the sanest I had ever been.

Here is what I know. There is life after death and that life is spectacularly, wonderfully, fantastically idyllic. I know that exactly as I know that I exist and my family exists and the world exists.

I met God. God was in Doug as Doug was in Him. God exists and He is a loving God and good.

I looked in the Bible and found this passage, which I knew was the right one:

"Hear, O LORD, and be merciful to me; O LORD, be my help. You turned my wailing into dancing; you removed my sackcloth and clothed me with joy, that my heart may sing to you and not be silent. O LORD my God, I will give you thanks forever." Psalm 30:10-12

That was at less than two years of sobriety. And what did I do with this miracle? I transformed a message of eternal bliss into gloom and misery. I turned a wondrous gift into a prophecy of death. I was unable to remain in the light: I was comfortable only in darkness.

By my eighteenth year I was better able to see. Slowly, God's light came to shine on the darkness in my soul.

My question: I am told to help others achieve sobriety. My sponsor and others encouraged me to sponsor other alcoholics. Without years of sponsorship I remained in darkness. I thought I had a huge hole in my soul that I wanted to fill. I had no hole, only darkness.

I had no light, for, without intending to, I had blocked the sunlight of the spirit from my life. Through helping others, through prayer, and through meditation, I learned to see. I learned to listen. I learned how to be. My soul was healed and my burdens were lifted.

I am sad to say that I am still not humble. I still am filled with longings for material things. I am often short tempered and unhappy, dissatisfied with my lot in life. I am judgmental and intolerant all too often. I am better able to be a sponsor, but am far from being able to be a good one.

I do the best I can, and it is a lot better than it used to be. I suppose progress not perfection is my mantra, as woman, as alcoholic, and as sponsor, providing that I am progressing forward most of the time. You can't get to be a good sponsor without a lot of experience, and you can always become a better one. At the least, I do my best not to do harm.

Understanding the infinite: I can't measure the ocean with a six inch ruler but I don't conclude that the ocean doesn't exist. My mind is too limited to grasp the infinite, let alone understand it.

Gilbert Ryle, a noted philosopher of his day, made fun of someone who came to Oxford University and kept asking 'Where's the university?' His point was that there was nothing other than the buildings and the grounds and the people.

During the Second World War the administration moved Oxford to Canada. Young people studied there. Older people taught there. Degrees were rewarded and knowledge was acquired. Mr. Ryle was wrong.

The University was more than the buildings and the grounds and the people.

Maybe God is like that. Maybe God is like the wind that you only know exists by its effects on trees and leaves and flags flying in the breeze. I've seen the effects of God on my fellow alcoholics. They are transformed. I have been too.

The important thing is to keep an open mind and know that you can get sober if you believe in some higher power and live by spiritual principles. I guarantee that your beliefs will change as you continue on a spiritual path. Where you will go, I do not know, but you will be in a better place.

I'm sure of that.

For me, life was strange. My inventories showed me I held many mutually exclusive truths. I was the victim of conflicting perceptions, judgments, and beliefs, which coalesced into a booming, buzzing confusion. When I pray now and meditate, the noise disappears. The world is quiet. In that peace I can hear God.

CHAPTER EIGHTEEN: A VERY SHORT DISCUSSION OF THE STEPS:

Steps One, Two, and Three

I see my situation. I have no power over alcohol and I can't manage my life. I learn that I can't distinguish the true from the false. I am demoralized and hopeless. Then the First Step assures me that I am not alone. If I want to change, or stop suffering, or live, I need to get some power outside of myself. I see all the people at the meetings who are sober. I'll just do what they do, which is to put recovery first.

I learned that if I want to stay sober, my primary purpose should be to stay sober and help other alcoholics achieve sobriety. I don't debate this. I accept it and move forward.

    a. Hit a point of incomprehensible demoralization.

    b. Admit my powerlessness.

    c. Know I'm not alone and that there is an answer.

    d. See that AA has worked for millions of people. All I have to do is what they did.

    e. I see that there is a power that will help me, although my concept of that power will

change as I stay sober. I stop thinking of problems and start finding solutions. I need help in finding the truth and becoming sane but it is possible. A lot of people have done it.

f. I prepare myself to act so that I can get the power I need, never forgetting where the power came from and how easily I can lose it. I'm beginning to see that I need to stay within my job description. I have to rid myself of the notion that I'm in charge. I decide to move forward. I'm in AA and I'll do the rest of the steps.

Step Four: I came in here damaged and traumatized. I need help to clean myself up. I need to learn who I am and what's holding me back. I learn a method that will change my life. I also begin the process of forgiveness. That power that helped me stop drinking is in my life. I will not forget that. I find the origin of my fears.

Step Five: I've seen a lot that's wrong with me. I tell my Higher Power, myself and another human being the exact nature of my wrongs. I was looking in the wrong place for satisfaction. I see how my character defects keep me from getting closer to God.

Step Five and a Half: I look back over the Step work I have done and make sure it is complete.

Step Six: I ready myself to ask for help in removing all the impediments to a contented and useful life. I'm so used to doing things my own way that it's difficult.

Step Seven: I ask for help in changing my values and perceptions and removing my short comings. I admit I can't do it alone. I'm starting to become right sized.

Step Eight: Now I have to clean up the harms I've done. I begin by seeing who and how I hurt someone or something. I continue the process of forgiveness. I make an extensive list and go to my sponsor for help. The purpose of the housecleaning is to become of maximum service to God and others.

Step Nine: I do my housecleaning, even if it causes me discomfort. I ask my Higher Power for strength and direction and ask my sponsor for help. If I don't, I may cause more harm than good. It doesn't matter if I'm forgiven. It doesn't matter if it doesn't make me happy. That is not my goal.

Step Ten: I continue doing the first Nine Steps whenever I'm upset. I pray that God's will (or Higher Power's) be done. Not mine. Every time I'm disturbed I remind myself that I'm not in charge. I don't forget to admit when I'm wrong. I may have to say I'm sorry. I may owe an amends. Whatever I do, I do it promptly. Step Ten is a way to continue to do the first Nine Steps as a way of life.

Step Eleven: The Inventory is so important that I check up to see if I've done it completely before I go to sleep. In the morning I ask for help in clearing my thinking, so that it remains sharp, without undue influence from me. I pray and meditate to remove the noise in my head, the truths that are lies, and the misperceptions that lead me astray. I try to get closer to the power that has gotten and kept me sober.

Step Twelve, The simple formula, which I had thought silly, that is, what my primary purpose is, was the beginning of a new way of life. I have had a spiritual awakening as the result of the Steps. I practice the principles of the Program and carry a message of depth and weight. I had been promised to be happy, joyous and free. That promise came true.

CHAPTER NINETEEN: THE STEPS IN MORE DEPTH BEGINNING WITH STEP ONE

Step one-'We admitted that we were powerless over alcohol-that our lives had become unmanageable.'

I think the First Step is the most difficult for the sponsor. I don't find anything written on how to take this Step in the *Big Book*. I think that's because there is nothing to say. You either see or you don't.

Many of the women I sponsored wrote very comprehensive autobiographies for their treatment facilities. They detailed what they did, who they hurt, and the consequences of their drinking. It didn't convince them they were powerless over alcohol. It didn't stop them from drinking again.

A counselor told one of my sponsees she had done the best First Step he'd ever seen. She showed it to me proudly.

I asked her where the 'We' of the Step was and added, 'By the way, do you know what the dash means? 'We didn't do that,' she told me. 'Is it important?'

'Yes, Virginia, there is a Santa Claus, and yes, it's important,' I told her.

In the *Big Book*, Bill Wilson described his feeling of self-pity and woe. He admitted that alcohol was his master and that he was doomed. He didn't stop drinking. Bill was the last person who made this admission WITHOUT the possibility of being able to stop drinking because of Alcoholics Anonymous. At that time there was no 'we' to sustain him.

One way of looking at the First Step: I believe that the 'we' is the most spiritual word in the entire *Big Book*. The dash is telling me that even if I don't drink, I can't manage my life. The 'we' were the first almost hundred alcoholics who got sober when the book was written. Actually, there were ninety four people who had gotten sober but few of them were continuously sober. I think it could be argued that the 'we' expands to include all the alcoholics who got sober in AA.

The 'we' is what gave me hope when I came into the rooms of AA. Without the 'we' there is no First Step. All there is despair and desolation, as described by Bill Wilson in his story.

People just like me, who drank like I did, and acted like I did, stopped drinking and led good lives. If they could do it, so could I.

Some people want autonomy and freedom so much that they can't accept being one of a large number. Sad, really. They don't understanding that thinking you're free doesn't make you free; thinking you're different doesn't make you different.

I've met many individuals who refused to accept their powerlessness. Some might have stopped drinking. Some returned to drinking. A lot died. Sad to die in the name of freedom when there is a way to become free. Too many individuals could not see their irrationality and believed they were right and the rest of us sheep were wrong.

We had good lives, only went to jail when we brought a meeting in, and were loved by those we loved.

And those who continued drinking: Jails, long term treatment facilities, supervised housing. Now, where's the freedom in that?

I think I can safely say that if I'm an alcoholic and powerless over alcohol, the only way I can get sober is if I find a power outside of myself that is stronger than I. I also believe that I have to lead a life according to spiritual principles, rather than the materialistic values that caused me so much harm.

It is factually correct that alcoholism is fatal, directly and indirectly. It kills the alcoholic and ravages all those around him.

'But that isn't about me': The newcomer agrees with everything you say about the other guy. The only thing is he isn't an alcoholic. Yes, he drank too much and got in trouble, but he can stop whenever he wants and he can take a drink or two now and then.

What convinces someone to accept his alcoholism? It takes what it takes and it comes when it comes. There's nothing you can say or do that makes any difference.

How bad does it have to get?

Pete L described his life while drinking. He was living in an apartment with no heat, electricity or water. He had sold the appliances and the furniture. The toilet didn't work because he sold the pipes. He had a single, dirty blanket that he covered himself with and slept on the floor. One day he woke up and said to himself, 'If it ever gets really bad I'll go to AA.'

That's sort of funny. It took Pete another year plus a jail sentence and a stay in a psych ward before he figured that out that it really was that bad.

I'm just another drunk. I'd been lying to myself about how much I drank, what it did to me and what it did for me. I can't explain how I went from an occasional half a glass of wine to a bona fide fall down drunk. I did though.

Pete had a very low bottom. He didn't see he had a problem.

I came to a point where I saw that I had a problem, that I had no power and couldn't manage my drinking or my life, but it happened after I came to AA and got sober. Some say we've been graced with the ability to see. We can see without seeing. Some say we got 'sick and tired of being sick and tired.' Maybe we finally hit bottom. Sadly, some who have seen the truth lose the insight. They 'forget' how bad it had been.

Dr. Silkworth, in 'The Doctor's Opinion' in the *Big Book*, said the alcoholic could not distinguish the true from the false and thought his way of living was the only normal one. That's another way of saying that the alcoholic cannot see. It's a way of saying he's crazy. He doesn't know what's real.

I believed that I was doomed. My life was horrible and I felt miserable. I kept saying 'It hurts to be me.' It did. I have no idea why I was willing to do whatever it took. I didn't think I was an alcoholic and I didn't believe in God. The *Big Book* told me it would be good for non-alcoholics as well. I believed that until I was finally able to see that I was an alcoholic.

When I got sober I had no trouble staying sober. That made me think I was doing it myself. Still I stayed, mostly because I understood that there was something very wrong with me, drunk or sober.

I made a promise to myself that I would do AA fully and completely for one year and then I would decide if I'd give up the Program. It's been more than twenty years and I'm still in AA. I didn't fake anything. I looked to find someone who was staying sober and did what he did. It worked very well, not only about not drinking, but about having a better life.

Admitting you have a problem is good but it won't solve anything. Some deny the truth of what they have experienced or forget it. Drinking a lot may result in permanent brain damage, making rational thought impossible. Others just drink.

The alcoholic is 'different in mind, body and spirit' from normal drinkers

Neuroscientists have found that the brain of an alcoholic is dissimilar from normal drinkers and teetotalers. The alcoholic smells or sees alcohol and becomes obsessed with the idea of a drink. He has to have that drink. No matter how bad things had been before, the alcoholic must take the drink.

The part of the brain that commands the person to take a drink is not the part of the brain where rational thought resides. Thus, believing you shouldn't take a drink won't stop you from taking a drink. Appeals to reason will not work, because another and very different part of the brain is involved. That's part of the powerlessness. We can't will ourselves into being sober. We can't convince ourselves not to drink.

Give up trying to convince someone that alcohol is bad for them, even in the short run. The problem for me, and for any sponsor, is how to convince someone that he's an alcoholic. I've learned you can't. All the autobiographies and all the psych-social histories of someone's life don't convince anyone. Well, they do. The counselors believe it. The families believe it. The only one who doesn't is the one who can't give up drinking.

Times have changed. At the time the *Big Book* was written it was taken for granted that everyone entering the doors of AA believed they were powerless over alcohol and couldn't manage their own lives. Bill and Bob were taking new people through the first three Steps before their first AA meeting.

Some scientists are upset that AA defines an alcoholic as someone who is powerless over alcohol. 'AA,' they contend, 'is teaching weakness.'

'I'm sorry you feel that way,' I reply. We're not teaching weakness, we're just acknowledging it. We need a power outside of ourselves or we can't stop drinking.

This isn't theology or religion. It isn't psychology or learning to understand yourself better. It's just the facts of life-nothing about God at all.

Neuroscientists, psychiatrists and many rehabs are not convinced that AA has it right. They have 'statistics' to back them up. One more time: Do they have statistics on the number of people who followed the directions in the *Big Book* and stayed sober?

Scientists have statistics that show that AA doesn't work. One reason the success rate in AA is so low is because a lot of the people in AA are court mandated and don't want to be here. Also, very few people, these days, have a clue as to the solution of the problem. It takes Twelve Steps, time and a lot of work. It requires doing things which you don't want to do. You find yourself doing things you absolutely are sure won't work. Above it, it takes courage.

WILAA: 'It takes balls to stay sober,' says a friend of mine with fifty two years of sobriety.

That is, simply, the truth.

More of my story

I was standing at a podium, four years sober, speaking for someone's seventh anniversary when I suddenly saw the progression of my drinking. 'Oh no,' I thought. I was an alcoholic. I was too weak to look at myself. I was too weak to see the truth.

When I took my First Step, I lied. Fortunately, that didn't matter. I was doing what I had to do, and that was a lot more important.

Here are the Principles of the First Step

My way stinks.

If there is something that I feel is essential for me to do, something I just have to do-DON'T DO IT!

Conversely, if there is something that I just can't do, and I don't even have a reason why, JUST DO IT.

I'm not all that. Stop thinking of myself as the center of the universe. I'll be a lot less tired if I don't have to solve the world's problems, and be a lot less frustrated too. In case I haven't noticed, I don't even have the power to take care of myself, let alone the rest of the world.

Stop figuring everything out. Save myself the trouble and just find someone who has the answer to your problems.

Ask what to do. Listen. Follow the advice. Sure I can read and study the *Big Book* but don't forget I need input from someone else as well.

Using my brain is good; using my feet is better.

Excise 'Yes, but' from my vocabulary.

Try to be as honest as I can be. DON'T LIE. Don't be slimy.

CHAPTER TWENTY: STEP TWO. 'Came to believe that a power greater than ourselves could restore us to sanity.'

I glad I did the Steps quickly. Once I saw that I couldn't get myself out of the hole I dug, I admitted there was nothing I could do. I could say that I was restored to sanity at that point. I knew I might die if I kept on drinking and I knew I could do nothing about it. I could indeed distinguish the true from the false.

A Power greater than I is the Power that got me sober and keeps me sober. This isn't a question of faith. The AA meetings furnish quite a bit of empirical evidence. I go to a meeting and see people in the rooms. Remember, I promised to look and try to see. I stare into the eyes of a newcomer and think 'nobody home.' In a few weeks, or maybe months, the individual is laughing, talking and participating in the meeting. I can see his soul through his eyes and his soul is smiling.

I know I can't stop drinking. These people were just like me and they have stopped, for a month, a year, or multiples of years. It isn't faith I need, it's a spirit of adventure, a spirit of experimentation, and courage. The method is experiential, not cognitive or religious

The only faith I need is that what worked for others will work for me.

It's just like Step One. You can't see until you see. What I tell people about Steps One and Two is that they should do the best they can and move on. Things will get clearer.

In the early days of AA it was taken for granted that the new member had done the first two Steps. Often Bill or Bob would do the first three Steps with a man before he came to his first meeting. It was short and sweet. It isn't like that today. I think they expected more of the alcoholics in the early days.

I saw as best I could. I got some principles under my belt. That was sanity. That was the foundation for staying sober. Sobriety was iterative and incremental. Awareness was as well. I couldn't handle all of reality at once, but I could manage some of it.

I sponsor that way. It works very well. You can't see until you can see but I was seeing more and more all the time. I had to learn not to share my view of reality, except where absolutely necessary. Sponsees have to find their own way.

Some things are self-evident to most people. I've observed that when people want to drink they have many reasons for doing what they do, and none of them make sense to anyone else.

One quick example: many people who have ignored familial responsibilities for years, feel they have to leave a rehab to get a job and take over supporting their family or get enmeshed in little league, soccer, or school work. Really?

It's especially difficult if the family members need help. Of course, leaving precipitously never works. The counselors know it. The sponsors know it. The family would rather their relative would stay put.

One of the principles of the First Step is making sure that if there's something you just have to, have to, have to do, particularly in early sobriety, that something is the last thing you should be doing.

Let's be sensible here. Sometimes there is something a person absolutely does have to do, but it is very rare and usually it's something that everyone agrees should be done.

I continue my practice of the principles of the steps. I practice so that I can do something well. I also practice so that it becomes a habit that I'll perform on a regular basis. You might say I'm internalizing better ways to behave. You might say I'm restructuring my neuronal pathways. All I know is what I do, which is practice the Steps so that doing things in this new and better way becomes second nature to me.

AA has no dogma, no compulsory ritual, no single way to behave, and no common deity. In Step Two the only commonality of the Higher Power is that it has the power to help alcoholics stop drinking.

If we don't see that we're alcoholics we might be a little, or a lot, crazy. That's why we need so many inventories. When I came into AA I had no idea of what I wanted or why I acted the way I did. I had insights and theories but I really didn't have a clue.

I used to try very hard to get people to understand the situation they were in. I don't do that now. I try for a bit and stop. I'm powerless over someone else's ability to face reality. There's nothing I can say or do if a person is determined not to see herself as she is.

So what's a sponsor to do? Bill's Story is a good starting point. Talking about the people who got sober is worthwhile. You can try to make the person see how crazy he is but it seldom works. A sponsor can give worksheets and talk for hours but the sponsee isn't listening. How do you know your mind's impaired when your mind is impaired?

I know people go to Alanon. This works just as well. The experience of working with sponsees teaches me how much power I have. It's the amount of power I have over alcohol, none.

More of the process of AA

I can see how AA works in Bill's Story. It's like a mini-video. Bill relates how he couldn't stop drinking. Then his friend, Ebby Thatcher, invited himself over to Bill's home. In the *Big Book*, Bill describes his meeting with his good friend, Ebby Thatcher as they sat at Bill's kitchen table. Bill and Ebby knew that this was a matter of life and death. If either one of them drank, he would end up in an asylum or die.

Bill was amazed. He had heard that Ebby's drinking had gotten so bad that he was in a mental institution, probably for life. Ebby walked into Bill's house, clear-eyed, smiling and sober. Bill couldn't believe his eyes. Ebby sat down at Bill's kitchen table and explained 'I got religion.'

Bill's heart sank; first a drunken nut and now a religious fanatic. Bill was no friend of religion.

Bill had a moment of moment of clarity. Ebby had found the power to stop drinking. He was sober and he was happy. Bill couldn't deny the evidence of his own eyes: whatever Ebby had really worked.

The telling line is that Bill saw Ebby. Ebby had the power to stop. It didn't come from him. In the old days Ebby had no power and neither did Bill. Bill was ready to listen.

Ebby told Bill it wasn't religion. Some men had visited, Ebby told Bill, and given him a way to stop drinking. He had to follow spiritual principles. They included being honest about his problems and what he'd done wrong, correcting the mistakes of his past, getting closer to the power he needed to stay sober, and helping others get sober by telling them about his new way of life. That was why he came to see Bill. Ebby didn't judge Bill. He didn't tell him what to do. He just told him what he had done.

I've seen the insanity of the first drink many times. People crawl back into AA after having been sober for a number of years and then drink. Sometimes it's because of dental pain, sometimes surgery, sometimes life gets too hard. Then they get sober again and after a few years drink again. I met someone who went through DT's three times. Now that's staying power.

Here's an example of craziness. I was sponsoring a woman and we were talking about insanity.

'I don't get the insanity,' she said. 'My life is pretty normal. I think the *Big Book* exaggerates a lot.'

'Oh,' I said. 'You owned your own business. You had a nice car, a driver's license, and nice friends. You visited with your family all the time.'

'What's your point?' she asked.

'You were in jail for eleven months, are homeless and jobless, your family won't talk to you and your only friends are convicted felons and their low rent friends. You really don't think that's normal, do you?'

Well, if you put it that way,' she said, laughing.

Everybody doesn't fall that far. Some people manage to hold on for many years, spreading terror and misery wherever they go, but hanging on, one way or another.

The Second Appendix to the *Big Book* tells us that the best way to stay in ignorance is to have 'contempt prior to investigation.' This was probably first said by Rev. William H. Poole, Anglo-Israel. (The Book incorrectly attributed the remark to Herbert Spencer, who never said it.)

That kind of contempt allows you to do as you please. You may not believe this. That's because you haven't the foggiest idea what your motives are. It's just another brand of craziness.

What can a sponsor do? Talk about the inability to see the craziness in the sponsee's life. Lots of luck. That's why I tell each sponsee to look at people who got sober. I can't define the wind and can't see it. I know it exists by its effects on material objects. I can't define God and can't see Him, but I know He exists by His effect on human beings.

Principles of the Second Step

Stop wallowing in the past or daydreaming about the future. Be here. My life is right now.

Look into the eyes of those I encounter at AA meetings. See if I can find their souls. Do my best to see, hear, and learn all I can.

Ditch the 'I have all the answers' mode. Wake up and smell the coffee.

Look at people who are further along the path of sobriety. Ask them what they did. Do what they did. I won't be like the sponsee that had a lawyer for a sponsor and told her what the law was.

Continue to be as honest as I can.

Vow to get a sponsor and work the Steps as she sees fit.

Believe that I'm not unique. When it comes to alcoholics, we're all the same. Don't say that I am such a sinner that God will not forgive me. God's forgiveness is irrelevant to the process.

Check to see if I'm drifting back into craziness by doing daily inventories. Remember my difficulty in distinguishing the true from the false.

CHAPTER TWENTY-ONE: STEP THREE: 'Made a decision to turn our lives and our wills over to the care of God as we understood Him.'

I really need a sponsor here. Otherwise things get too complicated.

The short form of Step Three is (a) I couldn't stop drinking; (b) I found something that worked for others; and (c) I decided to try it.

I said I'm in and I meant it. That kept me mo++ving forward. I think my Higher Power was the process of AA at that point.

After I'd been sober for a while, I revisited Step Three and found it much more complex.

A Sponsor has a lot more to work with in the Third Step. She helps set the pace of how deep to go and when. Some people want to define 'God.' This can be fine or it can be an excuse to keep on the Third Step and not do a Fourth Step Inventory.

Don't forget the cell phone with only one number on it. The analogy is clear. Everyone would say that self-reliance in the extreme is crazy but it pops up again and again. With time the feelings for self-domination and control are less urgent and the perceptions less intense, but they will return, particularly in times of stress or fear.

What God is and what God's will is are talking points. What does it mean to turn something over to God? How would we do it? I'm not sure I know.

What I'm sure of is turning something over to some external power was beyond me when I did the Third Step for the first time. All I had to do was make a decision to do the rest of the Steps and that's what I did.

You see it's not about what I say but what I do. When I make a decision it's about making a promise and keeping it. Parts of my brain stop me from going forward or propel me in a different direction. The problem is that my conscious and unconscious desires are at war with each other. I stand in the battle field, confused and unable to proceed.

Pathology trumps rationality.

Deciding to practice spiritual principles as a way of life, means practicing acting in ways that are spiritual and not materialistic. My goals are 1) to carry the vision of God's will in all my affairs and 2) to practice the presence of God.

Do I ever decide to act selfishly? We all do. That's the human condition. I can recognize what I'm doing and laugh at myself. Then I do what I have to do.

Sometimes my decision is about getting out of trouble. Do you remember the people jumping out of windows from the World Trade

Center on September 11th? Horrific, but they figured anything was better than burning alive.

I made a decision to follow God's way because I felt like I was burning alive. My soul would die if I didn't do something. I decided to learn a new way of life. *Mirabile dictu.* I wasn't leaping to my death. I jumped into a safety net. I knew that. I saw how millions of others made doing God's will their primary purpose and flourished.

I begin with a decision but hope to end in joy. I begin with grace, that undeserved gift from God. I think it is a loan.

Part of making a decision is due diligence. I have to find out what's involved and what the consequences of my decision would be. That's called making an informed decision. Once I've done that, I can proceed.

The decision to turn my life and will over to the care of God in Step Three is one which grows in intricacy and depth as I stay sober. I came back to my decision again and again. I didn't do it all at once because I couldn't.

You could probably write a doctoral dissertation on the meaning of the Third Step. I truly am keeping it simple.

WILAA: *After I've gone through the Steps, my understanding of them grows.*

I may understand that self-reliance doesn't work. I may intellectually understand that I'm not in charge and shouldn't act as though I were. The problem is that understanding something and believing it are two very different things. Knowing I should do something and doing it are likewise non-related.

Think of all the people who want to lose weight. I think the statistic is that 95% or more of people who go on a diet gain back all the weight they lost and more.

Step Three helps me see that I can't 'just say no.' The Big Book is very clear: I'm not in charge. If I want to change, I'll have to do a lot more than want to change.

The beginning of change is twofold: first you see and then you make a decision. The rest of the Steps give the instructions for implementing the decision.

Take this on faith: start small. Spirituality comes from subtraction (your ego, your dishonesty, your selfishness). Step Three is like taking out the trash.

The Set Aside Prayer

'Dear God please help me to set aside everything I think I know about people, place or thing so I may have an open mind and a new experience. Please help me to see the truth about the people,

place or thing. AMEN.' (This prayer comes from the Chapter to the Agnostic.) Please see: http://friendsofbillw.net/twelve_step_prayers.

I've had a few sponsees who were very pious. They knew they were alcoholics. They believed that AA could help. They believed in God. They had a very good grasp of the tenets of their religion. The only problem was that they couldn't stay sober.

They had a lot of trouble finding sponsors. They thought they needed someone who loved God, someone who went to church, weekly or daily, somebody who understood. There are many individuals like that in AA, and the pious newcomers find them. If these worthy ladies tell them they still have to do the Steps, they find new sponsors.

'Stay with the first three Steps for the first year. God will take care of you.' That's something I've heard often. That's a nice thought and might have surface plausibility. It's not the Program of AA.

Some religious women feel that they love God. They can't understand why they're having trouble. They listen faithfully to their carefully selected sponsors, calling every day, going to meetings every single day, and praying a lot. Then they drink. They can't understand why. Sometimes they get DUI's and are sent to ASAP. Sometimes they end up doing a little time in jail. They go to court ordered AA meetings. They believe that all they need is church.

Sometimes they sign the slips that are given to ASAP and not go to the meetings. They keep drinking but make sure they don't drive. One day they get in their cars for some reason or other. They end up in jail for a year, and still scoff at the people in AA. They call them Godless.

AA members call them drunk.

Alcoholics who continue drinking may not be homeless but I've never met a happy active alcoholic.

The Third Step Reality Check

It's easy to believe my little stories. One of the nicest things about Step Three is that the *Big Book* gives me a reality check. After I've gone through the Steps and have been practicing the principles embodied in them, I come back and ask myself these questions, based upon the Third Step Promises.

- *Have I quit playing God?*
- *Do I have a new Director who is the Father, while are I am His child?*

- *Am I less and less interested in myself, in my little plans and designs and more and more interested in seeing what I could contribute to life?*

- *Do I feel new power flowing in?*

- *Do I enjoy peace of mind as I discover that I can face life successfully? Am I conscious of the presence of my Higher Power?*

- *Have I begun to lose my fear of today, tomorrow or the hereafter? Am I reborn?*

- *Think about what I and my sponsor talk about. Think about myself and how I act. If I spend my time talking about my boyfriend/husband, family, job, or residence, I'm still interested in myself, and my little plans and designs. No problem. I either go back to Step One and go through all the Steps again, or move on to Step Four and do the remaining Steps.*

I had trouble with the 'Higher Power thing', especially being reborn. Here is where I suspended my disbelief. I decided to substitute my concept of a Higher Power which was the Power of Peace, Love and Joy. That worked for me at the time.

Pascal's wager: Pascal was a French philosopher who proposed making a bet that God exists and living as though He does. If He doesn't, you haven't lost anything. If He does, you're ahead of the game.

Why not quit the debating society? You can always argue later.

The *Big Book* tells me that my decision will have little lasting effect, if I don't immediately do Step Four. My deep seated problems won't go away no matter what I decide.

Think of all those people who advocate only doing the First Three Steps the first year of sobriety, and the few who believe you should do a Step a year. Do they think it's okay to substitute their reasoning for the experiences of the millions of people who've gotten sober in AA? I would assume so.

'I turned my will over in the morning and took it back at night.' Silly. This Step is about making a decision.

Many newcomers think freedom is doing whatever you want. That kind of freedom isn't worth dying for, even though you may. Some people think resisting all the directions of others is a sign of freedom. I think it's more like a two year old saying no. Where's the freedom in that?

So many things influence my life: genetics, my brains, my upbringing, what sex I am, the time and place I was born in, etc. My freedom is limited by who and what I am. I already know that what I think

I want isn't what I need and isn't really what I want either. I'm driven blindly by desires for material goods, fame, fortune, prestige, and think I'm rational. Where is the freedom in that?

Maybe the only true freedom I have is in choosing to pursue a spiritual path. I have to find a way of living that leaves me 'happy, joyous and free.' For some it's finding a God that is personal to them. For others it's doing good works and behaving well. Whatever my path, my journey makes me, least partially, free.

AA provides new ways to behave that become habits. It's becoming more mature. By the way, I'm not trying to find my inner child. I'm channeling my external adult. AA does help me grow up.

The belief that things will make me happy is a delusion. I'm out of touch with reality and consequences. I wonder why I still cling so vigorously to things rather than matters of the spirit.

How interesting. I turn my life and will over to You, God. What will happen? I have to trust in the process.

Sex, prestige, and security are what I wanted, although not necessarily in that order. I had all of that. My life was unbearable. Love was the only answer, love of God, self, and others. It wasn't the love of things. That's not love but avarice.

Third Step Prayer: *'God, I offer myself to Thee- to build with me and to do with me as Thou wilt. Relieve me of the bondage of self, that I may better do Thy will. Take away my difficulties, that victory over them may bear witness to those I would help of Thy Power, Thy Love, and Thy Way of life. May I do Thy will always!'*

I remember reading the Third Step Prayer when I first got sober. All I cared about was having my difficulties taken away. I remember that clearly. As for the rest of it? I ignored it.

This prayer sounds like I'm turning something over to God. I think it's more about asking for help in doing that. Notice that there is no Amen at the end of the prayer. I found the reason for that later on.

I believe this is the only Step where the reader is encouraged to write her own version of a prayer.

Make sure you make this prayer with 'complete abandon.'

It's like jumping from the burning building. Some sponsors insist that their sponsees 'know' all about God, or their conception of Him, before they proceed to Step Four. How does that fit with 'complete abandon'? Besides, if God is omnipotent, or omnipresent, or ineffable, how can you ever know Him?

Can you measure the ocean with that six inch ruler? Can you ever understand God, even the God of your understanding? I think Step Three is about you and what you do, not about an intellectual conception of God. Most people are not theologians nor do they want to be.

Even theologians have to take this step with abandon, and, for me, that means not thinking about who or what God is. It means jumping into life and trying to get rid of self-sufficiency. Isn't understanding God a way of being in control? Isn't it, after all, one more way of holding on?

The principles of Step Three:

> When I learn what works in other people's lives, I try it in mine.
>
> Look at all the facts and consequences before making a decision. Sometimes even ask for help. Hold my course.
>
> Learn my job description. Stay within my pay grade. Remember the actor who wants to rewrite the script, do the lighting and tell cast members what to do. It never works.
>
> Find trustworthy people and follow their suggestions.
>
> Do the Program as well as possible, with all of my heart and soul. Don't think a Third Step Decision means expecting God to take over.

For a newcomer: How do know you've finished Step Three? You're on Step Four.

CHAPTER TWENTY THREE: MORE ABOUT THE THIRD STEP

The difficulty with decisions. Three Ladies

1. The lady who swears she is going to visit her children, who are living with her mother. The third time she drives down to see her boyfriend instead of up to see her mother you know she is (a) lying, (b) unable to control her impulses, (c) unaware of her true feelings, or (d) has a very bad sense of direction.

2. The lady who just didn't get how difficult it would be to climb Mt. Everest: she doesn't have the money, the physical ability, or the determination. She might be able to make the climb if she worked hard, trained hard and did some motivation course. Maybe. If she is eighty years old and has one leg, you do have to wonder about her sanity, but, hey, some eighty-year-old one-legged women just hit the summit.

3. The lady who decides to fly to Las Vegas but thinks she doesn't need a plane ticket. She'll just flap her wings and concentrate. Ain't gonna happen.

I don't always know whether I'm a 1, 2, or 3.

That's where reality checks come in. (Reality checks may be called short form inventories). Sometimes I just have to look at the disparity between what I decide to do and what I end up doing. Sometimes I have to ask someone. Sometimes my reality check bounces. If that happens too often, I'm really in trouble. ***Ephesians 4:18 –'Having the understanding darkened…because of the blindness of their hearts.'***

I work on seeing myself clearly. I look at the consequences of my actions and see what I did well, and what I did badly. I think about what I could have done differently. I talk with someone about the divergence from what I think I want and what I end up getting.

I used to call that divergence the unconscious, that which was unknowable. I know differently now. I can see more about myself but I need a lot of courage to look at myself full on. It's just a different kind of frontal nudity.

The Serenity Prayer, attributed to the Christian theologian, Rheinhold Niebuhr, is very useful. The words do not change but my courage, serenity and wisdom can. I can increase my physical strength by going to the gym. I learn to lift by using leverage and by slowly increasing the amounts of weights I use and the techniques I employ. I can similarly enhance my ability to see more clearly. I practice daily and in equally different ways.

I train my capacity for acceptance the same way. How often have I prayed for patience and found some very annoying co-worker slowly performing tasks which I needed completed so I could do my own work. This, indeed, was not the kind of answer I was seeking, but I did learn patience. Thus my prayers were answered.

I used to live the Serenity Prayer in reverse and accepted that which should have been changed, struggled mightily to alter the immutable, namely the character of someone I thought I loved, having no insight or intelligence, let alone wisdom in identifying my problem.

For me modification of my beliefs, perceptions, and judgments requires practice of various disciplines, discussion with a person I trust about my assessment of situations, and courage.

Sadly, the more I need to change the less able I am able to act rationally. Pathology doesn't always trump intelligence, but it generally does. The more pathological I am, the less able I am to engage in healthy activities, which would facilitate modification of my behavior.

And I am not looking for alteration but transformation.

I know radical revolutions of thoughts and deeds occur. I am ready to be transformed.

'People often say that this or that person has not yet found himself. But the self is not something one finds, it is something one creates.'
Thomas Szasz, *Personal Conduct, The Second Sin*, 1973

The actor in a play: The following rarely happens in a show on Broadway. The actors are grateful to have a part and aware that a hundred other actors are standing in the wings, eagerly waiting to replace him. The following, however, does occur in different forms in daily life and is a very helpful analogy.

The actor decides that different words would be better. He speaks these words in the middle of a performance, alternatively confusing and enraging his fellow cast members. He leaps off the stage and changes the lighting, walks into the theater in a new and very different costume, ignores stage directions or changes them, and does whatever else he feels will improve the performance.

Even if his thoughts are correct, his actions are not. He sows confusion, not improvement. And his ideas probably aren't correct. He's looking at this from his standpoint, generally trying to expand his part and aggrandize himself. He's also an actor, not a writer, or director, or costume designer.

He attempts to go it alone, but he is a member of a cast and is acting outside of his job description. Self-reliance is not merely inappropriate here but leads to confusion, poor performances and maybe loss of a job.

Well, he could, quietly, go to the director and make his thoughts known. The director, perhaps after consultations with the writer, lighting director or costume designer, will say yea or nay.

That's it. The actor has made his thoughts, wishes, desires, foolish fancies, or well-constructed, useful suggestions known. Again, that's it. Move on, actor, or move out.

All suggestions are not followed, or, sometimes, not even heard. Sometimes the answer to a prayer is silence. That's the way it goes. Move on, actor, or move out. Move on, honey, or be prepared to take the consequences. They won't be pretty. Then again: 'Perhaps the truth depends on a walk around the lake.' Wallace Stevens

CHAPTER TWENTY-THREE: THE FOURTH STEP: Made a fearless and thorough inventory of ourselves.

WILLA: The Fourth Step gives us a method which we'll practice for our entire lives, namely, rigorous self-scrutiny.

It began my transformation from a frightened, angry, broken female into a compassionate, kind and loving woman.

I did my first Fourth Step in rehab, a California Fourth Step with hundreds of questions. It got me very depressed. I did my second Fourth Step two months later, sorta, kinda, by the *Big Book*. I wanted to use my computer because my handwriting was so bad. My sponsee said no. I dutifully went off, read the *Big Book*, wrote the Inventory by hand, and did a terrible job.

My sponsor had a lot of problems at that time. Her new restaurant was failing. Her husband, a heroin addict, had relapsed. She was pregnant. She told me that she just couldn't sponsor anyone because she had too much on her plate, so we never did a Fifth Step. It seemed reasonable to me, but I was four months sober. I had no idea she was not following the AA way, which is to do more in stressful times, not less.

Should we call it the Tao of AA? We could but one of the principles of Alcoholics Anonymous is keeping things simple (and unpretentious) so we won't.

I found another sponsor and did the Fourth Step with her. She sent me on my way, saying 'Read the *Big Book*. It's very clear.' I didn't have a clue. I was miserable, though, because I saw what a loser I was. I didn't believe in God. I didn't know how I could change. My God was 'the process of AA' and I assumed doing the Steps would help me. I missed the origin of fear and the need to forgive others.

I did another Fourth Step at three years of sobriety, which was better but not fearless, thorough or searching, and another one a year or so later. Several years later I was in a *Big Book* Study Group. We did the Fourth Step according to the *Big Book Awakening Work Book*. You can find it at thejaywalker.com.

Later I went over my last inventory with my sponsor. It was very painful. I've done a few more inventories, a lot of mini-inventories on specific issues and countless Tenth Step inventories.

Helping someone do a Fourth Step

I've heard a lot of Fifth and Tenth Steps and appreciated the courage of my sponsees. I've told them so. Some of my sponsees came

236

from wealthy families. Some came from living in a series of foster homes and having nothing and no one to love them. Most came from somewhere in between. They all wanted to find out who they were. They all wanted to change. They all wanted, most of all, to stop drinking.

I wasn't a substitute mother. I wasn't a cheerleader. Most importantly, I wasn't a critic sitting in judgment.

I told a few of my embarrassing moments so my sponsee would know that we were doing this together. I listened to what she said without out disapproval, condemnation of censure. I listened and began to care about her, as I began to care about all my sponsees.

They got what they got out of it. They were looking for insights and they found them. More importantly, they found truth. I received a great deal. I became a person who listened. I cared and I became kind.

That was another gift that AA gave me.

I was a critical, fault finding individual who felt that I had to be smart. I really liked it if you were very intelligent too. It was my essence. When I went over the Fourth Step and heard my first Fifth Step, I was kind and encouraging without really trying. If that doesn't prove God exists, I don't know what does.

None of my inventories showed me how abrasive I was, and how destructive to people's self-confidence and self-esteem. Working with a sponsee on the Fourth and Fifth Steps prevented me from acting that way. It would be a betrayal of her trust. I was learning who I was and what I could be.

I can't tell a sponsor what benefits she will receive. I can tell her though that she'll have the unique experience of walking with a frightened individual and giving her support, hope and courage. I can tell her that the benefits she will receive will be enormous. In this interaction, the sponsor becomes acutely aware of her character flaws, and very interested in stifling them so that she can be a help rather than a hindrance.

There's a lot about God in the Fourth Step: I want to mention something I didn't look at for four or so years, namely the presence of God in this Step. My first sponsors didn't think it was important and didn't bring it up. I read the *Big Book* assiduously, but, like my drinking, I just didn't notice.

Again, I didn't do the Fourth Step very well, but I did it well enough to keep going. I couldn't see what I couldn't see until I could see it.

How to do the Fourth Step according to the *Big Book*: The *Big Book* tells you to make three columns and go back through your life. I can begin in the present. I've found it's more effective if you start with the past and work your way forward. To paraphrase Eugene O'Neill, the past is contained in the present and the future as well.

WILAA: Patterns of behavior are more recognizable if we start with our early childhood and go forward, but whatever works is fine.

Cheat sheets: You can find a number of 'guides' for the Fourth Step. Most of them are very clinical. I don't object to them as long as you do it the *Big Book* way first. This is a good method to use throughout your life. Writing things out makes them more personal. Checking things off is clinical. It helps me avoid my feelings. I can't imagine doing an inventory according to *The Twelve and Twelve* every time I get upset. I know people who say they do.

The *Big Book Awakening Work Book* I spoke about earlier shadows the writing in the *Big Book*. (You can get it at thejaywalker.com.) This is a great book to use for a step study group. It is also helpful for a sponsor to use with a sponsee in her Fourth Step, provided the sponsee has done a complete Fourth Step first.

Please note that the Fourth Step examples in the *Big Book* are not very detailed. Short and sweet works very well.

Are there three columns or four?

There is a debate as to whether there are three columns or four in the Fourth Step. The *Big Book* tells us that after we finish the three columns we go back and write down our part in things, whether anger, selfishness, self-centeredness or fear. You would think that would be the Fourth Column, but-whatever.

As long as you talk about your part in things, it doesn't matter whether you designate it the fourth column, or just make room for the column. It is more convenient to make four columns so that you can see the whole resentment in one place.

WILAA: Step Four enables me to look at myself clearly, feel my emotions in real time, and stop being a victim.

People delude themselves and don't know it. Otherwise it wouldn't be a delusion. Because I was so good at reading other people I thought I understood myself. I didn't. I can be objective about everything but me.

Proposal for a new kind of therapy

(1) Videotaping a person's surroundings and filming him for two weeks. (2) Cutting the tape until it's eight hours long. You might hit some confidentiality issues with the incidental players but most people won't mind. The director must not insert himself into the action. Then show the final product to the patient-participant.

The Fourth Step is like that, up close and personal. It's not a video but it helps you see.

This Step brings up a lot of distressing memories of what others did to me and what I did or failed to do. I believe that if the Inventory isn't painful, I'm not getting it right.

The Bankruptcy Theory of the Fourth Step

When you file for bankruptcy you do it so that you can have a chance at a new life. Your debts are "forgiven" and you start over with a fresh start. If you forget to list a debt in your court papers, that amount of money is not forgiven and must be repaid.

The Fourth Step is similar. It is the beginning of being forgiven. God removes the defects of character and also the feelings of guilt and shame but if you "forget" to list your wrongs, they stay with you. You will probably drink again. You will definitely be filled with shame and guilt.

To Review: Why are we studying the Steps? Why do we practice the principles in the *Big Book*? Sure, it is so that we stay sober, but if that is all you see, think a little more.

When I took Step Three I was cautioned that my decision would have 'little lasting effect' unless at once followed by trying to get rid of the things in myself that had been blocking me. Drinking was a symptom of my disease. I had to get down to causes and conditions.

Some results of this Step

- I won't have to have temper tantrums or explode with all of the resentment and anger stuffed inside.
- Secrets will be acknowledged and I won't have to drink to forget. I'll identify my need for self-reliance, and see how it has hurt me.
- I'll be able to know what I'm feeling in real time-and able to check motives. I will know why I am doing what I do and look to see if my actions will get me what I really want.
- I enter into the process of forgiveness. I am being forgiven and I learn to forgive.
- I'm beginning a lifetime of inventories. I'm learning the best format for looking at myself.

Eventually I had the method down pat. I wasn't totally honest when I did my first two Fourth Steps. Doing a lot of Ten and Eleven really opened my eyes.

Business inventory: If we own a store, we have to look at our merchandise: do we have enough of what we need and too much of what we don't? Think the Gap-how about having 200 pairs of jeans in size 2 and 200 pairs of jeans in size 20. It looks like we have plenty of jeans. They're filling the store.

We just don't have the sizes that will sell. We've got to get rid of damaged goods, even if we like them and they're our size.

That's how it is with the inventory. I want to find the flaws in my makeup which caused my failures. The *Big Book* suggests starting with resentment. Resentment means blame and mostly blaming others. That way I can keep on doing what I want. When I'm resenting someone else, I'm not looking at myself and don't have to change. It's always about what someone did to me or what I think they will do to me later on.

Instead of looking for help from God, I am concentrating on others, what they did to me, and what they should do now. That way I don't have to look at myself and that way I don't have to look at my situation as it is in real time. That means I can stay in my problems and keep doing what I am doing instead of finding the power to change.

Resentments keep me in a place where alcohol and drugs are the only answer. Once I see my part in things and see exactly where I am, I see a way out and drinking and drugging stop being solutions.

How am I set free from the bondage of self? How do I learn to forgive myself?

I trusted no one, certainly not a being I didn't believe in. I began by trusting the process of AA and doing an inventory of my resentments. I moved on from there. I began by forgiving those who had hurt me and then I was ready to forgive myself. It was all intellectual for me until I worked with a sponsee and moved from my head to my heart.

The time has come not to learn, not to think, not to act, but to be. I can only do that by learning, thinking and acting.

I am learning who I can be. I must learn how to be that person.

The Fourth Step helps me accept who I am and what I want and gives me the courage to face my situation and the truth about myself. Checking motives and being willing to forgive others and myself becomes part of my life.

How do we get rid of the feelings of resentment, shame, guilt, remorse, despair? Just follow the instructions in the *Big Book*. Take a large piece of paper and put four columns on it.

The Resentments Inventory

The First Column: We list everyone who ever hurt us. We list all institutions (like schools, Churches, youth groups, Governments, the police) that have caused us harm. We list all the people who have made us angry or resentful.

Stop for a minute: Look at the people who have harmed us. They look pretty sick. We need some help here because if we don't we will be filled with anger and rage and probably not be able to continue.

The Fourth Step Prayer in its entirety

> *'We realized that the people who wronged us were perhaps spiritually sick. Though we did not like their symptoms and the way these disturbed us, they, like ourselves, were sick too. We asked God to help us show them the same tolerance, pity, and patience that we would cheerfully grant a sick friend.*

When a person offended us we said to ourselves '…This is a sick man. How can I be helpful to him? God save me from being angry. Thy will be done.'

This prayer is a form of forgiveness, helping us let go of our pain.

The Second Column: Now we go back and next to each name write down what the person did to us. (In a few words please.) Think of the man who told someone's wife about her husband's mistress. Sure the husband resented him. Mmmmh. Maybe he shouldn't have been unfaithful. It might have made his life a lot more peaceful.

The Third Column: We write down what was affected; self-esteem, security, sex relations, ambitions, personal relationships, and the way people look at us in the world. In early sobriety everything is affected. That changes as we become more sober. Then we are affected specifically by specific people as they interact with us.

The Fourth Column (or not): Forgetting what the other person has done to us, we list where we were selfish, dishonest, self-seeking and frightened.

I believe being selfish means you think only of yourself; seek-seeking that you seek to aggrandize yourself.

The inventory is that simple. Even so, I had a lot of trouble filling in the columns. That is why I needed a sponsor. After I listed selfish, etc., I would write a few words saying how I was selfish or dishonest, self-seeking or saying what I feared. I put it on the same sheet as the columns. Some people prefer a separate sheet.

The Fear inventory is based on what I think I'm afraid of. Inserting a Fifth column in the Resentment Inventory helps me see fears in relationship to actual situations. It is not a theoretical endeavor. I see that I am afraid, and what I fear.

That means wherever I've put frightened or afraid or just the word fear in the Fourth Column, I write down (do we dare call it a Fifth

Column? what I was afraid of. I look at my fears. I ask myself how much of fear came because I was self-reliant and trusting myself to solve my problems.

A sponsor may question the efficacy of self-reliance. I would point to areas where I couldn't manage the people, places and things in my lives. I had to have help. This is where the strength of the bondage of self can be weakened.

To get rid of fear

The *Big Book* says the answer is God. That's one of the things I didn't see for a long time. I don't think a sponsor shoving God down my throat would have gone well, but who knows? Maybe my sponsors didn't talk about God because they knew I wasn't interested. Maybe they did and I didn't listen. I don't think so, though, because I would have argued with my sponsor and I didn't argue.

Although the *Big Book* is speaking of 'God' here, let's keep it to the God of our understanding. That would be more consistent and more palatable.

The sponsor's job is to note that fear that comes from relying on myself. After all, if we have to rely on ourselves, it's like that cell phone with only one number. I know that I can't do it myself. If I proceed on the fuel of self-sufficiency I have to be afraid: I am not enough.

We can find mention of self-reliance in all the Steps, and in each case it is to our detriment. If I forget that I don't have the power to stop drinking, I've thrown Steps One, Two and Three out the window. Self-reliance and reliance on God are mutually exclusive. This isn't to say that I shouldn't take responsibility for my actions but at some point I must acknowledge my limitations. Then I work on finding some power outside of myself so that I can function.

> *'Perhaps there is a better way-we think so. For we are now on a different basis; the basis of trusting and relying upon God. We trust infinite God rather than our finite selves. We are in the world to play the role He assigns. Just to the extent that we do as we think He would have us, and humbly rely on Him, does He enable us to match calamity with serenity.'*

> *'We never apologize to anyone for depending upon our Creator. We can laugh at those who think spirituality is the way of weakness....It is the way of strength. The verdict of the ages is that faith means courage. All men of faith have courage. They trust their God. We never apologize for God. Instead we let Him demonstrate, through us, what He can do. We ask Him to remove our fear and direct our attention to what He would have us be. At once, we commence to outgrow fear.'*

Atheists deal with this as best they can. A sponsor can help with that. By the time a person gets to the Fourth Step, the sponsor should have a pretty good idea of what the sponsee is about. That will help immensely. The point is that sometimes the writers of the *Big Book* lapse into the Judeo-Christian concept of God, but okay. We have the right to use the term 'Higher Power,' or 'the Force of the Universe' or 'Fred, as long as that power can get and keep us sober and restore us to sanity.

WILAA: *Sometimes you have a sponsee who says she, or he, has nothing to put in the Fourth Column. She, or he, did nothing wrong.* (Lots of luck, honey.)

I ask my sponsees to pretend they are three or four of the more significant people in their lives, e.g. spouse, children, boss, and best friend. Then the sponsees are to say what the others would say their character defects are.

Reflections on the Fourth Step

We have the work we have done plus preparation for the Sex and Fear Inventories: I want to be careful and not pretend to trust God but continue doing what I had been doing. If I'm raging at people and looking down on them, or hurting them, lying, stealing, and doing immoral, illegal and slimy things, I'm not trusting God. I'm acting badly in God's name. If

I say I'm relying on God and still doing what I had been doing, I'm giving myself a mixed message. Something's missing.

What do I do when I'm afraid and acting badly? The rest of the Steps.

I take comfort in this. Once I realized my part in things it became much more difficult to continue doing them. Telling God, myself and another person my character defects (shortcomings, exact nature of my wrongs are really all the same) is the beginning of having them removed.

The rest of the Steps get you even closer to God and further from your fears.

Isn't it clear now how Step Four helps you with Step Three and why you must do it immediately? So it will be with the rest of the steps.

The Sex Inventory

This isn't about becoming perfect or imposing my moral judgments on others-my place is not to be in charge of other people's sexual conduct. I need to clean up my act, not anybody else's. So I see: 'We all have sex problems. We'd hardly be human if we didn't. What can we do about them?' Now we're ready to do the Sex inventory and it basically is the same as the resentment inventory. It's worded a little differently.

How much trouble did I get into because of sex and my desire for it? Could I tell the difference between love and sex?

Think about the people I had sex with or wanted to (it might be a good idea to put in dates as well as when I met the person and when I first had sex with that person as well as how long the relationship lasted and why it ended.)

Here a sponsor can add some questions that might point the sponsee in the right direction. For example, I might ask (1) what the sponsee wanted from each relationship and (2) was the other person a good prospect for such a relationship and (3) What were you thinking!!!

I put down the Three or Four Columns (plus possible a fifth of what I was afraid of), looking again to where I was fearful, selfish, dishonest, self-seeking-when I were inconsiderate or damaging to the other and when I had aroused jealousy, suspicion or bitterness.

I check to see what I should have done instead of what I did.

I make sure my sponsee writes a paragraph or two about an ideal sexual partner and an ideal sexual relationship.

The Main Questions: Was the relationship selfish? Was it all about what I could get out of it? Was I dishonest about this? How? Why?

I asked God for help in shaping a sane and sound ideal for my future sex life, asking who I should pick, how I should go about finding a mate, partner, whether I should be satisfied with one night stands, whether I understood I had the power to say 'No' or 'Maybe' or just plain 'I don't want this.'

As an AA sponsor, I'm careful to let God be the final judge. I avoid hysterical thinking or advice. As in most things, I stick to the steps and avoid giving advice, unless my sponsee is making a particularly insane choice. Even then I just suggest the sponsee do some more thinking before going forward.

What does someone do when sex is very troublesome? I know the answer. 'We throw ourselves the harder into helping others. We think of their needs and work for them.'

Vital for the Sponsor: I make sure I'm careful to be of service and listen before speaking. I want to engage in dialogue and not give advice.

Above all, I tell, in a way I consider appropriate, what worked for me as opposed to voicing my opinions of what will work for the sponsee.

The Fourth Step resentment list

When I looked at my resentments I saw what a waste of time and energy they were. They kept me from looking at myself and doing the things I needed to do. I learned to have tolerance and patience towards others (even my enemies). I'm willing to take responsibility for what I have done in the past and try to make it right. It is here that I make a simple list of all the people I've harmed, even if there are no resentments involved.

Last but not least

I have to talk about what was left out. Hopefully I've established a close relationship of trust. I can ask if there something that the person feels is so shameful she doesn't want to tell anyone about it. I can ask if there one last secret she don't want to share? Some sponsees want to put this down on a separate sheet of paper and not include it in their Fifth Steps; they'll tell God and themselves, but not anyone else, at least at this time.

To the Sponsee: My suggestion is: keep the secret and make sure you can trust this other person. If not, promise yourself that sometime you will reveal all of your secrets, just not yet.

WILAA: A sponsor can tell the sponsee not to let the one secret she can't tell, sometimes for valid reasons, prevent her from doing the rest of the Fourth Step. The sponsor can explain that people find that they tell things they'd never thought they would divulge to anyone. That's how it works.

WILAA: If you don't do a Fifth you'll probably drink one. I didn't do a good Fourth or Fifth Step in the beginning, but it was good enough.

Step Twelve in *The Twelve and Twelve* talks about that one secret you haven't told anyone. Many people keep some secrets and stay sober. Is this heresy? It's just saying do as much of this as you can and see what happens.

Of course it is better to tell everything, unless there's a statute of limitations that hasn't run yet, but sometimes you can't. I am not advising anyone to keep something from a sponsor, but many people have and it apparently worked out. Do so at your own risk, however.

The *Big Book* tells me that this is a good beginning for I have seen my 'grosser handicaps.' That means that I will have to do more inventory work, mostly because I can't face all of the truth about myself. At least I can see that my way did not work (Step One)-that I was insane to think that I could change anything but that there was Power that could bring me to reality (Step Two)-and that I really was willing to have that Power help me (Step Three).

As I finished my Fourth Step I realized that I believed that everyone was basically honest and didn't tell intentional lies. Now this is strange. I wasn't young and I had been a trial lawyer-enough said. I was giving everyone the benefit of the doubt. Here's what I realized: an honest person thinks every person tells the truth. A liar thinks that everybody lies.

A wise man knows that some people lie and some people tell the truth. When I realized this I was beginning to find self-awareness.

With Step Four I'm ready to move on and admit what are bigger defects are. Looking at myself and seeing the truth is difficult but admitting it to someone else is far harder. The danger of not doing so might make me drink. That's why I immediately do Step Five.

Acceptance comes before change and truth comes before acceptance.

I do not like accepting life's limitations and the consequences of my actions. I need not 'accept' them, but they don't care. They aren't going anyplace.

The process of acceptance: I could consider things like old age and death as negative and try to avoid them by not thinking about them. That is like thinking that I don't need air by not thinking about it. Try as I might, old age and death will come to me. Thinking my attitude will conquer them is foolish.

Accepting them, however, is quite different. I won't conquer them but I will feel more comfortable as I grow older. My efforts to 'not care' are futile and insane.

Acceptance is the only form of not caring that succeeds. I can embrace old age and death only as far as old age and death allows the contact.

The way I begin to learn acceptance is writing down my character defects and then telling them to God, myself and another human being. There are as many levels of acceptance as there are of powerlessness and freedom. It takes a long time to accept my lot and to accept myself. Acceptance is honesty. Acceptance is humility.

As you can see, the sponsor has a lot of work to do here. This isn't being done for what I get out of it. It's really all about the sponsee and how I can be of service.

The Principles of the Fourth Step

- Being honest as I can be.
- Facing life and the truth about myself and others. Checking my motives.
- Being willing to forgive others and myself.
- Not reinventing the wheel: keeping to a simple formula.
- Not lying, by omission or commission, not shading the truth and being as clear as possible. Giving up being the victim

- Learning how to follow directions.

- Keeping an open mind and bringing God into the equation. Always watching for self-reliance when self-reliance won't work.

Not being slimy (again). Some call this the Thirteenth Step.

CHAPTER TWENTY-FOUR: STEP FIVE: 'Admitted to God, to ourselves, and to another human being, the exact nature of our wrongs.'

This is another Step which furnishes an opportunity for immense spiritual growth for sponsor and sponsee.

Part One: Doing a Fifth Step

Alcoholics are dishonest, often leading double or triple lives I thought I was honest until I finished my Fifth Step. Not only was I dishonest but I found that I was self-destructive and afraid.

The pathology of me

I was a woman filled with self-hatred. I thought I was worthless no matter what honors I received and what successes I achieved. I tried to be a good and giving person and a noble soul. I thought I helped others for the sake of doing good, without expecting gratitude or a medal.

When I finished my Fifth Step it became very clear that I wasn't noble, giving or good. I was profoundly selfish. I did things for others to validate my existence. If I did good things for others, I could look at myself and judge myself worthy.

In Step Five, I have the sponsee reread her Fourth Step, write down her character defects and think about them. I ask her to tell her Higher Power what they are. If she doesn't believe in God, no problem. Just pretend there is someone or something listening and proceed. It usually makes for a shorter Fifth Step.

I ask her to write about the patterns of behavior she discovered. I also have her write down what she did that hurt others or herself. I ask her how far she is from the person she wants to be. If she wishes, she can pray for the courage and honesty to see herself as she really is. She then is ready to tell me the exact nature of her wrongs.

I've observed that many controlling people think they need to oversee people so that things get done right. Let's call the controller Sally. Note, Sally has the ability to do those things herself BUT that isn't what's important. Getting things done isn't important, because Sally could do them. She wants someone else to do them. Sally may be a bully and enjoy people doing her bidding. She may be passive aggressive and govern through apparent weakness. I have a lot of trouble with passive aggression. It's like eating Jell-O with your fingers.

I ask the following questions: (Here's where a Sponsor helps the sponsee learn the Steps, work the Steps and practice the principles of the Steps.)

How people respond to the attempted management.

If the sponsee is really the best person to run the enterprise.

I might point out that a part time temp worker rarely has the knowledge or experience to be in charge.

Sometimes the sponsee does have the ability to be in charge but she isn't. She has to accept that. She just does her job to the best of her ability.

I gently suggest that the sponsee has no idea of what is important to her. This is where I bring up the Florida-Alaska disparity. Character defects take me farther away from what I think I want and farther away from what I need.

I talk about how character defects make experiencing God or the Higher Power very difficult.

I hint that if the sponsee wants to be in charge, she is trying to take over God's job. Sort of arrogant. I ask the sponsee if she realizes what she's doing and what the effects of her actions are.

This step won't solve all our problems-and the rest of the Steps don't always solve our problems either. A good Step Five puts me on the right path. I am actually honest with another person and find I don't have to be a saint. I am not so special that I deny my humanity.

The insights I gain (as sponsor or sponsee) convince me that I have to keep doing more inventories. I'll continue to do them as the *Big Book* directs. I've learned more about myself when hearing the Fifth Step of others then doing it myself.

Part Two: The second aspect of the Fifth Step is hearing it

I have an obligation to be tolerant, loving, and nonjudgmental. If a sponsee is blind to her faults, I think about how much I should say and how I should say it.

Often I think the person is very self-centered and personally dishonest. Thinking back to my own early days, I have some stories of my own self-centeredness and dishonesty. Talking about them may make it easier for the sponsee to proceed.

It's not easy pointing out someone's character defects like dishonesty or selfishness. It takes a lot to do it without the other person feel like I'm attacking her/him. It isn't a fine line between telling the truth and punching them in the face. I have to know what to say and how to say it.

Some people are so fragile that anything less than thousands of words about the greatness of the sponsee is seen as criticism. The Steps are the way to become less grandiose and less fragile. A newcomer doesn't understand anything about the negative side of her, and thinks that even a word about her less than stellar qualities is a global rejection.

So what's a sponsor to do? (Less than you want to)

You listen as the sponsee reads her Fourth Step or talks about the exact nature of her wrongs. You learn how to be encouraging and non-judgmental without dishonestly presenting the only view that the sponsee wants to hear.

Think dancer, musician or athlete. I lose myself in the music, the dance, or the sport. My focus here is on communicating insights to someone. I'm not trying to be smarter, better than the other person, or look good to somebody. I'm listening with purpose.

I leave my judgment at the door. I begin to find the words that will convey truth, love and kindness. This isn't easy to do. I have to, for my sponsee and for me. I'm convinced that this is a portal to my transformation.

Bill Wilson spoke about 'emotional sobriety'. There's even a movement in AA which concentrates on this.

I need to be a sponsor as well as sponsee to get the full benefit of the Steps. If I'm doing the steps right, I achieve emotional balance, psychological growth and spiritual harmony. I don't need to do anything more.

Principles of the Fifth Step

- Pick one trustworthy person for confiding secrets. Proceed with discretion at all times
- Work on learning that trust is a precious commodity, not to be randomly distributed. Give up telling everyone everything. This isn't Blabbity Anonymous.
- Try to have kind, loving people in my life. Get help practicing honesty.
- Learning how to have compassion and kindness.
- Learning how to listen and how to speak so that I can be heard.
- Experiencing the freedom of being with another person and not using her/him.
- Beginning to see the spirit of the other and being able lose sight of myself.

The need for external things disappears in this spiritual experience. I experience joy

I try to expand all of this to my daily life, harder perhaps, but necessary. I practice these principles in all of my affairs, not just when it's convenient.

CHAPTER TWENTY-SEVEN: STEP FIVE AND A HALF:

When one of my sponsees finishes her Fifth Step I ask her to go home and think about the first four steps. I ask her to write a little bit about what she learned about herself in each of the first five steps. I also ask her to write about the principles of each step as she has been practicing them. We go over that the next time we meet and then proceed immediately to Step Six.

I believe that every sponsor should do this with all the steps at least yearly. It's a good spot check inventory of her emotional and spiritual growth.

Here's a sample:

What I learned

Step One: One I learned that I was delusional and couldn't manage my own life, drunk or sober.

Step Two: I saw the possibility of losing my delusions and becoming sane.

Step Three: I learned that it was hard for me to give up control of my life, even though I knew I had no control. I was willing to try AA and see where it took me.

Step Four: I learned that I was selfish, self-centered, dishonest and afraid. I wasn't particularly nice. I stopped blaming others, which was how I had lived my life.

Step Five: I felt the kindness and compassion of another human being, who wanted only to be helpful. I realized that I had never felt that before.

What I practiced

Step One: I stop thinking I'm the center of the universe. That's part of my being as honest as I can be.

Step Two: I look around me with new eyes and see life differently. I don't trust my perception and judgment but do some reality checks.

Step Three: I practice making informed decisions. I give up trying to run the show.

Step Four: I always check my motives and see where I'm selfish, self-centered, etc.

Step Five: I stop telling everyone my personal business. I try to listen to what others say and I do so as best I can, without being judgmental.

CHAPTER TWENTY EIGHT: STEP SIX: 'Were entirely ready to have God remove all these defects of character.'

When I did Steps Four and Five, I became discouraged. I recognized that I had been filled with self-hatred and fear. I wasn't who I thought I was. I was much worse. In my experience, I have had to help the sponsees through similar feelings of depression and pain. After all, they had just found out that:

They had been dishonest with themselves.

They didn't see any way that they could correct the wrongs they'd done. They had lost faith in their judgment and perceptions, which weren't reliable.

They saw that they've been trying to run the show, with no ability to do so, even though the results are poor.

They saw no way out.

Yes, we're back to the twin demons: the inability to be honest and the need to be in control.

WILAA: Dishonesty is not just about our drinking (or overeating, or drugging or excessive sexual behavior). It permeates every area of our existence. We learned that we didn't have a clue, no matter what our age or experience, as to our ability to recognize who was dangerous and what situations to avoid. We didn't know what we wanted, or if we did, were too afraid to go for it.

The *Big Book* talks about a feeling of lightness and freedom, of no longer being isolated, of being part of the wondrous beauty and grace of a fabulous universe after finishing the Fifth Step. Some people feel relieved once they talk about their secrets. Not all feel better.

As far as I can tell, Bill never had a feeling of lightness or freedom. This is one of the instances where Bill uses a carrot rather than a stick to motivate the reader. I think he just got carried away.

I wasn't filled with joy after completing Step Five (or Five and a Half). I was profoundly disturbed. Once again, I felt doomed: I knew my judgment was impaired. What more didn't I know?

I saw that many of my prized attributes were disguised needs for approval or safety. I discovered the deepest darkness of my soul.

Step Six was the turning point. I wanted to change. I wanted my character defects to be removed. Wishing does not make it so. Just think of all the people who purchase lottery tickets.

The sponsor helps the person understand that that being depressed makes Step Six easier. I wanted to change, partly because it was so unpleasant being me and hurt so much. I wanted to change because the good part of me, the best part of me, wanted to have a better life.

If I had known what it would take, I might have returned to drinking. Being good means acting, well, unselfishly. And when I stopped drinking, new compulsions, the so-called soft-addictions sprung up and had to be dealt with.

The rest of the steps take me further along the road. The sponsor can explain that things will get much better. I make sure that my sponsee knows that I've struggled with my troubles exactly as she is struggling with hers. I tell her some of what I've done and continue to do. I don't, however, lay everything out as though I were telling her my Fifth Step. I tell her what is appropriate for her to know under the circumstances.

I've seen a lot of sponsors use their sponsees as emotional Band-Aids. It isn't fair to the sponsees and it doesn't work. Emotional Band-Aids never do.

My unfamiliarity with loving behavior: I didn't know what loving behavior was, because my parents didn't know how to behave and didn't know how to love. When I was in the presence of people behaving lovingly, I didn't recognize what I was seeing. I thought they were fakes. This was a closed system which kept me unloved and unloving.

My parents taught me to find fault with everything and everybody. In my family we all talked behind each other's back. I had one aunt and one uncle who loved me and behaved lovingly but they were quite strange. I thought their shortcomings caused their kindness.

My aunt and uncle's love was what saved me from the self-centered pit of vicious spitefulness of the rest of my family. Their nurturing, flawed though it might have been, kept the best part of me alive. I thank them for that, always.

An early amends I made: I heard that my uncle was dying. At the nagging of my daughter, I flew down to Florida to see him. I had been brainwashed never to change my plans for anyone. I had been trained never to say 'I love you.' I had neglected him because I was too busy. He had always been good to me and I wasn't even going to visit him before he died.

During the long flight I planned what I would say to him. When I got to his hospital room, he was so happy to see me. 'If there was one person who would come, I knew it would be you,' my uncle said.

I didn't give my prepared speech about what a lousy niece I had been. I just said 'I love you.' It was true. It made him happy. It made me happy.

That was my Ninth Step. I told my uncle I loved him.

How do I start to behave better and how do I behave better? You just saw a little bit of how it happens.

Step Six is the rallying point. Six and Seven are the break in the Program, the Intermezzo-the place where Bill Wilson plugged the gaps in the Oxford Program and removed the wiggle room.

I want to have my character defects removed and I pray that God will help me.

Some people believe that you have to list all of your short comings in Step Six. I think I did that in Steps Four and Five.

If you hear someone say, 'The only thing a person can change is himself.' smile and go on with your day. They don't get Step Six or Seven. That's for them and their sponsor, not for you. You're not the Chief of Inventories-R-Us, or the arbiter of what is correct.

I've tried to be a good person my entire life. I wanted to be noble and found I was self-hating. I wanted to be good and found I was afraid. I went to therapists, took anti-depressants, read self-help books, psychology and philosophy, and tried attending religious services. Nothing helped.

My religious phase didn't include believing in anything or understanding anything-about God, myself, or others.

I've said that I'm flawed. Anyone who knows me can tell you that. I make a lot of mistakes. Sometimes all I can do is say 'well that was stupid' and file it under E for experience.

'Progress not perfection' has often been used as an excuse for not acting well. It's a thought used to comfort the flawed alcoholic who's struggling with an inability to change. It encouraged me. I remembered how I had acted and how I could have acted better. I saw how far I had to go. Progress helped me see far I had come.

I've seen a few meticulous people who strive, rightfully, for perfection in their chosen field(s). Trying to be perfect in everything you do whenever you do it comes from a belief that you are truly special, if not spectacular. It is self-defeating. You learn from mistakes, not victories. You learn from failure, not success.

WILAA: *Striving for perfection in all things can be an excuse for not doing anything.*

To sum up Step Six: My character defects prevented me from behaving well and getting closer to God. I readied myself to ask for help in having them removed. I promised myself that I would follow the directions in the *Big Book*, even if I thought they were wrong or didn't feel like doing them.

For years I believed getting character defects removed would make me happy. That may happen, but often doesn't. Being of service to God and others can be a bitch. It's time consuming, hard work and sometimes thankless. It may not make me happy but it will set me free. This step opens the door to a great new world.

There isn't much you can say about Step Six. You want your character defects removed and you can't do it, so you ask your higher power to help. This is where you take a breather. You're getting ready to make a fantastic journey so you take a little time to pack and get ready to go.

WILAA: I guess that's why Step Six is only one paragraph in the Big Book. I take the step and move on. Even so, I want to keep on talking about it.

Principles of the Sixth Step

- Be of maximum service to God and others.

- Do all of the Steps for the rest of my life.

- Watch for the errors of my ways, no matter how strongly I want to hold onto old ideas.

- Remember that prestige, security and sex are never enough.

- Remain honest in my appraisal of what I can and can't do.

- Take a minute before charging ahead. Don't blindly follow my instincts. If I am, pause, say a prayer that the truth becomes manifest and that I have the power to act on my new perceptions.

- Try to keep my self-will in check.

CHAPTER TWENTY-EIGHT: STEP SEVEN: 'Humbly asked Him to remove our shortcomings.'

My shortcomings have caused many difficulties in my life. I was willing to go to any lengths to keep my husband, have a nice house, clothes, and my job. I was looking to get more from these things than was possible to obtain. I wanted them to make me happy. I wanted them to make me feel as though I had a wonderful, loving parent, who cared for me and protected me. It never worked.

I had to evaluate my goals and my values. I had to see they prevented me from participating fully in life. I wanted to be happy. My old values didn't work. Prestige, security and sex were not able to give me what I wanted. Chocolate candy didn't work either.

First I have to acknowledge my misperceptions. Going against a lifetime of habitual behavior, perceptions and judgments isn't easy. I hear all too often that we have to work on ourselves. What I do, again, is act in ways that enable me to change. It takes a lot of effort to implement my insights. It takes some prayer. When I didn't believe in God or doubted His meddling in human affairs and, more specifically my affairs, I began to think of prayer as a way of restructuring my brain.

Step Seven says 'that we humbly' ask God to remove our defects. If my goals are materialistic in nature, I'm in trouble: No matter how much I have, it's never enough. I am, despite my fine thoughts, consigned to seeking ends which cannot ever satisfy me.

I can't do this myself. I can still be driven blindly for my need for sex, prestige and security. Insofar as I'm driven blindly by my desires, I have no clue as to what I'm doing or why. It's an insane way to behave. I'm not sure what 'God's will' is. I do know that when my desires drive me, I am very far from God's will for me.

I didn't know the difference between my wants and my needs. I confused sex with love, and often for a person who wasn't present. I had great convictions. The problem was I believed that what I wanted was what I needed. What the *Big Book* tells me is that I can't change my values without help from an outside power. I may try to fool myself and say what I want and what I believe in. This is all noise. I can't pull myself up by my own bootstraps. I can't work on myself.

It's like being a brain surgeon and operating on myself. It can't be done. For one thing, you usually have to anesthetize the patient before commencing the surgical procedure.

Whatever got and kept me sober is what I pray to. It may be a deity named Fred. It is definitely something real, because I can't stop drinking and I haven't had a drink in a long time.

I don't take pride in my sobriety but I do have gratitude for it. I know that even my immersion into the steps and into service didn't come from me. I can feel good about what I did though, because it was often difficult. This isn't about false pride but the enjoyment in a job well done. It might be a joint venture, but I did my part, and pretty well I think.

WILAA: *Self-centeredness isn't thinking too much of myself. It's thinking of myself too often.*

I came to realize my shortcomings got in the way of my being useful to others. It got in the way of my attaining those goals which enabled me to have what I needed. When I first got sober, I thought Steps Six and Seven were all about becoming happy. They're not, but the thought kept me going for a long time.

WILAA: *An impaired mind cannot fix an impaired mind. How do you know your brain isn't functioning when your brain isn't functioning?*

The Seventh Step is one paragraph in the *Big Book*. I did the first Six Steps and saw that I needed help in changing. I had tried for so long and in so many ways and I basically was exactly where I had been when I started. I first asked that those defects of character which stood in the way of my usefulness to God (or Fred, or Higher Power) and to others be removed by…whatever. I pray now to God, who is a meaningful and experienced entity in my life. That God has answered all of my prayers.

Of course the answer wasn't always yes.

My values are shifting from what I want to what is good for me. How do I know what is good for me? It makes my soul sing.

WILAA: *Humility is just honesty in a more pleasant form.*

So I'm not humble. I try to be honest. That helps me. I know what humble is and I'm not it. I've gotten as far as not pretending to be something I am not, so that you, whoever you are, will be impressed. Humility doesn't mean pretending I'm not good at something when I really am. Humility is accepting that I've been given a gift through no action of my own.

Humility is realizing that I've been given willingness and the focus and intensity to pursue excellence. How can I not be humble in the presence of that power which enabled me to do what I, after years of effort and study, and therapy, could not do for myself?

Humility is understanding that my gifts could be removed in an instant, by disease, accident, or violence. It's also knowing that each person has gifts. Who is to say which is most valuable?

At the end of the Seventh Step, I ask my sponsees what their deeper objectives are. I tell them to think about this for a while, maybe a week or so and put down three goals they wish to achieve in the coming year. I am always surprised by their answers. Can you imagine why?

There's a men's meeting I've heard about. A lot of old timers attend. They bought a large, gold plated loving cup, engraved with the words, 'Humility Cup.' The rule was you had to nominate yourself and the group would decide if you deserved the cup. In their fifty years of existence no one nominated himself.

WILAA: All my character defects derive from my inadequate relationship with God.

The Seventh Step Prayer:

> *'My Creator, I am now willing that you should have all of me, good and bad. I pray that you now remove from me every single defect of character which stands in the way of my usefulness to you and my fellows. Grant me strength, as I go out from here, to do your bidding. Amen.'*

There is no Amen at the end of Step Three. It's just my opinion but I see Steps Three through Seven as part of the process of turning everything over. That's why the Amen is at the end of the Seventh Step Prayer and not the Third.

The Fifth and Sixth Steps showed me over and over again that I constantly demanded more of things and people than they could provide. I wanted the itch to stop but kept using itching powder.

Principles of the Seventh Step:

- Look at what I want and see if this is just more itching powder. Think of the consequences of striving for what I want.

- Try to see myself as the best person I can be and try to become that person. Lose the idolatry of self-reliance.

- Strive for humility.

CHAPTER TWENTY-NINE: ENTERING THE WORLD OF THE SPIRIT- THE EIGHTH STEP: 'Made a list of all persons we had harmed and were willing to make amends to them all.'

Once I stopped seeing everything from my point of view, I saw how much damage I'd done. That was disturbing. I guess I developed a conscience.

'Seeing' is nice, but doesn't get me anywhere. The time has come to rectify my wrongs. This isn't about feeling better about me. It's about doing what I can to fix what I had broken.

Who do I owe an amends: I owe an amends to anyone I had harmed. I do not owe an amends if I had acted badly but did not harm anyone. In this Step I am looking outward, rather than at my motives or feelings. I learn to look carefully at what I did to others. This Step is not about my actions but the consequences of my actions.

At a meeting someone said if he saw somebody and crossed to the other side of the street he owed an amends. I worry more about the person who crosses the street to avoid me.

This Step helps me be humble: I'm not so important. The person I'm avoiding may look at me and walk on by, not even remembering who I am. Let's say I make a joke at someone else's expense. The other person laughs but could care less about what I said. The other person might have a great sense of humor or, more likely, doesn't believe that my remarks have any effect on anyone else. I'm just (like the First Step) not all that. Here's just one more person who doesn't take me seriously.

One more time, Step Eight helps me see who I am in relationship to others. It enables me to see that many actions, perhaps unintended by me, cause hurt or harm to others. Naturally, I look at my actions and see if I did intend them but didn't admit I did. In either case, if I've harmed someone, I owe an amends.

What is an amend or an amends?

Some people say it's changing our behavior. Others, taking a more legalistic approach, talk of reparations or making the person whole. (Or at least as close as possible to what he/she was like before I harmed them.)

The truth is the amends depends upon what I did, how it hurt someone, and what seems to be the best way to proceed. Sometimes it's no more than apologizing or paying someone back the money I had borrowed or stolen. It's a little more difficult when the theft is peace of mind. Giving someone peace of mind is a lot more difficult than paying money.

The idea of a living amends

Some people talk about living amends, namely, leading a decent life and behaving with love, kindness and tolerance. I wonder about that, since living a principled life is the basic element of the AA program. Don't give yourself credit for making an amends when all you are doing is behaving the way you should.

Sadly, sometimes when you have harmed your child badly, the only thing you can do is behave as well as you can. Whether you speak to your child and apologize is something between you, your sponsor and your conscience.

The purpose of Steps Eight and Nine: to help me become of maximum service to God and others

I must see who I have harmed and do my best to restore that person to what they had been before I hurt them. If they have harmed me, I let my anger and hatred go. I forgive the person or pray for forgiveness. The Fourth Step Prayer has always helped me.

Sometimes I justify my actions because the other person hurt me. That's not the way we do things in AA. I look at my actions and see if I've hurt anyone. If I have, I owe them an amends. If having anything to do with this person will cause the other person or myself harm, my sponsor and I find a way to make an indirect amends. No matter what, I have to forgive this hurtful person.

Forgiveness entails being honest about the harm that was done to me, otherwise it isn't forgiveness

Sometimes I'm harmed by not admitting the damage that was done to me. I can't admit that someone I loved behaved badly. Until I face the fact of the mistreatment, I can't forgive the other person. That's because I don't know (can't see) how much I was damaged.

Part of the process of forgiveness is admitting how and why I was hurt, and then forgiving the person who hurt me. When I forgive someone else, I am more able to forgive myself. Forgiveness is a pardon but not a free pass. Someone did something wrong. I forgive them. It doesn't mean I have to love them. It doesn't mean we have to be best friends.

The way to make amends

The *Big Book* doesn't help us much in giving us rules or specific direction in making amends. There are a few guidelines though.

I'm told to ask for direction and power. A sponsor is absolutely necessary in the amends process. So is a Higher Power.

I'm cleaning up my side of the street, not the other person's. Sometimes I have so much bitterness for what 'they' have done to me that it becomes impossible to proceed. That's where I need the help of a sponsor who will guide me towards the forgiveness I must extend to the other and to myself.

I begin by making a list of people I've harmed. It is imperative to go over the list with my sponsor before proceeding. It will get rid of many names and maybe add a few.

The index card method

- Take an index card for each person.
- Write down the person, institution, or other people I've harmed. Write down the specifics of the harm.
- Write down the way to fix the harm. That's the Amend I'm making.
- Put the cards in piles of doing immediately, doing soon, doing when it can or should be done, and not doing at all.

What's a sponsor to do: I did my index cards with a sponsor. I made sure my sponsor had a sponsor. This is real life, with real life consequences. Maybe we in AA are less able to make amends than anyone, but we have to do it. That's why we need a lot of help and a lot of guidance, sponsor as well as sponsee.

I'm very careful with my advice for how a sponsee should do amends. I've seen women tell their sponsees to tell their husbands about their affairs or their out of control spending. I've heard women advise their sponsees to confess everything to their bosses. That may not be a good thing and may inflict unnecessary harm on others.

I've heard one sponsor tell her sponsee to go to all the women that she had talked maliciously about and say she was sorry. Most of them had no idea that she had spoken ill of them. Lovely. You can imagine how the women felt. We don't make amends that would hurt another person.

WILAA: *We can't buy our own peace of mind at the expense of someone else.*

I must acquire a spirit of forgiveness. I'm not condoning someone's actions when I forgive the person. The bitterness and hatred I feel poisons me and continues for a longer time than the original damage. Am I not perpetuating the other's evil deeds when I hold on to my resentments, reliving what 'they' did to me, feeling the venom of the hatred that prevents me from loving myself or others? The deed is over but the pain lingers on. Only I can excise it. I do it by forgiving the other. It is sort of like an exorcism. I'm casting out my anger. I often need a lot of help, although a sponsor might be able to do the deed rather than the parish priest.

Forgiving someone is letting go of the hurt and moving on. This is the Step where I enter the world of the Spirit

I ask for God's guidance and strength and proceed, no matter what the cost to me. I always make sure I'm not perpetuating further harms.

The price of admission to the world of the Spirit is releasing my anger and forgiving the other person

I give up my persona as victim. The cost of the ticket is facing someone and admitting I did wrong, and trying to correct that wrong.

Without that, I can't forgive myself. Self-hatred is as much a killer as alcohol. This is the Step where I learn to forgive others and love myself. It is also an extension of the humility we sought in Step Seven.

Do I put myself on the list? It doesn't matter if I do, or if I don't. When I finish my amends, or at least most of them, I've made my amends to myself. I've cleaned up my side of the street. Now I'm ready to be of service. What more can I do to heal myself than that?

The Twelve and Twelve tells me that the goal is to have the best possible relations with every human being. Sometimes that means I cut off all contact. Sometimes it means that I'm in for a rocky ride and I limit contact. This isn't an automatic one size fits all solution. Each situation and harm is different. The spiritual precept of making things better depends upon the facts and circumstances of each case.

I have a friend who spoke about his amends to his wife. He told her he had cheated on her and gave her a few details. I asked him why he did that because I felt it would hurt her.

He told me that she knew he had been unfaithful. If he denied it or sidestepped the issue, she would not have trusted him or believed him. He had to validate her suspicions, tell her how very sorry he was, and promise not to do it again. This is what I mean about the absence of unthinking, routine solutions. There are no cookie cutter solutions; no one size fits all amends. As a sponsor I have to know all the facts before I can consider suggestions for making amends.

And I know that sponsees, just like me, don't like to tell all the facts. Usually that's because it doesn't make us look good. I have to do it anyway. As a sponsor, I have to be clear and careful, and not do a rush job, to make sure I'm getting all the facts.

The method of the index cards: Don't procrastinate. Write the list, get the index cards and talk to my sponsor. Delay may be fatal so please get started…now.

I do my best to make the person I have hurt whole. When I make my amends I am courteous. I know that walking in with a surly attitude and a lot of anger when trying to right a wrong will never accomplish my goal.

I go in a spirit of peace. Can you imagine walking in and punching someone in the nose when you are trying to right a wrong? I'm sure it's been done. A metaphorical punch? Often.

WILAA: When making an amends I do not go with anger, but I also don't proceed with an attitude of shame. As a child of God I crawl before no man.

I continue this process from the first time I make an amends until the day I die. It is inevitable that I will hurt others even if I am on my guard. Hopefully I'll hurt others less and less often. The consequences will not be as dire.

In the spirit of forgiveness and righting my wrongs, I learn more about practicing the presence of God or whatever my Higher Power is.

I am, again, fitting myself to be of maximum service to God (the power that is the center of my life, whatever it is) and to others. I begin with forgiveness.

I ask for direction-what do I do? I ask for power to do it.

I proceed and do what I should be doing no matter what the consequences to me; after having established that this is the best way to proceed.

We must, one more time, forgive: Forgiveness is paramount. If you look on the Internet you may be surprised to find how much is written about it. That is because the human condition requires forgiveness. If we can't forgive others, we are doomed to experience painful experiences again, and again, and again.

'Forgiveness is God's Way' Matthew 18:21-35

'The weak can never forgive. Forgiveness is the attribute of the strong.' Mohandas Karamchand Gandhi

'Forgiveness is the fragrance that the violet sheds on the heel that has crushed it.' Mark Twain

'I think that if God forgives us we must forgive ourselves. Otherwise, it is almost like setting up ourselves as a higher tribunal than Him.' C.S. Lewis

Martin Buber and the Concept of *I and Thou*. I can treat others as objects to be used or I can love then, When I use others, I have a relationship which is I-It. The tragedy is that this relation is one shared by two objects. I am an 'it' as much as the object I use.

I can never be in a relationship with another person that doesn't have an element of using the person that doesn't have an element of using the person no matter how much I love him. I strive for it to be otherwise, but I am human.

The only relationship that is without ulterior motives is that between a person and God. That is an I-Thou relationship. Both parties love the other rather than use the other.

When I try to do is make every relationship as close to an I-Thou relationship as I can. I look for the godliness (or goodness) in the other and love the other for that. As my love becomes purified by my desire to love rather than use, I become a loving being rather than an insensitive object.

When I forgive myself, I'm more capable of love. If I'm filled with self-hatred there's no room for love of any other person. Self-disgust prevents me from getting close to anyone.

Anger lies underneath disgust and fear underneath the anger. When self-forgiveness vanquishes self- disgust, the anger disappears. I see my fears for what they are: neurotic perceptions of an injured child who doesn't want to be hurt.

The walls I erect are not mere self-protection. They include all kinds of weapons to keep people away, most of which I know nothing about. I have to see who I am and what I do. Then I can see my 'instinctive' actions as foolish, based on misperceptions, self-justification and the need to perpetuate my discomfort.

Inventory reveals my folly. Some external power permits it to be banished. God? Perhaps. The process of the actions of a shared community and ethos? Often.

Forgiveness is a dynamic process which, like fear, feeds upon itself, but works in exactly the opposite way.

WILAA: *The most effective beauty treatment is forgiveness-of others and yourself. The world becomes more beautiful and you do too.*

The hard part is seeing who I've hurt. I want to be noble. I want to be good. That won't happen until I right my wrongs. I don't do this to feel good about myself. I do it because it's the right thing to do. I no longer feel the guilt and shame that has dogged my existence since I was a child.

Ironically, those feelings didn't prevent me from acting badly. My dishonesty afforded me the opportunity to continue with my hurtful behavior. Knowing I did wrong or wanting to do the *right thing means nothing until I act righteously.*

WILAA: *Whether believer or atheist, it's my task (1) to clean up the messes I've made and (2) to practice forgiveness. I'm not looking for it from anybody except from God.*

Remember, doing Step Eight, is preparing me to be of maximum service to God and others. I will get a sense of peace and well-being but that isn't my goal. I keep that in mind. I'm to right the wrongs I've done and move on.

If the person says 'Go away,' I leave quietly. I make amends where possible. If the person rejects me, I speak with my sponsor and find another way to do the amends. When making amends, I may or may not explain what I'm doing and why I'm doing it. I behave with love and kindness. I don't defend myself or blame the other. I do what I came to do, am polite, and leave.

Sometimes I can't make the amends, even though it would give me peace, because it would too hurtful to someone else. Sometimes I can't make direct amends because the other person is too dangerous. I have to use the brains that God gave me, as well as listen to my sponsor's advice.

Principles of the Eighth Step

- Look back and making sure my side of the street is clean.
- Scrutinize my behavior and thoughts to make sure I am enhancing opportunities to be of maximum service to God and others.
- Try not to cause harm.

- Act in a spirit of forgiveness and humility. Get it all done, not just the easy stuff.
- Ask for direction when necessary, from God or other human beings.

CHAPTER THIRTY: STEP NINE. 'Made direct amends, wherever possible, except when to do so would injure them or others.'

If I want to escape the prison of self-will, I have to clear the way. I have to repair the damage I've done before I can move on.

If I can't bring myself to do this, I ask God for help. If I don't believe in God I ask whatever my Higher Power is to help me. I promised to do whatever it took to stay sober and that includes making amends to the people I've harmed.

I'm going to people on a spiritual basis, even when they have harmed me. The first thing I've got to do is let go of my anger. One more time, it's ludicrous to go to someone with my fists clenched and a sneer on my face and tell them I'm going to make amends. Same thing with punching them in the mouth. Not too spiritual.

Making amends prepares me for daily life. Once I've gone to someone I had hurt in a spirit of love and tolerance it's a lot easier to act that way on a regular basis. This helps me towards a sober and fulfilling life. A life of bitterness and resentment inevitably leads towards drinking and away from God.

What does it mean to say 'God forgives you'? It can't mean He lets go of anger. Maybe I'm forgiven when I admit my wrongs and try to do better. I may find peace in doing this; I may not. If my God is the process of AA, the force of the Universe, or the Spirit of Joy, I have even less understanding of what constitutes God's forgiveness.

Maybe it's about having guilt and shame removed. Again, I may not be able to define God but I feel his effects, in this case on me. One more time, I feel the sense of ease and comfort I have been looking for all my life.

No matter, I clean up my side of the street. I might get involved in philosophical debates about the nature of God's forgiveness, but not while making my amends.

What if I've borrowed or stolen from people and don't have to money to pay them back? Making amends is not meeting them and telling them that I'm not drinking and have God in my life. I can't just say 'Sorry, can't pay you back, no can do.'

I can go to them and say, 'I know what I did and it was wrong. I know that I have to pay you back. I don't have a job now but I am going to get one and I promise that I will start paying you back the minute I can. It may not be much, but I will make more money and then will be able to pay you back all the money I owe you-sooner rather than later.'

Of course that means as soon as I start earning money, I begin sending some, no matter how little. I also ask if I harmed the person in other ways than financial I ask if there's anything else I could do to make amends. Many people have many skills that they could use to help someone else even if they don't have money to repay their debt.

It doesn't matter if I'm not forgiven by the person I've hurt. I'm not there to be forgiven but to make things right.

The questions you can't answer but have to

I was about three years sober. The AA meeting was very small and ended early. I was cleaning up afterwards and saw a woman lingering, as though she wanted to talk to me. I smiled at her. She responded somewhat nervously. 'I need help. I have to make an amends,' she said.

'If I can help,' I said, 'I'd be glad to.' How thankful I am that I didn't give a lecture on needing a sponsor or doing the Steps in order.

'I have AIDS,' she said, 'and not much time left. I'm a crack addict. I don't want to take any treatment. I just want to die. I took my fourteen year old daughter with me to a crack house and sold her for a rock.'

'That's pretty bad,' I said. I tried to speak in a gentle voice. What could I say? What did I know?

'Here's what I think,' I told her. 'If you look at the Ninth Step in the *Big Book* it says that **'As God's people, we crawl before no man.'**

'That's what it says. The early members of AA did bad things. Making amends sometimes is trying to fix things that can't be fixed.

'I don't know about that. I know you shouldn't crawl.

'Say how much you regret what you did. Tell her that you pray that she heal despite what you did. Forget about explaining that you didn't know what you were doing or making any other excuses. Tell her that you did it, it was horrible and that you are very sorry.

And the other amend you make is that you get treatment for your AIDS. You owe that to your daughter as well.

She said thank you, I think, and walked away. I never saw the woman again.

WILAA: When you don't know what to say, think Big Book. There's always something there.

I need a sponsor, and I need a sponsor who has a sponsor. I don't get do-overs so I consult with my sponsor if I'm not sure of what to do. And for the times when a sponsor is not close at hand, nothing helps like something from our basic text.

I made my list of those I harmed. I tried to forgive them. I brought my list to my sponsor, who added people I had forgotten, or who I felt I hadn't hurt. My sponsor deleted some names. I may have had a desire to bring about some end (bringing someone in my life, hurting them, or showing them how wrong they were to leave me).

My sponsor and I thought about the best way to make the amends. The *Big Book* is not particularly clear. It doesn't give specific directions.

That's probably because matters of the spirit can't be quantified. Each situation is different and requires thought and care. If there were a list, I could check it off and move on. Frankly, I would like that but it wouldn't work. It's like the Fourth Step: I have to internalize what I've done. It's part of developing a conscience.

The amends process in Step Eight requires a great deal of thought. Who did I hurt? What was the harm? How can the person be made whole? How do I make an amends if it would hurt someone? How do I forgive someone who has hurt me so badly? As a drunk, I could always slide by, not looking at what I had done, or who I had hurt.

Now I'm experiencing what I've done in real time, here and now. It is painful. It's very instructive, though, and hopefully will prevent me from repeating the same mistakes.

Sometimes I'm at a meeting and say something that sets someone off. I don't intend to hurt the person but the person is hurt. If I'm making fun of children being in beauty pageants in a room full of mothers whose girls are in pageants, I might very well owe an amends.

If I say that the meetings in California are great and someone in New Jersey gets upset, I don't owe an amends. It's not reasonable for the guy to start crying. Maybe he's off his meds.

I'm never free of my responsibility to make amends. Step Ten tells me that each day, each time I'm upset, I have to check to see what's going on. If I owe an amends I must make it as soon as possible.

What happens if I've been involved in a relationship where I never asserted my rights and the other person acted badly? Do I owe an amends? Maybe so. Maybe not. Again, it depends upon the specific facts of the specific case.

Some of us adored being victims. In Step Four I learned I chose situations and people that would predictably hurt me. How could I blame someone else, when I was the person who put myself in harm's way. It was difficult to get angry at someone else when I could have prevented the whole thing by not getting involved. That's when my temper tantrums stopped. Weird. Once I saw who the real cause of my difficulty was, I stopped getting mad. I guess I knew, underneath it all, that I was mad at myself, and once I acknowledge that I caused what happened, the anger I felt (really at me) disappeared.

I felt hurt. I felt impotent. I needed help in changing but didn't know how. The resentments I felt towards others had served a purpose that also disappeared. I learned that my resentment was preventing me from moving on and living a better life.

Why do I wallow in self-pity and despair? Why does anyone? Isn't it an excuse for not moving forward? Doesn't it justify my fearful behavior? Underneath my resentment and anger, again, was the corrosive fear that paralyzed me and deluded me into believing others are out to get me. I really believed that my paranoia was being perceptive.

Others have wronged me. Do you know that some of the inmates of concentration camps stood around the camps after the guards left, even if it meant disease, starvation and death?

I can be like that. The war is over. I could say that I have PTSD, but I'd be better off if I found some food and clothing and move on.

Steps Four and Nine set me free

I thought that I discovered my part in my pain in Step Four. Some people do. I did stop having temper tantrums.

I needed to forgive those who hurt me, and for that I needed physical action. When I corrected the wrongs I had inflicted on others, something profound happened. I was finally able to forgive those who hurt me because I understood, viscerally as well as intellectually, that I participated in the harmful activity, either by choosing the people or by failing to let go of my anger.

I was able to move on. I could make decisions rationally. I could see the world as it was and not as I had thought it to be. I was relieved of the bondage of self.

Another philosophical non-issue: how could God, if all good, allow such evil? For me, I care more about getting some food. If God gave humans free will, He gave them the ability to choose evil. The concentration camps were not God's work. I don't think God was teaching the Jews, Gypsies, homosexuals, and the intellectually challenged a lesson.

I hear that in the rooms. God was teaching someone a lesson. I know there are biblical passages which support this, but I can't believe that God causes the death of millions of people to teach one person a lesson.

WILAA: The feeling of setting things right stays with us long after the deed is done. We are truly getting rocketed into the fourth dimension.

The Steps are not linear. When I do Step Nine, I'm drawing on my insights in Step Four. Just as Step Seven is not about becoming happy,

Step Nine is not about feeling good about myself. I make amends to make myself more spiritually fit.

Principles of the Ninth Step:

- Pay debts promptly or acknowledge them and pay them as soon as possible.
- Scrutinize my actions and the consequences of my actions. Remember that remorse is an action word. She who rights the wrongs in her path demonstrates remorse. Wringing my hands, crying how badly I feel, is clatter.
- Listen to my conscience. There's nothing like the Ninth Step to develop it.
- Make my feelings and desires manifest, making sure that I am trying to align my will with the will of God.

CHAPTER THIRTY-ONE: STEP TEN 'Continued to take personal inventory and when we were wrong promptly admitted it.'

The *Big Book* gives explicit directions on how to do Steps Ten and parts of Step Eleven. These inventory steps have a great deal in common with Step Four and, similarly, are about taking specific actions. This Step is a proven, effective, method for dealing with my emotions, my beliefs and my perceptions. I will, hopefully, use this technique for the rest of my days.

I learn to practice the first nine Steps every time I'm upset. I might be angry, resentful, selfish, afraid, or all of the above. I may not know what I'm feeling except that I'm uncomfortable.

The rule is, if I'm upset, I have nine or ten things to do. That's a lot of work but the focus is on me. I only have to be upset and talk about myself. That's always intriguing. I can do it for hours.

I've observed that a newcomer generally believes that his life and his feelings are fascinating to everyone, especially his sponsor. He also thinks he might write a book about his life, or AA, or the Steps. He might, actually, become a substance abuse counselor. (He has so much to give others.) When I at about a year sober I took courses at the New School on

Substance Abuse. I planned to own and manage a substance abuse rehabilitation center. (Talk about grandiosity.)

Should I write out my inventories? My feeling is that it's a very good idea. The *Big Book* stressed the need to write the inventory on paper in the Fourth Step. I wrote my Tenth Step inventories down for a few months. After a while, in most cases, a mental inventory worked as well. I write the inventory if I'm particularly upset or am dealing with a deep-seated, recurring issue. I found that writing helps me internalize the process and the insights I gained: this wasn't just an intellectual exercise.

Basic Tenth Step Directions

Whenever I'm upset, I do a mini-Fourth Step about the situation, with all four columns.

Talk about this with God, myself and someone immediately. (Step Five) Ask that it be removed. (Steps Six and Seven)

I might say the Seventh Step Prayer. I might pray in a different way. How I pray and what I say are my prerogative.

Make amends when necessary. (Steps Eight and Nine) When I'm wrong, I promptly admit it. (Step Ten) If my wrong involves another person, I usually admit my wrong to them, but not always. (This can bring our relationship to a new level. Mostly people admired me for my admission. It is a sign of strength rather than weakness.)

I move on, thinking about who I can help. **Love and tolerance is my code.**

I stop being a fighter and begin being a reconciler.

Sometimes though, it's like going into the wrong office building. It's not about apologizing. I have to recognize I made a mistake and find the right building. Notice that this is emotionally neutral. Making a mistake is not the end of the world. Refusing to admit it could be.

(It's often helpful to think of what I did right.)

I often write down what I did wrong; what I could have done better then; what I can do now.

And there's more, a lot more. The *Big Book* is about inventory, but not as an intellectual exercise. When I finish the Fourth Step analysis, there's a lot more I have to do.

I say, 'Thy Will (not mine) be done'; that's a prayer too

We don't have a common Higher Power. The vision we have is the same though, bringing joy and light into the world. How we do this depends upon us. Again, there is no set of rules. We do what comes to us.

I can be as willful as I want here. It's not about my ego. Will power is great as long as we have the right objective (back to Steps Six and Seven).

No one graduates from AA. Self-scrutiny, prayer, meditation, confession, restitution, and service hopefully continue through the life time of every member of Alcoholics Anonymous.

A cautionary note: a lot of women I've sponsored used the Tenth Step to feel better and do better at home or at work. It's useful but in the long run won't be effective. Using the wrong tool can backfire. Prayer is a spiritual tool which doesn't fit mundane situations. It works best if your mind is in the right place and you're trying to set yourself up to improve your conscious contact with God.

Some Promises

- 'Our obsession with alcohol will disappear…We will recoil from it rather than seek it.'
- 'We don't fight the urge to drink; the urge to drink has disappeared.'
- 'This new state of mind continues as long as we maintain our spiritual condition.'
- I will be spreading less confusion and more harmony in all areas of my life.

WILAA: Part of my inventory is checking to see if I had spread chaos or joy, confusion or harmony.

Read pages 84-88 in the *Big Book*. I think these pages are the most neglected pages in the entire *Big Book*. They are, at least for me, the most important. Please remember that generally we don't 'use' these directions to solve a specific problem or change a particular character defect. The process is one of transformation and how it plays out can't be determined or controlled. The end result will be good, but not in the specific way we wish it to be.

Directions: The *Big Book* has a series of specific instructions, easy to read but difficult to do, actually a lot like running a marathon. The concept is simple. (I put on some running gear, get some water, and run 26.2 miles- easy to understand; difficult to do.)

I've heard people say that you can start doing Step Ten at any time. Certainly you can admit you've done something wrong promptly. Most of the Step, however, requires having done the first Nine Steps, which is difficult to do without having done them. On the other hand, a quick run through of the Steps was all I needed to do Step Ten with some degree of rigor, another reason to do the Steps quickly.

The *Big Book* says we must:

'Continue to take personal inventory...'

I wrote my inventories down at least until I was sure that I had the process down. Even then, if something is particularly troublesome and some character defect shows up repeatedly, writing the inventory down can't be wrong.

'*...and continue to set right any new mistakes as we go along.*' Okay, (1) I have to determine what mistakes I'm making and (2) I have to set them right 'as I go along.'

'*We have entered the world of the Spirit...*' Oh yeah? Well, let me not do a 180 and run out the door.

Great. I'm willing but I haven't been good at it to date. Not to worry, I'll improve.

'*This is not an overnight matter…It should continue for our lifetime.*'

'*Continue to watch for selfishness, dishonesty, resentment, and fear.* 'Here is the hint that makes all the difference: Any time I feel upset, I do a little inventory-who or what bothered me; what happened; what it affected and my part in it. If I'm afraid, I write down what I'm afraid of. I use one line with the four columns, last column, fear, anger, resentment, selfishness. (If afraid, what I'm afraid of.)

That's just the beginning.

'*When these crop us, we ask God at once to remove them.*' That means I immediately ask God to remove them, not ask God to remove them at once. I don't wait. I might say the Seventh Step Prayer.

'*We discuss them with someone immediately…(and) make amends quickly if we've have harmed anyone.*' I wrote the answers down in the beginning partially so that I could bring them to my sponsor because I often forgot the incidents within a day or two. In a few words, I indicated who I discussed them with and maybe what the other person had said.

I sometimes felt that no amends were necessary or needed help in finding the right course of action. This is where I needed my sponsor.

There are at least two ways I do this.

(1) In Step Eight, I find forgiveness of others essential for making amends. This spirit of forgiveness extends to me and to my entire world.
(2) In Step Nine, I seek guidance and power to do what is right, and do it, whatever the consequences, although mindful of not hurting others to achieve peace for myself.

A lot of people stop here. Please remember this isn't therapy. It's not about finding myself or building my self-esteem. Read the black letters.

'We resolutely turn out thoughts to someone we can help' This means I think about whom I can help.

'Love and tolerance is our code.' Doing a lot of amends where I acted with contempt and intolerance serves as a deterrent to continue doing so.

'We (have) ceased fighting anything or anyone.' I look at what upset me and think about how I practiced love and tolerance. I check to make sure I have ceased fighting and what I have ceased fighting.

I understand that I'm not cured of alcoholism and acknowledge that I *'..have a daily reprieve contingent upon the maintenance of our spiritual condition.'* I have to see if my spiritual condition was harmed by my character defects and see if it still is.

'We carry the vision of God's will into all of our activities, asking ourselves 'How can I best serve Thee-Thy will (not mine) be done.

No kidding-in all of my activities.

Mother Teresa on carrying the vision of God's will into all of our affairs

If you are kind, people may accuse you of ulterior motives. Be kind anyway. If you are honest, people may cheat you. Be honest anyway. If you find happiness, people may be jealous. Be happy anyway. The good you do today may be forgotten tomorrow. Do good anyway. Give the world the best you have and it may never be Enough. Give your best anyway. For you see, in the end, it is between you and God. It was never between you and them.

I can't allow myself to be sidetracked by what others do. I act as I do because I'm trying to carry God's will in all of my affairs. I may be discouraged or disheartened by those I love, who do not reciprocate by treating me lovingly or with kindness.

Sometimes I have to remember that I'm not doing anything for the approval of others or their following my suggestions. It's difficult being giving and kind and good when I know the people don't value me or my efforts, very difficult indeed. How many times have I gone to the aid of someone who needed help? How many times did they then lie to me or persist in acting poorly or in ignoring performing prayers, meditation and service? More than I can say. This goes to my expectations, which are often quite unreasonable.

I know that it's not between these people and me. It's about God and me.

And thus I pray and I meditate I continue on this path. I have good friends, very good friends. As for the others, I learn that being self-protective is not selfish and I remember my rule: don't take what sponsees do personally. I cannot go back to what I had been. I cannot go back, and the only other way is forward. And so I go forward.

I do a check off-if something came to me about God's will or how I could serve God (HP, authentic self, etc.). I occasionally write it down. I check to make sure that these thoughts go with me constantly, that I am God conscious. Prayer is an excellent way of getting closer to God, as is meditation. That means that I go forward and improve my conscious contact with God's will. That means that I move on to the Eleventh Step.

Principles of the Tenth Step:

- Admit errors promptly; apologizing, changing behavior or making amends when necessary. Check my motives and use Tenth Step as soon as possible.
- If too upset and knowing that I can't behave well, try not to say anything take a break. Be willing to leave someplace if absolutely necessary. Have exit strategies: going to the bathroom, taking a little walk or a cigarette or snack break.
- Practice restraint of pen, tongue and email.

- Always say 'Thy Will, Not Mine' be done, when upset, and know that it's a prayer. Work to recognize my feelings.
- Love and Tolerance is my code, something I work on all the time. Unacceptable behavior is unacceptable but be careful to makes changes only when it directly concerns me and sometimes not even then.
- Work on carrying the vision of God's will into all of my activities and always remember to continue on with Steps Eleven and Twelve, which are essential for finding the vision and carrying into my daily life.

CHAPTER THIRTY-TWO: STEP ELEVEN. 'Sought through prayer and meditation to improve our conscious contact with God as we understood Him, praying only for knowledge of His will for us and the power to carry that out.'

I continue doing the Tenth Step. I don't stop because I'm at Step Eleven. The following is my take on what the *Big Book* tells us to do. We first improve our conscious contact with God by doing further inventory. The inventory gets me further into God consciousness, even before the intimacy I get from prayer and meditation.

Again, the *Big Book* is very specific: **Before going to sleep** '…I constructively review my day:

- *'Was I resentful, selfish, dishonest, or afraid?'*
- *'Did I owe an apology?'*
- *'Did I keep something to myself that should be discussed with someone else at once?' 'What could I have done better?'*
- *'Was I thinking of myself most of the time?'*
- *'Was I thinking of others and what I could do for them?'*
- *'Did I think about what I could pack into the stream of life?'*

- *'Did I try to stem my worry, remorse, and morbid reflection?'*

After a while I need only think about my answers. In the beginning, as in Step Ten, writing things down really helped. By the way, do you see why some people call this the Eleventh Step inventory?

'After my review I ask God's forgiveness.'

I must be very specific here. God please forgive me for…and be sure I know what I'm asking forgiveness for.

In the beginning, my character defects were so flagrant that I'd often behaved badly. I needed forgiveness for my actions, my thoughts, and my overt and subtle behavior. At that time, I didn't receive much peace from seeing how I, over and over again, acted badly.

I forgot the truth that what I had seen, learned, and wanted from others or from life was not theirs to give. In short I had no acceptance and want to redesign life to suit my little plans and designs.

Later on as things got better it was more about me forgetting who is in charge (metaphorically, what is my job description) and what I can and can't do, physically, spiritually, emotionally and logically).

I tended not to be grateful. I forgot that God exists.

I was being very considerate and tried to lessen God's burdens when I didn't have the ability to do so and when nobody asked me to anyway.

After this prayer for forgiveness, I ask what corrective measures should be taken

Please note the passive voice.

This wasn't about the situation but about me and my character defects. Every evening I basically review my Tenth Step. I'm making sure I practiced Step Ten accurately. To help me even more, there are other things the *Big Book* has me do. This takes me from looking at what I had done to seeing what I should be doing.

'Upon awakening...' That means as soon as I get up-not after my first cup of coffee.) Getting on my knees is a lovely way to do this, but is not specified-it is my choice.

'We ask God to direct our thinking, especially asking that it be divorced from self-pity, dishonest or self-seeking motives. We remember that God gave us brains to use.' Note: this is to clear thinking, and is not asking that self-pity, dishonesty or self-seeking be removed.

The prayer concerns contaminated thinking. Also, when sponsees call asking for advice about a thousand things nobody cares about, I've been tempted to quote the line '...God gave us brains to use.' I never have.

'We think about the twenty-four hours ahead.' I usually first think about what meeting I am going to, what things I have to do, what I would like to do. Sometimes I make a to-do list. Some people make a gratitude list to get themselves in a better state. When I try, all I get is an attitude of platitude. I'm better off following exactly what the *Big Book* says.

If we '…are not sure what to do we ask God for an inspiration, intuitive thought or a decision. We try not to struggle and just wait for an answer.' So much for doing the 'next right thing,' as though a newcomer, who has done no step work, would able to do so.

I don't obsess over what I should do but calmly go about my day and generally the answer comes to me. In the beginning, I waited a bit before acting on my 'thought.' I used to check with the Oxford's Group's four absolutes. If my great insight had far reaching consequences, I checked with someone else before acting on it.

'We pray that we will be shown all through the day what our next step is to be, that we be given whatever we need to take care of such problems.' So much for telling the newcomer facilely to do the next right thing.

'We specifically ask for freedom from self-will, and make no request for ourselves only but ask for ourselves if others will be helped. We are careful never to pray for our own selfish ends.'

This one is very tricky and requires some amount of experience because it is difficult to know which are selfish ends and which aren't.

The rest of the morning mediation is left to the choice of the practitioner of this Step. I try to do at least thirty minutes of meditation, sometimes guided by CD's, sometimes mindless meditations and sometimes listen to music. I love Gregorian Chants.

Since the *Big Book* indicates that its readers should do inventories many times each day, the writers of the book must have realized that no one would be able to surrender easily or permanently. I can only do better and better as I reprogram my mind and soul into a more spiritual way of living.

There are a number of promises associated with Step Eleven

'We are in less danger of excitement, fear, anger, worry, self-pity, and foolish decisions. We become more efficient and don't tire so easily.'

The *Big Book* says 'It works-it really does.'

This section of Step Eleven reminds the reader that there is more that I must do to stay sober, to get closer to God, and to be of maximum service to God and my fellows.

The Rest of Step Eleven

I'm okay on the first part of the Step, which is inventory. I pray and meditate daily. I'm still waiting for the white light experience.

I once saw a woman who must have weighed two hundred pounds. Everyone said how wonderful she looked and how well she was doing. I mentally sneered until I learned that she had lost three hundred pounds seven years ago and had never gained them back.

That's what maintaining my spiritual condition is. If I have an old jalopy, it can only get so much better. I am maintaining it as best I can. I don't have to be a saint to stay sober, just to maintain my spiritual condition as best I can. Of course, if you keep a car long enough it becomes a classic.

The spirituality of AA is very simple. When I read the *Big Book* a few times I wanted to investigate other paths to the God of my understanding. AA encourages me to get 'outside help.'

I love AA's pragmatic approach: No one need go to a desert or a mountaintop to find God. An alcoholic's spiritual path is found in his daily life. I find God in the here and now. I do not reject all attachments but learn how to have healthy ones. Love of others is one of the greatest joys of Alcoholics Anonymous.

AA tells me I prepare for my spiritual journey by doing-more inventories! If someone prefers a different set of practices I urge them to follow the *Big Book* directions for thirty days first. If they wish to dispense with earthly attachments, that, too, is their choice, provided they act in a rational manner, and not from fear.

In the evening I go over my day

I check to see if I've done the Tenth Step Inventory and the other actions that have been spelled out in the *Big Book*. After that, I look at that inventory and see how well I'm doing.

I asked God's forgiveness, first for acts I've done, second, for acts that I didn't do. I may discover that I haven't loved God enough, trusted him enough, or even, in my consideration for God, have taken over some of His tasks so that He could rest.

After that, I ask 'what corrective measures should be taken.' I don't need to know God's job, nor do it. I'm not asking God what I should do. I'd like to know what should happen next and hope that I can wait for an answer. I don't, one more time, have to put on my white cowboy hat, get on my white horse and charge ahead, even though I don't know where I'm going, what I'm doing, or what would be the right thing to do.

Here is where I learn how to self-calm. A parent teaches an infant learns to do this very early on. Otherwise he is beset by unfulfilled desires, anxiety and apprehension. Step Eleven teaches me to let go of the need for action, no matter what.

I have no responsibility to do anything other than ask 'what corrective measures should be done.' That's my only responsibility. I ask the question and go to sleep. I'm freed from the need to do anything, at least that evening. My obsessive thoughts are quieted. I sleep like a baby.

In the morning, during prayer, meditation, on my morning walk or in the shower, I receive one of a set of responses

Dearie, it's out of your pay grade. Forget about it; or, let it rest; or even, don't you have something better to do? Occasionally, I receive specific instructions on what I should do, usually during prayer or meditation. I have no anxiety associated with this. There's something I have to do and I do it. I think that is the vision of God's will that I carry with me in my daily affairs.

Just as in Step Ten, I find myself gently guided to practice the principles of the Program.

The Eleventh Step turns to traditional methods of spirituality. The NIH has reported that twelve weeks of meditation can help a person stop drinking for a prolonged period of time. That may be true.

People sometimes feel that they can mandate what the results of going through the Steps will be. They feel that they have the power to help someone become psychologically fit and more capable of daily living. They view Step work as therapy and believe that that they are the best practitioners of this new art.

Nothing could be further from the truth. What is true, and what I must recognize as true, is that I can demonstrate, by my thoughts, demeanor and actions, how a person can become and stay sober. I hope I can demonstrate, by my thoughts, demeanor and actions, how a person can get closer to God. I'm not doing therapy and I'm not sure of the results.

I've experienced the possibility and actuality of immense psychological growth. The Steps affords the newcomer the simplest way towards permanent sobriety. Not to beat a dead horse, it's better to have a sponsor to help.

Problems arise when someone who has been sober for some amount of time comes to a person seeking what has been described as 'emotional' sobriety. There are some who are seduced into thinking that taking someone through the Steps will result in the kind of peace and happiness this person wants. Usually the person does not wish to change his values or goals, and is actually seeking for help in having his 'little plans and designs' be fulfilled. Now we know that doesn't work.

Thinking that doing the Steps per the *Big Book* will enable me to help someone achieve psychological health is a delusion. It only works if people are willing to surrender to the Program. I derive benefit from going through the Steps but after a certain amount of time being sober, what I think people need is action, service, and more service, and more inventories. Prayer and meditation. That is the avenue to spiritual transformation.

People study the *Big Book* obsessively. It's fun. It may be useful when I'm sponsoring someone, but after a while it's time to practice the principles in all my affairs. Besides, I can't pick and choose what results I want from my spiritual practices. I know I'll get something wonderful but it may not be mental health.

I'm sober. I can talk about what I did. If I want to help someone else get the peace and joy of a spiritual life, I must be sure that I have the peace and joy of a spiritual life-at least some of the time. (I can't give away what I don't have.)

The problem comes when I think I'm a magician and can cure the person's psychological problems. The side effects of the Program come when they come. For me, it is arrogance to take over God's role. I, personally, don't have a clue how to help someone with their psychological problems. All I can do is take someone through the Steps and wish her well.

Improving conscious contact with God

Praying and meditating are more important than understanding. Getting close to God doesn't mean getting insights into His nature.

The spirituality of the Steps is not separate and apart from life

It doesn't discount the problems of my day to day existence. I find my God in the world. It occurs within the context of my life. The foundation of my beliefs is the absolute knowledge that I couldn't stop drinking on my own and that some power outside of me has enabled me to remain abstinent for a significant period of time.

This power is real and demonstrable. I must continue with daily scrutiny of my actions, my motives and the consequences for myself and others. I know that trying to assist God or substitute my judgment for His demonstrates that I don't understand my place in the Universe. The Eleventh Step process spotlights my faulty judgment, over and over again. It also shows me how inadequate my relation with God is and helps me improve it.

Analytically I think you can be an atheist and not find the language problematic. A sponsor's job is to help with this. The 'God of my understanding' had been the Process of AA, or an authentic soul, the

Power of Love, or Fred, at various times in my sobriety. All are consistent with Eleventh Step directions.

Sometimes I think my Higher Power is an infinite source of love. I learn to plug into that power and become a good and loving person. My theology can be that simple.

The *Big Book* leaves the specific type of prayer and meditation to the alcoholic. It must, because each person's God is the God of his understanding and there can be neither rules nor directions in how to find, communicate, or love that God. That does not mean I'm on my own. I've checked out books, religious groups, new age sects, philosophical tomes and books on neurophysiology. I never ignore or reject advice or guidance from those further along the spiritual path. Guided meditations are good to listen to; various books on prayer and meditation are invaluable.

The practices of prayer and meditation have become precious to me and very rewarding in terms of happiness, joy and serenity. I have seen many truths and none of them were true. I've had many conflicting perceptions of people and ideas. Despite all of my inventories and all of my discussions with my sponsor, I still can veer off into the clatter of my mind.

Prayer and meditation turn off the noise. I can hear better or see more clearly. In the silence, I can begin to practice the presence of God.

Here is where I find out if the words I said and the prayers I made in the Third Step meant anything. In Step Eleven I'm actually able to keep the promise I made early on. That decision in Step Three is strengthened and enhanced as I continue to practice the principles and actions of the rest of the Steps.

Dr. Bob, his wife, Anne, and Bill Wilson had a period of 'quiet time' every morning. They believed it was very useful. The Smiths were devout Christians. However, they did not include their beliefs in this step. The admonition to use outside help is as relevant here as with therapists. There's a lot of outside help getting to God. People should use it.

The maintenance of my spiritual condition becomes more difficult and easier as I proceed. What was little more than a hope becomes deep and abiding. I remind myself if agitated or doubtful to ask for the right thought or action, fairly secure in my knowledge that I'm not being driven blindly by fear, self- centeredness or selfishness, and, again, fairly secure that I'm seeing things clearly without the haze of dishonesty. It's here that I remind myself that I'm not running the show.

This is all good but, again, the answer does not lie within me. Prayer and meditation are not enough. I have to go forward. I can't stop here. First I must do all of the actions as found in the *Big Book* and then I have to engage in carrying the message and practicing the principles of AA.

Step Eleven leads me to Step Twelve, working with others and practicing these principles in all my affairs. Steps Ten, Eleven and Twelve, are distinct but taken together enable me to maintain and improve my spiritual condition. Concentrating on any one to the exclusion of the other two gets me dancing to a different tune, and one which I composed. That's a formula for dis-ease and discomfort.

I can eat only at McDonald's or I can partake in the banquet of life

Doing any one Step to the detriment of another means that I'm engaging in microwave sobriety. Could anything be less appealing that a reheated Big Mac? Go to it as you choose.

There are a lot of Tenth and Eleventh Step study guides, some written for profit, some not. I don't object to anyone using any study guide they want as long as they first do the Step the way the *Big Book* lays it out for us, and with a sponsor. Check off sheets are too clinical. They don't afford me the opportunity to internalize what I'm reading or experiencing.

The question of whether someone is ready to sponsor another person comes up periodically. If I believe that I'm able to help others reach a fourth dimension of reality, I must check to see if I am spiritually fit

I would like to direct your attention to the Spiritual Inventory found earlier. The inventory was very useful in helping me along my spiritual path. I've done it a number of times. It's worth the effort.

Principles of Step Eleven:

- Never forget that I find God through subtraction. Work on practicing the presence of God.
- Do not get sidetracked or become complacent. Accept my need for more as something good. Remember, always, my place in the universe.
- Keep enhancing my vision of God's will and make sure that I carry that, and not my ego driven wants, in my daily life.
- Stop to smell the roses.
- Never take credit for the work of others.

-

CHAPTER THIRTY-THREE: STEP TWELVE. 'Having had a spiritual experience as the result of these Steps we tried to carry the message to alcoholics and practice these principles in all of our affairs.' (You will find a full discussion of the Twelfth Step in the earlier section on sponsorship.)

As I continued on the path of spiritual growth, I experienced a sense of freedom. I acted out of love because I loved myself. I acted out of kindness because I had forgiven myself. I respected others and tried to behave truthfully, honorably and wisely.

My daily practices of inventory, prayer and meditation, enabled me to deal with successes and setbacks with equanimity. My ailments and the deaths of loved ones were not of my own making. All I could do was accept them.

I felt the presence of God, a God not of my choosing or creation, but one who took me out of the gutter of alcoholism and transformed me into a responsible, useful member of society.

Lately I've been assailed several times by the pseudo-intellectuals of AA, who inform me of studies of brain stimulation where the subjects feel the presence of God. Apparently, certain brain lesions cause similar experiences.

'Ho!' they cry triumphantly. 'You see, you talk about God but God doesn't exist. It can't. It's all in your head.'

'I'm sorry you feel that way,' I reply. There's no point in refuting illogical 'arguments.' Brain stimulation is a sufficient condition for the 'spiritual' experience but not a necessary one. When you are in the presence of God, you will feel His presence. You don't need your brain stimulated for that.

In the *Big Book*, Bill Wilson had a 'white light' experience. He reports that he was thrown from his bed and felt transformed. 'Am I crazy?' he thought.

He questioned the director of the Hospital to which he had been committed. The director replied. 'I don't know if you are, but you're doing a lot better this way. Hold on to it.'

Generally speaking, the artificial experience as well as the hysterical one is not long lasting. Meeting God will change you forever.

Parenthetically, there are those who report that Bill borrowed the experience from another alcoholic. It wouldn't surprise me. It doesn't matter because, again, it's about what I do. Although I have to say that lying is a lot more than stretching the truth or poetic license. I wonder if Bill's habits are what kept him depressed and unhappy.

A little more about the God thing: Anne Smith, the long suffering wife of Dr. Bob Smith, kept journals for many years. Although they were donated to AA, only one volume remains: the tale of Anne, her husband,

Dr. Bob Smith, and Bill Wilson. Apparently Anne would read philosophy, psychology, and theology and then relate the gist of her studies to the two men. It gives a good picture of their talks about God and recovery.

You can obtain a portion of the journals at http://hindsfoot.org/annesmth.html. It's very interesting.

In the old days in AA, the wives did a lot of the heavy lifting. Bill Wilson's wife, Lois, was the sole financial support of the family. She would come home from work, clean the house and cook for the assorted crew of alkies who were residing in or visiting their home. It's been suggested that she even did some of Bill's amends. Didn't she start Alanon?

Those who are atheists make their accommodations with the language and meaning of Steps Ten, Eleven and Twelve. I work with atheists but beg them to keep an open mind. I was an atheist but experiences in my life forced me to change my mind.

A sponsor can help me see how far I am along my spiritual path and encourage me to proceed, in my own direction and in my own way. It is sometimes easier for the non-believer or the uncertain one to make strides. They only have to learn. The believer has to unlearn some of what had been taught to her.

What I've experienced in meditation has its own reality. It has opened the portal to an alternate universe. It helps me see, and in seeing I find what I didn't even know I was looking for.

At the end, Alcoholics Anonymous is not about theology or metaphysics but allows me to lead a good and productive life. This means that I must act well, always. I become a loving individual and a kind one. I am set free and can be useful and help to others. Yes, I learn how to practice the presence of God but my goal is to carry the vision of God's will in all of my affairs so that I can be of maximum service to God and others.

I experienced joy and happiness, and lived, finally, in a beautiful universe with wonderful people. I, too, was able to contribute to the joy and happiness of other. In humility and freedom I became a channel of God's love and grace.

And with all of the blessings of this new life, I sometimes find myself slipping backwards into my old ways of self-sufficiency and materialism. I wish it were otherwise. I am just not that spiritual.

Steps Ten, Eleven and Twelve anchor me

They bring me back to my primary purpose and back to my need for practicing the presence of God. The brilliance of AA is that it propels people like me, shallow, materialistic, and fearful, towards this wonderful life, and that it reels my ambitions and fears in each time I stray.

I spoke mainly about the Twelfth Step in the portion about sponsorship above, because I think that's where it belongs. Here I will just give a very brief summary.

There are three part of the Twelfth Step: having a Spiritual awakening, carrying the message, and practicing the principles in all my affairs.

Part one: 'Having had a spiritual awakening as the result of these Steps...' Why not think or write about some of your spiritual awakenings or of those you have heard about, rather than hearing, one more time, about mine?

Part two: 'Carrying the message' There are many ways of carrying the message but few are verbal. Think here of how you and others have carried the message well or badly, and maybe even write about it.

WILAA: It's hard to carry 'the' message if you haven't done the Steps. That's one reason why it's good to do the first run through of the Steps right after you get sober.

Part three: Practicing these principles in all of our affairs.

(That, of course, is how we best carry the message.)

I don't know why AA worked for me. It didn't matter what I believed. It didn't matter what I felt. What mattered were the actions I took. What mattered was the way I lived my life. My heart knew much more than my brain. Fortunately I listened to my heart. I was doomed and dying twenty one years ago, and am neither now. For that I am eternally grateful.

That's why I'm a fanatic about learning what the *Big Book* says. That's why I'm a fanatic about following the directions in the *Big Book*. I've talked about my own gift of amazing grace. I hope that the reader of this book will find that grace as well.

Principles of the Twelfth Step:

- Do the Steps assiduously, working for that spiritual awakening. Think about what it is carefully. It is my message.
- Carry that message when and where it can be helpful.
- Practice the principles of all Twelve Steps in my daily life. I become my message.
- Make sure I know what the principles are and use my daily inventories to check that I am on the beam.

The serenity, courage and wisdom that I need in order to behave rightly doesn't come easily. It requires time, energy and work-basically the work of learning what the principles of the Step are and then practicing them in my daily life.

Pretty awesome. The answers to all of my questions are in the *Big Book* and *The Twelve and Twelve*. I just have to know where to look. The answers to all my problems are there too.

CHAPTER THIRTY-FOUR: A SHORT SET OF QUESTIONS FOR THE SPONSOR AND SPONSEE TO TALK ABOUT (If you feel they are not complete, you can use the Step Worksheets or make up your own questions.)

A very good set of short questions for someone who has been around for a while and would like to do more work

This is for someone who has trouble working some of the later Steps. If someone has trouble with Steps Ten or Eleven, there's nothing like going to back to Steps one and do.

Create a new prayer and promise that would help you practice the Steps. In no more than a page, explain the Step to a newcomer. Also, in as much detail as you can, tell how you practice the Step in your daily life

You might want to use the Worksheets found below as the basis of a *Big Book* Study, or instead of these short worksheets if you want longer assignments. I don't think it's down, but there far fewer questions. I give them to my sponsee, ask her to think about them, write a little bit and then meet with me and talk about her answers. **There are no right or wrong answers. There's no A in AA.**

Actually there are some wrong answers

They're the hasty responses that scarcely merit attention. They're the jargon you hear at meetings which contradicts the *Big Book*. I don't want to discourage my sponsee but I don't want to encourage her to continue not thinking about these matters. The problem is that many people are so sensitive that they perceive everything that is not over-the-top unadulterated praise as harsh criticism.

You can look in the *Big Book*, *The Twelve and Twelve*, online or anywhere else you please. It's better to do a little reading before you answer the questions.

You can write out the answers but you don't have to if you will remember them. If you don't do the questions, you won't be able to answer the last question in each section. Please write out the answers to any questions where you're asked to do writing.

Step One

Where is the First Step in the *Big Book*?

Give three instances where you took charge. Can you manage your life? What suggests you can't? Did it hurt you?

What were you thinking?

Did you have any power here? What power did you have? What is your situation in life? Are you a free woman?

Give specific examples of ten things you're powerless over.

What do you think about the 'we,' the 'dash' and the 'pitiful, incomprehensible demoralization?' Do you really think you have to stop drinking? Be honest please.

Are you powerless over alcohol or can you take a few drinks now and then? Write no more than a page explaining the First Step.

For each of the following Steps, please begin with the ways in which you practiced the preceding Step.

Step Two

Write ten occasions where (sober) you saw something wrong, or heard it wrong, or knew you didn't understand something and pushed ahead anyway.

Ten times you forgot you were powerless and tried to take charge.

Did you know what other people thought was true and believed perceptions or ideas despite the evidence?

Was your drinking crazy?

How is 'thinking with our feet' a reality testing principle?

Give three examples where you said you wanted to do something and did something entirely different? Did your reality check bounce? How so?

What was the effect of your actions? Was this predictable?

Why didn't you predict it?

Write no more than a page explaining the Second Step.

Step Three

If you're powerless and find something that will give you power, do you say 'I'll try to get that?' Did you do that in Alcoholics Anonymous? How?

Short form: 'I'm in.' When did you decide you were in the Program and not around it? Maybe you haven't decided yet. That's OK. Just make your decision now. It does mean, among other things, that you'll do the rest of the Steps and be of service.

Give ten examples of opting out in your life. Why? (Think feet.) Was it your refusal to be powerless?

Your insanity?

Your desire to keep on drinking? Did opting out do any good?

Do you believe that an impaired mind can fix an impaired mind, or understand it?

When you are trying to understand AA, or what your sponsor tells you, as opposed to answer the questions or following directions, what are you doing?

What does it mean to 'turn your life and will over to the care of God as you understand Him,' and how do you do it?

Now write a page on the Third Step.

Step Four

Write a little about how you

Trying to manage things.

Staying outside instead of coming in.

Letting your impaired mind take over, so that you'll hear or see something that is probably or most likely wrong.

Setting the stage to drink.

Refusing to accept any idea or belief you didn't think of yourself. Not being able to keep an open mind.

How did it work for you?

Why do you look at yourself? How have your decisions divert you from what you thought you wanted to do? Have you learned a method to see yourself clearly? Do you think you'll be able to keep away from your earlier craziness? Here's where you study the *Big Book*, each and every word.

Write a page or less about the Fourth Step.

Now do the Inventory as written in the *Big Book*.

Why do you tell God first, then yourself and then another person the exact nature of your wrongs? Have you internalized the Fourth Step method and do it in spite of yourself?

Are you beginning to see? Are you catching yourself as you begin to distinguish the true from the false? Talk about your patterns of behavior and your motives.

Look at your relationship with God or your Higher Power. Does it come through in the Fourth Step? How? If not, go back and look at the Step, read the *Big Book, think about it some more, and maybe speak with your sponsor.*

Where are you with forgiving those who hurt you? Does the Fourth Step Prayer help you? What are your three most troublesome character defects?

What's the difference between character defects, shortcomings and the exact nature of your wrongs? Write a few paragraphs about the Fifth Step.

If you're a sponsor: Write a few paragraphs on how you learned to hear a Fifth Step and how it helped your spiritual and emotional growth.

Step Five and A Half

Have you gone back and made sure you've done the first Five Steps correctly. What have you learned from these Steps? How have you practiced each Step? Be very specific here. Write this out please.

Step Six

You've looked at yourself. How do you feel? Great? Well, try to keep on feeling great. How would you do that? Feel terrible? What do you do? Do you want to be happy? Is that the purpose of this Step?

What do you think about the statement 'The only thing you can change is yourself or your attitude?'

What's the difference between the values you have now and the ones you had before?

Write out your major character defects.

How about writing one or two paragraphs on the Sixth Step?

Step Seven

Do you know that you can't fix yourself? If you realize you're not the Center of the Universe and have very little power and none where you want it, you are? What's that word?

What are your new goals, if any?

Write down what character defects you want removed? Will this help you accomplish your goals?

What is the Seventh Step prayer telling you? OK, now please write about the Step.

Step Eight

What actions are important to take for you to accomplish your new goal? What is the purpose of this Step?

House cleaning? What does that mean and how do we do it? What do we get rid of?

Write down three things or qualities you would like to have removed from you or your life? What is essential for restoring the soul to health?

Write no more than a page about the Eighth Step

Step Nine

How do we clean up our side of the street?

How about three amends you've made in your life? The next three amends you're going to make?

What is the purpose of making amends? How does that fit in with Step Seven?

Write a little bit about this Step and your problems with it.

Step Ten

How would you characterize this Step? How would you do it?

Do you do it on a daily basis? Do you do it each time you're upset? Do you think it's necessary to write Tenth Step Inventories down?

How about the rest of the directions? How do you remember them or know that you do them. Again, do you write the entire Tenth Step Inventory and all directions down? Write down yes or no here, and if you don't, why not.

Let's say you're not doing Step Ten. What Step are you failing to do?

Step One? How?

Step Two? How?

Step Three? How?

Step Four? How?

Step Five? How?

Step Six? How?

Step Seven? How?

Step Eight? How?

Step Nine? How?

Do you still think you're running the show? Is that an illusion? A delusion? Are you capable of running the show?

List five factors that would convince someone else that you're not capable of running the dishwasher, let alone your entire life. This should be written, please.

By the way are you managing the things you're responsible for?

Are you the Serenity Prayer in reverse?

Include two or three written Tenth Step Inventories you've done fully (just like the *Big Book* says.) Do you try to bring God's will into all your activities or are you still doing things your way?

That's plenty to do. No need to write a page about the Step.

Step Eleven

Do you see the three distinct parts?

First, in the evening, do you check your Tenth step? How is that going? Would you state what you've asked forgiveness for in the evening?

Name a problem you brought to God. Did you get any answer to what corrective measures should be taken? Did you stop obsessing about the problem?

Second, in the morning, did you clear your brain, trying to stop being crazy? Plan your day? What are you planning? Is this about your new goal or more of your little plans and designs: Do you have a lifelong plan to getting closer to God? How close are you?

How are you doing with prayer and meditation? Would you please describe your daily practices?

Have you seen how the Steps help you see what is true? Have they quieted the noise and removed the confusion?

Whatever your God is, are you preparing yourself to meet that God? The more you practice the principles of all the Steps, the better able you are to face the truth, the better able you are to practice the presence of God. How close are you to having God in your life? Could you discuss how your conscious contact with God has improved?

Step Twelve

What are some of your spiritual awakenings?

What do you think is the primary spiritual awakening you have had as the result of the Steps?

How do you carry this message? Write this out, please, again based upon your work on the Steps? How do you practice the principles of the Program? Write out two ways for each step please. You might indicate how you are carrying your vision of God's will in your daily life.

CHAPTER THIRTY-FOUR: THE TRADITIONS. A VERY BRIEF DISCUSSION

TRADITION ONE: 'Our common welfare should come first; personal recovery depends upon AA unity.' And they say this is a selfish Program.

The Traditions are immensely practical. They are essential for the survival of AA and its groups. They are also relevant for the well-being of its members.

With Tradition One I discover that I am part of a world-wide community which affords millions of people the opportunity to stay sober and have a good life. My group is a spiritual entity which gives me the opportunity to have a spiritual existence.

Alcoholics come crawling into the rooms of AA, broken, shattered and incredibly isolated. The only meaning in our lives comes from bottles of booze. The first Tradition tells me that my recovery is important, but that the community is even more so. Each alcoholic is the keeper of the flame, maintaining that which is necessary for the survival of all its members.

This is the Tradition which teaches humility and reminds me that I'm not alone. If I want Alcoholics Anonymous to survive I must do more than not drink. I must be considerate of others. I must be compassionate. Newcomers learn not to monopolize meetings and to avoid confrontations. The meetings must be calm, healing and safe. That, too, is partially my responsibility.

This translates to being thoughtful and kind outside of the rooms of AA. When people marry, they practice restraint of tongue, pen and Email. They won't to throw the D word around lightly. When people have children they learn to be nurturing and warm, rather than critical and rejecting. I learn to give full measure, to behave well for myself and for the group. I learn to behave responsibly. My survival depends upon it. I learn how to 'be kind, be kind, be kind.'

I also learn when kindness is not appropriate. I must stand up for what is right, when it concerns me, my family, my AA group, and maybe even my God.

Not only am I learning to think of others, but I am happily invited into a community of those who love and understand me. Most alcoholics were not received anywhere while they were drinking, except to mental institutions, jails and prisons; and, strictly speaking, they weren't invited but coerced.

Gratitude is an action word. By doing what I can to insure the continued existence of Alcoholics Anonymous I'm expressing the gratitude I feel for what AA has given me. I learn to maintain the health of AA by being of service.

AA meetings give the alcoholic a forum to be heard, to learn of the experiences of others and the solutions they found so that they could stay sober.

A little discussion: Bill Wilson tells the story of riding on the subway thinking about taking a job which will relieve all his financial worries. He hears a voice saying the workman is worthy of his hire.

True, he thought. And it comes from the Bible, which makes it origin all the more convincing.

When Bill told his group about this revelation, they shook their heads. They agreed that the job would be ethical but ethics isn't enough when it's a matter of life and death. Only the best will do.

And this is true for all of us alcoholics. Good is not good enough. We must aim for the stars.

The story also shows me how I can fool myself into thinking God is speaking to me. Bill had a lot of trouble with the Bible but here the words from the Bible resounded in his brain. This couldn't be him; it had to come from someplace else.

An AA Sponsor's Handbook

Bill could have spoken to one person or two, who had been carefully chosen to agree with him but Bill knew how self-justification worked. That's why he spoke to his entire group and learned that he had neglected the most important thing, namely the survival of AA

It's pretty obvious what the tradition is telling me about AA. This isn't a rule for telling me how I should or shouldn't act. It's telling me what I have to do if I want AA to endure. What I do is my choice. I have the freedom to act as I please. The tradition informs me that if AA's survival is so important, I had better do what I can to keep AA vital and flourishing, even if I have to sacrifice some of my personal desires.

I can use this tradition in my relationships. I can see that by placing relationships above my own selfish needs I am learning a new way of life. I can't just do what I want when I want to. If I want to stay sober I have to live in accordance with spiritual principles. If I want a solid relationship I have to do this as well.

If I want to be reasonably happy, I can't just look to myself. That way brings me back to my state when drinking: isolated, unhappy and alone. 'The struggle for wealth, power, and prestige is self-destructive and futile. I can never get what I need if I'm looking for illusions. It really is just like drinking.

In Step Four I learned that I was driven blindly by fear. In Step Six I found that I sought more happiness and satisfaction from wealth, power and prestige, than I could ever get. By considering the needs of my fellows, my destructive impulses and false values can be kept in check.

I can't change if someone tells me not to do something. One example is 'just say no.' It doesn't work for anyone but for alcoholics least of all.

I am changing when I acknowledge the need for unity and fellowship and attempt to strengthen my ties with others.

The Twenty First Century may become known as the Time of Isolation. People are yearning to be connected and to belong. This Tradition emphasizes the immense importance of the AA community. As I guard Alcoholics Anonymous, I am emphasizing my commonality and affiliation with a large group which is striving to lead a spiritual life. In this Tradition I'm learning I am not alone.

TRADITION TWO: 'For our group purpose there is but one ultimate authority-a loving God as he may express himself in our group conscience. Our leaders are but trusted servants; they do not govern.'

In a sense Bill described the birth of the group conscience in Tradition One.

At my second AA meeting I looked around me and saw that people saw right through me. They immediately found out about the secrets I'd been keeping all my life. I believed+++ that that the AA group has an IQ of a million. Maybe that was a spiritual awakening.

In matters of the divine, I shouldn't go it alone, or with a few judiciously selected friends who would predictably agree with me. Bill learned what I have to learn. There are times when my personal desire clashes with my ultimate goals. I'm best off if I have a group of people who are trying to do the right thing and keep me right sized.

As long as I keep my goals in mind I'm better able to hear the truth. The truth will help me act contrary to my short term objectives.

The group is a spiritual entity, which means it exists and proceeds by spiritual principles. Without the group I can't stay sober. Thus I must adhere to these principles as well. My very life depends upon it.

What does it mean to make a relationship spiritual, or transcendent or divine? When I use people I can't have a spiritual relationship with them. I try to follow spiritual principles, either in a marriage, or with a parent or a child, or in any other relationship when I am trying to maintain a meaningful connection. I have to subdue my ego. Then I have the chance of creating a spiritual entity.

I begin with my AA group. I can expand my horizons by following the traditions as best I can, when at all possible. It's not always possible because of the world, because of human beings, and because of me.

When a group conscience is called, I have a duty to vote for what I believe is right rather than what I want. I'm learning integrity, something which is not usually found in bars.

TRADITION THREE: 'The only requirement for AA membership is a desire to stop drinking.'

I'm not sure that you have to be an alcoholic to be a member of AA. It doesn't seem like it. You also don't have to be a 'member' of AA to attend AA meetings.

Try signing up to be a member of AA. Where do you go and what do you do? I'm not sure anyone could tell you. There are no initiation rites, no application form, and no fees. AA is inclusive. If you want to stop drinking, you're in, even at closed meetings. And you don't have to sign a pledge.

On the other hand, there is a 'membership' within the fellowship: it is not exclusive and all can join. I made a mental commitment to be part of AA, both fellowship and program. I didn't really feel like I belonged when I started, but, oh, do I belong. I am part of a large, wonderful, spiritual enterprise. I work each day to keep my membership active. All I have to do is want to stop drinking, or continue not to drink.

For me, that means I accept my primary purpose: achieving sobriety and helping another alcoholic achieve sobriety. If I want to stop drinking, I'd better include the helping another alcoholic achieve sobriety. Otherwise, I'm my same old, clueless, selfish and self-centered self.

The cost of AA membership

Membership in AA means membership in the human race. The cost of membership is the smashing of the ego. The cost of membership is accepting that I am worthy of the gift of sobriety. The cost of membership is giving up self-hatred and contempt for others. The cost of membership is giving up the pain and despair of my drunkenness. The cost of membership is giving up my victimhood. The cost of membership is working towards being me without all the distractions, being the best me I can be, being the me I always wanted to be.

As a member of Alcoholics Anonymous, I can become happy, joyful and free. I just have to give up all the pain I had experienced, all the despair I felt, and all the bewilderment that beset my life. I don't know why I hold onto all that has hurt me. I just know I need help to let go.

When I become a member of AA, I trust that all will be well. I give up the need to understand and proceed according to the directions of others who, themselves not understanding all of the ramifications of the

Program, have been able to move on. We are truly a membership of the spirit.

An important question: 'Who dared to be judge, jury, and executioner of his own sick brother?' Alcoholism is a fatal disease. Banishment from AA can mean death or a long term sentence in a nursing home until death arrives. One of the cases talked about in the Third Tradition, as far as I know, involved a cross-dressing, multi-racial heroin addict. Bill first acknowledged, and then laughed at, the group's feeling that their reputation as self-respecting drunks would be tarnished.

The real question is why do we think we are the membership committee?

Maybe this Tradition is telling me that I should act with love and tolerance, and leave judgments, particularly life and death decisions, to those better able to make them. And make no mistake about it; alcoholism is a deadly disease, relentless, painful, and fatal. I can be judge, jury and executioner if I drive someone from an AA meeting.

It's also telling me that it's up to an alcoholic to say when he's a member. It's not up to me to make that observation for anyone else. That's a good thing to remember when I'm doing Twelve Step work.

TRADITION FOUR: 'Each group should be autonomous except in matters affecting other groups or AA as a whole.'

Once again, AA mandates as much freedom of choice as possible without harming anyone or anything. I'm getting used to the idea of thinking of others before I act.

See how this ties into the solution offered by the *Big Book*. 'Our very lives, as ex-problem drinkers, depend upon our constant thought of others and how we may help meet their needs.'

I hated this sentence when I first read it. It took time for me to understand I hadn't thought of others or their needs. I thought only of how I could make them stick around or love me or whatever. I wasn't thinking about their needs but only about mine.

The Fourth Tradition in Action: I was newly sober and attending CA, a different, very new fellowship I have never used cocaine but my rehab sent patients to CA meetings. I liked them a lot. The people were a lot like me, very wired.

For some reason I was voted the GSR (Group Service Rep) of my group. 'For some reason' I said. There was only one reason: the group had about six members and I was the only one willing to go to the area meetings.

I went to my first meeting. One of the GSR's had attended a meeting where the members were fundamentalists Christians and spoke about the 'blood of the lamb' and other concepts not related to our singleness of purpose. He spoke to the group about it.

Everyone agreed that wasn't a good thing, primarily because new members might attend the meeting and be frightened off. The problem was what to do. CA was a brand new fellowship and concerned about its survival.

The solution was to have such groups excluded from the Where and When (list of meetings) of the area. In theory, all was fine. The practicalities were another matter.

How would you decide who shouldn't be included; how would you tell the Group they were doing it wrong; what if the blood of the lamb group was a 'one off,' a never repeated phenomena of a few people?

Who would be willing to attend a few meetings of each group as policeman?

The discussion went on for a few months, by which time the problematic group had disbanded.

WILAA: One thing I've learned about the Traditions; when they're not observed, the group tends to die, sooner, usually, than later.

A good rule for me to follow personally came from the Middleton Group #1, Rule # 62. If you don't know what it is, it's just a single pungent sentence. 'Don't take yourself too damn seriously.'

Another gift of the program: being able to laugh at myself. Thus I can laugh at the 'for some reason' when I know the reason very well. Being able to laugh at myself might be a spiritual awakening. I don't mean sharing about things in my life that I make funny at the AA meetings. I mean looking at myself and seeing my life and I are just not very big deals.

TRADITION FIVE: 'Each group has but one primary purpose-to carry its message to the alcoholics who still suffers.'

The singleness of purpose has come under attack recently because many new attendees at AA meetings are multiply addicted. Many of them are graduates of rehabs which teach that 'a drug is a drug is a drug.'

I'm not so sure that's true. When I was first sober, my rehab took us to a number of meetings that were held in the same house. I quickly found that by looking at the people sitting outside on the porch at half time, I could determine whether it was an AA, CC, NA, OA or MA meeting.

You know, Dr. Bob Smith was addicted to pain pills. Bill and Bob were cognizant of the existence of the multiply addicted but espoused the concept of a primary purpose. They felt it was important that AA was for persons with the same problem. The 'we' of the First Step might be the most spiritual word in the *Big Book*. If I don't feel that this is my group and these are my people, who help keep me sober, I'm not sure I would care about the survival of AA.

Bill and Bob were amazing men. I say, if it's good enough for them, it's good enough for me.

Closed meetings, as determined by group consciences, exclude persons who do not have a problem with alcohol. Open meetings welcome everyone. Still the question of a person who has a different problem raises some issues. Many groups welcome such a person to attend open meetings, but not to lead the meeting, and sometimes not to share at the meeting.

You see, it's very difficult for an alcoholic who's gotten his fourth DUI, lost his job and family, and is living on the street, to identify with a compulsive overeater, a few pounds overweight, who is worried about eating an extra cupcake. The overeater might feel it is just the same and may even talk about a 'sugar blackout.' The alcoholic has trouble understanding this.

For an alcoholic, a blackout might mean falling asleep in Cincinnati and waking up in Peoria, married and naked, three weeks later.

On the other hand, if an alcoholic walks in and takes a ten year chip but casually mentions that he's smoked crack the night before, he is usually told that he isn't sober. Why, they'll even take his chip back. If the alcoholic has eaten a cupcake or two the odds are everyone will say 'no problem.

If use of another substance constitutes a relapse, doesn't that mean the singleness of purpose is perhaps not so single after all?

I understand the concept of singleness of purpose, particularly since I've never used drugs and have difficulty with identifying with the meth addict and the dope fiend. I have trouble with understanding rummaging through garbage dumps to get food. I don't get the need for lip balm at all.

Still, I have the feeling that using crack constitutes a relapse in AA. That could be a slight problem, one I'll leave for those more philosophically inclined than I.

TRADITION SIX: 'An AA group ought never endorse, finance, or lend the AA name to any related facility or outside enterprise, lest problems of money, property and prestige divert us from our primary purpose.'

What guides the group helps its members as well. Alcoholics can be a grandiose bunch, even when sober. They come into AA and are so in love with the Program of Alcoholics Anonymous that they want to proclaim their message to all. This enthusiasm is sometimes perverted. And don't forget we alcoholics don't become saints all at once.

Historically the founders of AA learned that people with other agendas wanted to use the AA name for their own purposes, which could have split the fellowship apart.

If I have a single purpose, then I do not deviate from my purpose, whether as member of a group, or as an alcoholic. AA shouldn't get involved with anything else. I wish to stay sober and carry the message of AA.

Alcoholics have the freedom to espouse any legal or ethical cause they wish, but not as members of Alcoholics Anonymous. They certainly shouldn't publicly identify themselves as being in AA and endorse a cause, implying that AA endorses the cause as well.

What I learn in my relationships of a familial, sexual, professional, or social nature, is that I can't be all things to all people. In my personal life I learn who and what I am. I don't compromise my values and my beliefs by pleasing others or trying to seduce them into my life by playing a part which is not mine.

When starting a new job it's a good idea to know my job description. In AA '…our primary purpose is to stay sober and help another alcoholic…' That's it. That's my job.

I also find a not very subtle reminder that problems of money, property and prestige divert me from my primary purpose. I have to follow my course. Money, property and prestige divert alcoholics from staying sober and helping another alcoholic achieve sobriety.

Money, property and prestige divert everyone. They're distracting, seductive and confusing. I'm allowed to be diverted or amused, seduced or confused. When the stakes are so high I have to be very careful.

I can talk about two realms, the materialistic and the spiritual. The former refers to things, or status, or lots of property. The latter concerns characteristics, attitudes and feelings of kindness, love, helpfulness.

I'm not talking about God here. I'm looking at grasping individuals who want to get to the top of the heap and will step on anyone who gets in their way. Is that who you want to be?

This Tradition is not only about the groups of AA. It's also about all of us, and how we see ourselves, hopefully honorable, honest, dependable and loving.

There are those who see Traditions as relevant only for the AA group. That's too narrow for me. Sometimes I learn more from the Traditions than the Steps.

TRADITION SEVEN: 'Every AA group ought to be fully self-supporting, declining outside contributions.'

Have you ever been part of an organization where fundraising was the most important function of it? The aims and principles of the group were often subordinated by the contributors to an enterprise or to the mindset or benefit of the 'benefactors.' AA won't go there.

In the beginning, AA had its share of promoters and flim-flam artists. The Traditions have been instrumental in keeping AA pure, protecting AA from the world and from its members.

At times a group or an AA Club accumulates a fair sum of money. You need only ask an old timer to tell of some of the wars that were fought over money. He might also tell you of instances where treasurers were able to embezzle goodly sums as well.

That's why a prudent reserve is so important: that means there's enough money to keep the group going, but not enough to steal. Adding donors and contributors brings in the prestige, security, outside influence. AA remains simple. It remains untainted by the materialistic demands of some of its members. A group supports itself or it dies.

Accepting only small donations puts the survival of AA in the hands of its members. I treasure AA and I keep it going.

People should be self-supporting as well. Circumstances may require me to accept outside help, but it's a tricky business. I should always speak with my sponsors when I go down this path.

Being fully self-supporting often means being humble; not seeking what I can't afford or obtaining it at the cost of debt or loss of something essential. Too much emphasis on property, money and authority weakens the group. Overvaluing property, prestige, and power detracts from my spirituality, and, often, from my sobriety.

Being self-supporting doesn't mean that I'm self-reliant. It means that I'm responsible.

TRADITION EIGHT: 'AA should remain nonprofessional- but our service centers may employ special workers.'

We pay people to do the jobs no one wants to do. In a sense these workers are being of service, but reality impinges upon ideals. They are actually doing jobs which are not service related but which can, or do, facilitate recovery.

Cleaning the toilets may be such a job. If you do it without pay, it looks like being of service. If you get paid for it, it looks like doing a job.

You may ask about becoming a paid counselor in a treatment facility, getting more than basic expenses and a little honorarium to speak at a meeting not in your area, or in any other way, earning money for doing Twelve Step Work. To me it's very simple; if you're getting paid, it's not Twelve Step Work.

Addiction specialists and social workers who are in AA have a serious problem. Primarily they are conforming to the directives of a non-AA group and following non-AA guidelines. They are not there to carry the message but to behave professionally and objectively. This can be very difficult for recovering alcoholics and, sometimes, detrimental to their sobriety.

For one thing, they're the experts. Everyone comes to them. Thinking you know everything is never a sign of humility. Here, it can be fatal. For another, they are not permitted to talk about AA very much.

How can they have integrity if they believe in AA but must talk behavior modification as a way to achieve sobriety?

Not having recovering individuals staffing treatment centers is problematic as well. Most non-alcoholics have a great deal of difficulty in dealing with addicts and alcoholics. They either mistrust them or are fooled by them.

So who staffs the treatment facilities? Do they work? Are they the best solution? This is a problem for another day and another venue. Simply put, for now, you don't get paid for service work. In non-AA facilities, which are most of the treatment centers, non-alcoholics are fine except for the being fooled or being unable to trust part.

A true story and one which demonstrates that experiences convey the truth more than words: I had been in my rehab for five days and the person who was supposed to walk us from the Hospital to the AA meeting across the street was very late. We were missing the meeting.

When the young man arrived, I used my take-charge marine approach and addressed him sharply. I blush to admit that I asked for the name of his supervisor, planning to report him for his dereliction to duty.

'Lady,' he said to me wearily, 'I work nights. This is the only day I can sleep in. I get up early to bring you guys to the meeting. I overslept fifteen minutes-on this bright and lovely Saturday morning.'

'I don't have a supervisor,' he said. 'And I don't get paid.' He calmly took the group over to the meeting.

That was an eye opener, maybe a true spiritual awakening. People were helping me (and the hospital group as well) for no reason other than to be of service, even at a cost to themselves.

This was very different from my experiences in the 'real world.' I learned that AA operated differently, and better, than what I had known before. It was one of the reasons that I stuck around.

'TRADITION NINE: 'AA as such ought never to be organized, but we may create service boards or committees directly responsible to those they serve.'

This structure is the reverse of corporate organizations. The boards and committees are directly responsible to those they serve and not vice versa.

WILAA: You can go to meetings any place in the world; they start on time, they end on time, they move along well and there is no violence. There is no president, sergeant at arms, armies, police and no organization. That's pretty amazing when you think of who the members of the organization are.

The Traditions emphasize that wealth, prestige and power can be detrimental to the well-being of a group, an organization, and an individual. *The Twelve and Twelve* explains that this isn't a practical matter. As the group is a spiritual entity, so too, is the society of AA, which '…is animated only by the spirit of service-a true fellowship.'

Many newcomers object to 'the God thing.' The opposite of spiritual is not ungodly but materialistic. The spiritual need not be connected in any way to God. There's plenty of room for the atheist and the agnostic.

A fellowship of the spirit is a fellowship of community, kindness and love, and animated by the spirit of service. I see no conflict with any religious beliefs. AA is the ideal society, a fellowship which enables all to exist together in harmony and amity. This group teaches every member to learn that kindness, love, and service are more important than prestige, wealth and power.

When I see what is possible in the rooms of AA, I realize that I can structure my life to be similarly joyous. The motivating force is respect for others who are travelling (and often struggling) along the same path. It becomes respect for everyone I meet. Parenthetically, I can have respect for no other person until I have respect for myself. The steps help me with this.

Like forgiveness, respect is a dynamic process: as I respect others I learn to respect myself. As I respect myself I am better able to respect others.

TRADITION TEN: 'Alcoholics Anonymous has no opinion on outside issues, hence the AA name ought never be drawn into public controversy.'

History has shown that no organization and no individual can be all things to all people. That is partially the basis of our singleness of purpose.

Step Ten promises '…that we will cease fighting anything or anyone-even alcohol.' So I don't fight. Why should AA speak about matters about which it knows nothing and has no interest in? As an individual I can have opinions about everything but that different.

As a recovering alcoholic 'my primary purpose is to stay sober and to help other alcoholics achieve sobriety.' In AA I have enough trouble carrying the message. I have no need to promote some point of view or some cause. AA has only one purpose. It needs no other.

In Step Three, I learn that I stay within my pay grade and stick to my job description. Here, members of AA, often tempted to use the AA name to promote some pet project, defer to the Tradition that keeps things simple and keeps all the members of the group sober.

Of course, no individual member of AA has the authority to speak for A.A. The New York Office of AA is often presented with questions concerning AA. Their usual response is: what do you think about it?

Dr. Bob Smith gave some good advice. One, written on his prescription pad, was 'Trust God, Clean House, Help Others.' The other, equally useful: 'Don't louse it up.'

TRADITION ELEVEN: 'Our public relations policy is based upon attraction rather than promotion: We need always maintain personal anonymity at the level of press, radio and films.'

Personal anonymity refers to newspapers, radio, films, and now TV and the Internet. In the early days of AA, celebrities would gush about how great AA was until they relapsed, which was not a testament to the efficacy of AA. In today's world, it is often impossible to keep membership in AA a secret. Intake workers at rehabs, members of AA meetings and media types reveal celebrities' affiliations to AA, sometimes for money, sometimes not.

That's not too good but it is a fact of life. Celebrities do the best they can. Remember '…we've ceased fighting anyone and anything.'

As an aside, I have trouble not going too far in the opposite direction and failing to protect myself when it is necessary to do so.

A sponsee of mine called from San Francisco. A man and wife were putting on a big show at her home group while giving out chips.

They were very funny. They sang, danced and told jokes. The purpose of chips is to acknowledge periods of time, let the group join in the celebration with the celebrant, and demonstrate that AA works. So the husband and wife team were usurping the functions of the chip 'ceremony.'

Besides that, people were snapping pictures and making videos of the two people as well as anyone near them. Maybe they wanted to show that AA was a lot of fun. Whatever their motive, however, they had no right to break someone's anonymity, particularly when they hadn't indicated that they were posting their pictures on the Internet.

This is a problem outside of Bill and Bob's experience, but one taken care of by the Eleventh Tradition.

My sponsee asked me what I thought she should do. As she was a new member of the group, I suggested she find someone she respected and ask his opinion of the chip show. She did. The chip-giving term was almost over so they didn't have to do anything. They might mention the need for anonymity and circumspection when the selection for the new person was made.

Anonymity does not belong at the group level. Some people take anonymity to a level never contemplated by Dr. Bob or Bill Wilson. As Dr. Bob pointed out, it's pretty hard to send a card or visit someone in the hospital when you only know him as Ten Year Steve, Thank God for God George or *Big Book* Ethel. We are a fellowship and sometimes have to be in touch with each other so it's nice if we know last names.

People complain about the AA telegraph. Sometimes it comes in handy. This story, possibly apocryphal, concerns a man who had moved to New York City and came to some AA meetings. His child was very ill and needed blood transfusions. He shared about that at the meetings.

A day or so later, twenty five members of AA came to the hospital to donate blood. If they had only known him as the guy who just moved from Chicago, they couldn't have found his child. If the members of AA didn't talk about this man, they wouldn't have known the kid was in trouble.

That reminds me of the blue card that is read at many AA meetings. It says something to the effect that what you see here and what you hear here should stay here. Well, no. Sure we shouldn't gossip about neighbors showing up at meetings. On the other hand, I often talk about the amazing things people said at meetings after the meetings. Heck, after three or four times, I might even think I said it first.

While I'm on this rant, that little blue card says keep your sharing confined to your problems with alcohol. I prefer to talk about solutions.

If AA has a public relations policy, I think it is anonymity, which is probably an oxymoron. AA doesn't need actors, actresses and other famous individuals to sell AA. Also, the concept of humility would deter promoting AA.

Nobody need promote AA, famous or not, nor should I make the attempt. When AA began, the founding members felt the need to tell everyone about this great new movement. They exercised restraint, but often did so reluctantly. AA enjoyed the attention of newspapermen, which was a good thing. No one knew what Alcoholics Anonymous was.

After the Saturday Evening Post article in the early days, a lot of people asked for help and there were not enough recovering alkies to go around. That's no longer the case.

AA has stood the test of time and conquered all that the early members feared. There are meetings all over the entire world. Almost everyone knows about AA and its usefulness in keeping people sober. AA need not promote itself now, if it ever had the need to do so before.

AA is a spiritual fellowship with no leaders and limited organization. AA members should not need the reminder that personal ambition has no place in AA. Once again, nobody can be voted President.

Instead, each member is, or should be, '…an active guardian of our Fellowship.'

This is yet another difference between most organized religions and AA. Alcoholics Anonymous weeds out those seeking prestige, security and power. If they are around, they are very, very frustrated.

AA has no hierarchy. The self-seeking member might become a group chair or have a position of some type. It never is a position of power and it is not prestigious. If I am lucky, I might become an elder statesman. Knowing me, I'm more likely to be a bleeding deacon, who no one wants to hear and no one likes.

I've learned that my actions are what counts and they define who I am. I don't have to praise myself. Self-praise generally comes across as unintended self-condemnation: I don't believe enough in myself to let others discover who I really am.

This is a good principle to follow in life. Rather than be a braggart, I let others tell how great I am. Self- promotion rarely works, and never gains friends.

TRADITION TWELVE: 'Anonymity is the spiritual foundation of all of our traditions, ever reminding us to place principles over personalities.'

WILAA: The short form of Tradition Twelve is that I place principles over my personality.

Anonymity is the highest form of humility. I don't engage in promotion. I don't require personal distinction. My aim is to be of service. Being of service requires listening, caring, having the courage of speaking when necessary, remaining silent when silence is required, and carrying the message always.

Individual aspirations have no place in AA. Exactly as no one can win the Humility Cup, no one wants to be the most spiritual. If they do, they have the sense not to mention it.

My personal ambitions always take a back seat to my primary purpose. I can accomplish great things. I'm convinced my greatest goal is being of service to God and to others. It's not about making a lot of money, becoming very famous, or having a lot of power. These transitory accomplishments are like my need for one more drink. One more drink is never enough and one more million dollars is never enough either.

I'm looking to practice the presence of God. Who could be grandiose in the presence of a loving God who is all powerful and all knowing? If someone does not believe in a Judeo-Christian God, the Higher Power still has a magnificence and splendor inevitably lacking in us humans. One of the reasons I'm afraid of searching for God is that I might find Him.

If others don't behave as I wish, that is my problem. I want my epitaph to be 'She knew it was between her and God.' I want to be remembered for what I have done, not what was done to me. I most certainly not want to have 'She did the best she could' on my tombstone.

When alcohol is no longer my master, when I am no longer fettered by the bondage of self, when I have learned to see and perceive wisely, I find better myself in a better place. Humility doesn't mean I'm never satisfied or that I'm satisfied with little. It means that I'm satisfied with who and what I am, exactly as I try to be the best that I can be.

Humility is the foundation of the authentic soul, which faces life bravely and brings love and joy into the world. I learn to practice gratitude and loving kindness. I stop being a chaos maker and start contributing to the delight of the world.

And most important of all, the Traditions, as well as the Steps, are often applicable for the alcoholic in his daily life and not about the group at all. We are reminded, one more time, to remind the God who 'watches over us all.' He is always with us, even when we choose to ignore Him. It is this God that is the basis of our lives, our loves, our relationships and our sobriety. This we should never forget.

SOME STEP WORKSHEETS (Which could be used in a Step Study Group)

Step One: We '...admitted we were powerless over alcohol-our lives were unmanageable.'

Recommended Readings: The Prefaces in the *Big Book* as well as The Doctor's Opinion; Bill's Story (pick out 'his 'Steps, which are a little different from the way we see them as written out now) and *The Twelve and Twelve*, Forward and First Step. Also, in the *Big Book*, There is a Solution, More about Alcoholism, and Appendix No. 2 in the *Big Book*.

A NICE WAY TO BEGIN

Write 100 good things about yourself, or fifty or even twenty five.

Find the prayers associated with many of the Steps and write them down.

Find the promises associated with many of the Steps and write them down as well.

WILAA: If someone is powerless over alcohol you can't ask them to try to stop drinking. What you can do is ask them to take positive actions.

Some questions

Why are the Steps so important?

How long is the longest time you have gone without alcoholic since becoming an adult? How many times have you been in rehabs or detoxes?

How many times have you said you would quit drinking? Has drinking had a negative impact on your life?

A few words only, please.

Write why you came to AA. Why you decided to do this Step work. Have you hit bottom? How do you know? By the way, what is a bottom? Who is the "We' mentioned in the first Step?

What does the dash mean?

What, if anything, are you powerless over? What are you willing to do to stay sober?

What are the problems you have with the Program of AA?

Do you know what the "Program of AA' is? Why do you want a sponsor?

How do you envision the sponsor-sponsee relationship?

Did you know that the brain of an alcoholic has been demonstrated to function differently than that of a non-drinker? Structurally different?

Are you able to distinguish the true from the false? Have you noticed that your perceptions are off about a lot of things, most noticeably your drinking, but other things as well? Think about the craziness of drinking, or maybe you don't think it's crazy. What's wrong with a cocktail or two before dinner?

How has your life changed in the last year or two? Have you changed as well?

Admission (here's that honesty stuff. This is the true beginning of a new and better way of life.). When you admit something do you mean it or are you just going through the motions? Does it matter?

Powerlessness: (obsession of the mind, compulsion of the body). Please check to see if you were able to stop, or if you even noticed that it might have been a good idea to stop drinking, or at least cut down.

Were you good at having one or two drinks and leaving the rest of the bottle on the table?

Unmanageability: How good were you at managing your life? Did your intelligence, education, common sense, help you? Was there a point when things stopped working?

If you feel you're totally capable of managing your life, why are you here, in a detox, rehab, AA meeting, or talking with a sponsor or just reading these questions?

Acceptance: Do you accept all of the consequences of your drinking (or drugging) and the need for help?

The most important question of all: Have you hit a state of pitiful, incomprehensible, demoralization? How so?

By the way, do you believe in any power greater than yourself? What is that power? Do you need help to stop drinking? To stay stopped?

If you still believe that you have all the answers or if you don't think you have a problem, you'll have a lot of trouble with the first Step.

Some more questions (you might want to write the answers down):

Do you identify with Bill or the patients discussed in the Doctor's Opinions?

In Bill's story in the *Big Book*, he seems to do a lot of the Steps. You might want to pick them out. Why is Bill's admission of powerless different from yours?

Suppose that someone takes you aside after a meeting of Alcoholics Anonymous and tells you not to come back because you are not an alcoholic.

Write a few paragraphs convincing that person that you are an alcoholic. If you're so inclined you can write a few paragraphs convincing your sponsor that you're not.

What do you think of the idea of telling someone to try some controlled drinking to see if he/she is an alcoholic?

Is that what you've been trying to do? Has it worked? How would you define an alcoholic?

How much, how often, or how long did you drink?

Why do you think there are no definite instructions in The *Big Book* on how to do the First Step?

Do you think being locked up in a room with a big glass of your favorite alcoholic beverage is a delight or a torment? Why?

Are you in or out? (AA, recovery, trying to stop drinking)

Write a little bit about your story and the powerlessness and unmanageability of your life (if any). No more than one page please.

Describe several instances that epitomize your powerlessness over alcohol.

Give some examples of when you were powerless over starting to drink, or once started, powerless over stopping.

Describe several examples of how your drinking has contributed to unmanageability of your life (job, relationships, health, finances, and sexual relations).

Principles you practice as part of the First Step: Your turn:

Anything else you would like to talk about in regard to the First Step? What do you think of the idea 'just don't drink and go to meetings'?

What do you think of the advice to stick with the First Step for a while, and maybe the first Three Steps during the first year of sobriety?

There are a number of web sites that can be very helpful. You may prefer to listen to speaker tapes, where people tell their stories or talk about the Steps. Some people do much better listening than reading. That's fine. If you are a person who learns by listening rather than reading, this may be the way to go for you.

Also think about iTunes and free AA Podcasts. All the great speakers are there. If you can't get to the Internet, try borrowing some CD's.

STEP TWO: 'Came to believe that a power greater than ourselves could restore us to sanity.'

See 'Bill's Story' in the *Big Book* and find Bill's Second Step. Take a look at Bill at his kitchen table when he sees Ebby. Are there other times in Bill's story where you see him doing (working) the second Step or elsewhere in the *Big Book*? Read the Second Step in *The Twelve and Twelve*. Take a look at We Agnostics.

['came to believe']: How did that happen for you? Or did it?

['power greater than ourselves']: Are there any powers greater than you? ['could restore us to sanity'] Were you insane? How were you going insane? What is involved in being restored to sanity?

Have you been practicing the principles of Step One? Jot down two instances of this. Please continue to do this for each of the rest of the Steps.

The *Big Book* is very insistent that an alcoholic has to believe in a power greater than himself.

Find the section where Bill does the Second Step in Bill's Story. Does it show the method of AA? Do you believe in a power greater than yourself (a) in regard to sobriety and (b) in regard to anything else??(Bill's Second Step: Bill saw that Ebby suddenly had tremendous power. He could only say, 'Why Ebby used to have as little power as I, and that was none at all.')

When did you realize how crazy your drinking was? Did other people point it out? That is probably the difference between the person who gets sober and the one who doesn't. The lie of self-reliance is a part of Step Two. Explain.

Write a paragraph explaining how a person 'takes' the Second Step. Is there anything about it in the *Big Book*, similar to the directions on many of the Steps?

More questions:

Were you good at some point in your life at figuring things out and doing them well? Give some examples.

Did you take such good care of yourself that you were admired for your good judgment and good actions?

Did you have good sense? What (if anything) happened to change that? What role did alcohol play?

The major areas of one's life include: self, family, sexual partner, friends, career, community service, recreation. How many of these areas are currently satisfactory to you? In which of these areas have you seen "insanity' play out? Think the bedevilments in the *Big Book*, p. 52. See the reality check below.

Think about the times when you were in places where you shouldn't have been, doing things you shouldn't have been doing, in dangerous places with people you shouldn't have been with and yet you are still here.

Thinking back on your life, were there any times when you have believed that there was a being outside of yourself taking care of you? If not you, how about other people?

Do you believe in God? What is your conception of a higher power?

Do you think God believes in you? Does some being have the Power to heal or help you? Do you want that to happen?

Were you "crazy' (a) in terms of your drug and alcohol use; (b) in terms of your life-then and now? How can you be restored to sanity? Have you been restored to sanity?

An alcoholic gets a feeling of 'ease and comfort' from drinking alcohol but when he stops drinking he needs more alcoholic to regain that feeling. Do you see the craziness in drinking something to give you a feeling of ease and comfort when drinking it just makes you feel ill-at-ease and uncomfortable?

Did you drink to cheer yourself up?

Did you drink because you were very anxious and alcohol calmed you down? Did you drink because you had a lot of trouble thinking?

Alcohol is a depressant and causes free floating anxiety and interrupted sleep. Doesn't that make it seem crazy to keep on drinking?

Write a few paragraphs explaining the Second Step to a newcomer.

> **Another reality check**: Does this describe you and your life? '*We were having trouble with personal relationships, we couldn't control our emotional natures, we were a prey to misery and depression, we couldn't make a living (which includes not being able to make a successful life), we had a feeling of uselessness, we were full of fear, we were unhappy, we couldn't seem to be of real help to other people*'... whether we are drinking or not. They

are the root of the problem.(The Bedevilments, Big Book)

When you are at a meeting do you listen to others or think about what you're going to say? Do you remember what they said? Do you know their names?

Have you realized that you were self-deceptive or in denial about many things? Do people ever tell you things about yourself that you just disagree with?

Do you recognize your feelings when you have them? Talk about times when you didn't. Do you perceive things accurately? Give some examples of when you didn't.

Was your behavior insane? Why did you drink or take drugs? Did it fill you with a sense of ease and comfort? Did you seem better and happier? Did there come a point in time when you needed to drink or drug-that you just had to have this stuff? That you felt worse when you didn't?

Did you ever realize that drugs and alcohol made you felt uneasy and in a state of discomfort but kept on using them anyway?

You may not be able to define insanity but do you know what it is? Were there other things in your old life that you would call insane?

Read all the questions. Then write about five of them.

Do your family, your fellow workers, your drinking buddies, etc., understand you?

Did you feel isolated and totally alone and only able to connect with others involved in the same crazy life style?

Have you ever felt the presence of God in your life? Do you believe in God?

Do you think God believes in you? Does some being have the Power to heal or help you? Do you want that to happen?

Has it happened to you?

Have you been restored to sanity?

Do you see yourself thinking, acting and being differently? How did it happen? If you're not, why do you think you're not changing?

Do you see people who are no longer enslaved by alcohol and can act freely and with love?

Do you see people who choose health and spiritual growth rather than self-destruction and despair? Are you so terminally unique that none of this applies to you?

The principles of the Second Step:

Step Three: 'Made a decision to turn my life and my will over to the care of the God of my understanding.'

What is the main thing about this Step?

Do you have to be able to define God to do the Third Step? Can you trust a God who has let you down?

How are you at taking directions? Being a team player? How about trusting others?

Can you give up the debating society?

Is there anything about not drinking in this Step?

Do you see that self-reliance is not a good thing? When isn't it and why?

Things to write about

Most alcoholics want to be in control. There are many reasons for this. Can you name a few? How well did you manage your life? If you think you did a great job, why are you answering these questions?

Don't forget the actor who ruined the play.

If you are the parent, child, or spouse of an alcoholic and are reading the worksheets, you might want to think about ALANON.

Think about doctors, lawyers, social workers, sponsors, family members, who clearly have more education and more experience than you.

Did you tell them all of your symptoms, all of the meds you're receiving from different physicians, your medical history and your terror? Did you heed their advice?

Have you ever followed people's directions even when you were sure that they were wrong? Looking back over your life, have you ever seen where God took over for you? How do you know? Talk about the times when you asked God for help and He ignored you.

How would you explain 'turning your life and will over to the care of God?' Is that part of the Third Step?

What is?

Can you make a decision to do something that you later realize you could never have done? Would it be a waste of time?

Have you ever decided to do something and do it? Did you say 'What was I thinking?' after the fact.

Do you know the difference between an informed decision and a wish that something will turn out the way you want?

What actions does the Third Step require?

How much does understanding God, His will or your own capabilities have to do with this Step? We're almost finished.

What do you need to be happy? What do you want?

If you got everything you wanted, would you be happy?

Now take a look at the Third Step Promises in the *Big Book*. Do they sound like a load of bull?

Are they in anyway similar to what you just wrote? FYI: take a look at the Third Step promises: You should be able to find them. Turn them into questions. Then ask yourself if they've come true. If not, no worry. Just hit the Steps harder.

And write out the Principles of this Step please.

Step Four: Made a searching and fearless inventory of ourselves.'

This is a very short worksheet. Just do the Fourth Step Inventory, even if you think you don't need to. If you're just finished one, why not pick the four most significant people in your life and do an inventory on them. Ask your sponsor about what to do here.

Why do we have to do the Fourth Step as soon as we finish the Third? What is the harm in waiting? At meetings people say 'don't rush through the Steps. 'They don't want the newcomer to graduate. Doesn't that make sense?

What are the reasons we do this Inventory? Why do we start with resentments?

What is the inventory of? Whose inventory is it?

Why is the inventory very painful?

Why do we have to bring up what we did in the past? Isn't the most important thing what we are doing now?

Why is doing an inventory so important?

Are we supposed to be robots and not have emotions?

The *Big Book* often talks about "ego deflation'. If I have very little self-esteem why should I want to deflate my ego even more?

Here are some concerns of my sponsees:

I'm afraid to tell someone else my secrets? Step Five makes me want to keep certain items off the list. The answer: How about sticking to the Step you're doing and not worrying about a different step?

Isn't this Inventory very mechanical? My counselor has me write an autobiography. Isn't that more thorough?

The answer:

In your discussion of the Fourth Step you add other questions to the Sex Inventory. If the *Big Book* is so wonderful, why do you think you can make it better? What's the point of adding how long I knew the person before I had sex with him/her? Or how long I stayed with the person and why we broke up.

The answer:

What's so important about knowing the truth? I think it's better to be happy. The answer:

The *Big Book* stresses a dependency on God as a way of removing fear. Isn't that just substituting one drug for another? Comment, please:

If we're doing this Inventory as a way of getting closer to God, why isn't there something about it in the *Big Book*?

Answer:

Last question: What's wrong with taking responsibility for your life and making sure you do things right?

Are you a controlling person? What would other people say?

Are you a passive aggressive? What would other people say? How is that a way to be in charge?

The principles of this Step:

Step Five: **'Admitted to God, to ourselves, and to another human being the exact nature of our wrongs'**

The main work in this Step is complying with it. What you see is what you get. Who do you ask to hear your Step?

Discretion: On the off chance that you've committed crimes with no statutes of limitations, or crimes whose statutes have not run, you should consider discussing the crimes with a lawyer, rabbi, priest, or physician. If you are involved in an on-going crime, choose very carefully. Perhaps you might consider stopping the criminal behavior.

If you don't believe in any Higher Power, you might talk to your sponsor about going back to Step Three, or even Step Two.

Some people talk to God, another person and themselves at the same time. Personally, I don't get how that works, but if it works for your sponsor, be my guest.

You also can talk to a deity you don't believe in. Why would you do this?

You look over your list. If you have no part in any of the drama of your life, pretend you are your Mother, Father, spouse, boyfriend or ex, children, boss and co-workers. What would they say about you?

If you think they would say that you're perfect, you might want to ask these people what they actually think. If you still think you have no part in the events in your life, ask yourself if you're a saint or very good at concealing your actions and your motives.

Ask yourself if you're engaged in a double life, one in which you do not tell yourself the truth, don't look at yourself, or are in total denial.

Do you know anyone else who is perfect? Talk about how you are just like that person. Are you spreading chaos or joy?

Assuming you've never done anything wrong, why are the consequences of your actions so dire?

You may have been abused as a child. The fault is not yours. How you dealt with your memories is your responsibility. Agree or disagree? Why?

Did you try to forgive the other person? Did you try to let go of the past?

Has the harm done to you become your defining characteristic, i.e., you're the girl who was raped, or hit by a car, or you contracted some terrible disease?

Think about the things you could have done to prevent the disaster.

Were the terrible people in your life there because you asked them to be? If you did, ask yourself why you were so trusting.

Talk about the nature of trust. Is it noble to trust everybody as soon as you meet them? I think we start at zero and let the other person work his way up. Trust is something to be earned, not given or thrown away.

When you were an adult: ask yourself if the events that occurred have been prevented if you had engaged in some thought before proceeding, particularly if everyone you knew advised you not to go ahead?

Ask yourself why you are so trusting. If you proceed after much advice, are you really 'trusting'? Are you just doing what you want to do and pretending you trust the object of your affection and not anyone else?

Do you trust others over yourself? Do you trust yourself over everybody?

Last Questions

Do you know the difference between defect of character, shortcoming, and exact nature of your wrongs? What is it?

How do you prepare to do the Fifth Step? Okay. Now do it.

By the way, why do you think the order is God, you and another person?

Do you know what the exact nature of your wrongs is? Where would you find it in your written Inventory? You can write them down if you wish.

To the Sponsor: Let's say this is the first Fifth Step you've heard. What do you do?

How do you remain non-judgmental and compassionate when the sponsee says something that really bothers you?

What helps you be kind, loving and tolerant?

How much should you talk about your own history?

Do you make sure you don't minimize something that's serious? How do you tell the truth without being very aggressive?

What do you do if you don't believe in God and your Sponsee does? (Or vice versa)

Principles of this Step:

When you do it; When you hear it?

Step Five and a Half: After you finish your Fifth Step you're directed to go home and review the first Five Steps in the *Big Book* and in your own writings. You might want to write this down.

Are you sure that you understand how to practice the principles of these Steps in your daily life? Will you make the practice of the principles a priority in your life?

Are you feeling connected to others in your Group? To God? Do you feel you can behave better and have a new peace and serenity?

To a sponsor

Make sure that you are clear about the First Five Steps. How about writing something here?

Read up on the Steps; speak to your sponsor; go to some Step and *Big Book* meetings; listen to Speaker Tapes on the First Five Steps.

What do you do if your sponsee is ecstatic and is sure she's got it?

What do you do when your sponsee is very depressed?

Some Results of doing this Step:

For the Sponsee

For the Sponsor

How do you practice Step Five in your daily life?

Step Six: 'Were entirely ready to have God remove all these defects of character.'

Which character defects do you want removed? Which ones do you want to keep?

Were you dishonest? Did you lead a double or triple life? How so? When was the last time you lied to yourself? To others? Give five examples of each, if possible.

How grandiose were you when you thought you were the worst person in the world? Are you grandiose, thin skinned, or childish?

Do you feel closer to the other people in AA than when you came in? Are you more comfortable with other people in general?

Reread the fourth column of your Fourth Step. How are you doing with forgiveness? What are your major character defects?

What do you do when stressed or unhappy-what did you do when drinking or drugging?

Did your character defects arise only after you drank or drugged or while you were engaged in drug- seeking behavior?

Write down which character defects have caused you harm or harmed other people? How far are you from the person you want to be?

What if you don't believe in God? How would Step Six work?

By the time you're at Step Six, what often happens is that you won't be ashamed of the terrible things you have done while sober. You may not become a saintly human being but you will be a better one who does not have such intense self-hatred.

Do you feel that you are actually practicing the first five Steps? Do you know when you are deviating from these principles?

Why is this Step so short in the *Big Book*? Are the additional writings in *The Twelve and Twelve* necessary? Why?

Does the expression 'separates the men from the boys' annoy you? Why? What do your character defects keep you from doing?

How about getting closer to God or closer to others?

What benefits do you derive from keeping your character defects?

How many of your troubles come from not wanting to have confrontations?

Here's a great prayer: 'Please God, help me to do those things that I know are good for me.'

We hopefully are trying to do those things which we understand, through our talks, and talks with others, that we know are good for us and things we should be doing.

Do you see yourself as giving or withholding?

Do you expect others to exert more effort or less in your friendships?

Did you learn from Step Four and Five that you did little or no giving which didn't have strings attached?

How much do you really care about your recovery and yourself? What is the difference between what you need and what you want?

Can you understand that as long as you thought you could take care of things yourself, you were filled with fear? Talk about that a little.

Were you wasting your time and the time of others as you played out your need for control? Talk about this a little.

If we don't rely on ourselves, who can we rely on?

What would it take to make you happy? Answer this honestly, please.

What are your three major goals for the next year?

How have you practiced Step Six in your daily life?

Even though we can't remove our character defects, we can do some footwork that makes things easier. Some examples?

If you're an atheist, how would you answer this question?

Step Seven: 'Humbly asked Him to remove our shortcomings.'

How much energy did you spend on getting, keeping or losing a boyfriend/girlfriend/lover/spouse-a nice house/clothes/job? If not any of these, how did you spend your time? If you say using alcohol or drugs, do you think you have no other shortcomings than your alcohol or drug use?

Were you willing to go to any length to get what you wanted?

How much time did you spend thinking, worrying, planning, and scheming to get more power and control, more prestige, more of many things, just plain more? By the way some alcoholics say alcoholism is a disease of 'more.' It isn't. It is a disease of wanting more of what we want. It doesn't include more Step work or more prayer and meditation. Trust me on this one.

Step Seven says that we "humbly' ask God to remove our shortcomings.

Why are we humble when we ask for help?

Sometimes we don't even know what our shortcomings are. We still can be driven blindly for our need for sex, prestige and security. Do you see that you can't be aware of what drives you blindly?

Do you know any humble people? Are you humble? Remotely humble?

> **The Seventh Step Prayer: 'My Creator, I am now willing that you should have all of me, good and bad. I pray that you now remove from me every single defect of character which stands in the way of my usefulness to you and my fellows. Grant me strength, as I go out from here, to do your bidding. Amen.'**

To write about

Why do you do Step Seven?

Do you believe that you had permanent values, sought for their own sake, before you came into the Program?

What were they? Is this consistent with the "true purpose of our lives?' as discussed in the Seventh Step?

By the way, did your actions demonstrate your purpose then? Do they now?

Do you see the ways in which you were playing God, against all logic and reason? Do you think that efforts at control are always the result of fear? Why or why not?

How about your character defects as the result of your inadequate relationship with God? Please note that this works as well if you define God as your authentic self, your soul, or a more traditional deity.

Are you still mired in self-centeredness, in the need to do things your way?

Do you think you will ever summon 'the resolution and the willingness' to get rid of your overwhelming compulsions and desires?

Are you finally willing to have the defects removed by a being capable of doing the job?

Those who talk about 'working on themselves' are destined to a long life of futility and woe. Why? Why is ego deflation such a peace gaining activity?

Are you free of the need to be perfect? What are your strengths and weaknesses? What do you really want?

Think about this for a while, maybe a week or so-write things down, and think again-put down the three goals you really have-goals that do not include any unreasonable demands (either on ourselves, others or God).

What do you want most in the coming year?

Be honest now. Yes, I know you did something like this in Step Six.

Did you constantly demand more of things and people than they could ever have provided you? How so?

Was there anything that could have given you what you truly wanted?

Step Seven is the Step where we hope to see what it is that we need and how we can get it. Why are some goals limited or self-imposed?

What are the principles of the Seventh Step?

Have you been practicing Step Six?

STEP EIGHT: 'Made a list of all persons we had harmed and became willing to make amends to them all.'

This is a Step that you understand as you do it. There's very little to think or talk about.

Do you have a sponsor?

Does your sponsor have a sponsor?

Why are you doing the Eighth and Ninth Steps? Do you find a lot of guidance in this step?

We are told to pray for knowledge of what the right thing is and the power to carry it out. Then we do what we have to do, despite its consequences to us. Have you ever done this?

What if you don't believe in God? Who do you pray to? Who do you think has the power to help you?

The *Big Book* says this is where we enter the world of the Spirit. What are your thoughts about this? Why do you have to forgive those who harmed you?

If someone has really hurt you and you hate them very much, how can you forgive them?

Do you know people who have been hurt so badly that they are scarred for the rest of their lives? Do you know people who have gotten over their trauma and are doing well in their lives?

What do you think they did to accomplish this?

Some Practical Questions

What do you do if you can't, or shouldn't, make direct amends? Common sense and your sponsor will help you. Any examples?

What are some amends you have made? Although you didn't call them amends, have you ever tried to right the wrongs you have committed? How did it go?

When do you start making amends?

Would you ever do an amends out of order? Should you put yourself on the list?

Making all of the amends to everyone else allows you to look every human being in the eye without shame or regret. You learn to forgive others; and to experience the forgiveness of others. Are you, right now, getting closer to the person you want to be?

Does that sound like you're making an amends to yourself? How valuable would it be to learn how to forgive yourself? There's not a lot to say about this Step. The point is to do it.

Principles of this Step: (and how you practiced Step Eight)

STEP NINE: 'Made direct amends, wherever possible, except when to do so would injure them or others.'

This is another Step that you do rather than talk about. You need a Sponsor and you need to proceed. Write down some reasons why you are reluctant to proceed. What can you do to move forward?

We are going to go to people on a spiritual basis, even when they have harmed us. The first thing we have to do is let go of our anger towards them. How do we do this?

Think of an example from your own life.

Write about your difficulties doing this Step. Or the difficulties you envision.

What is forgiveness? Is your forgiveness of me the same as God's forgiveness of me?

Principles of the Ninth Step

STEP TEN: 'Continued to take personal inventory and when we were wrong promptly admitted it.'

Here too, following the directions of the Tenth Step is how you do the Step. Although we're doing the Tenth Step by the *Big Book*, you might want to examine the Tenth Step in *The Twelve and Twelve*, which offers many oft quoted remarks.

Do you ever have emotional hangovers? What do they do for you?

Can you ever be wrong? Can you admit you're wrong to yourself? To others?

Give an example where've you've done this. By the way, would your sponsor agree with you?

Are you proud of the fact that you're stubborn? Is it a virtue? Is it the same thing as being committed to the truth? What are the character defects associated with stubbornness?

What do you think your sponsor would say, at least to herself? Do you know what the most difficult thing is for sponsors?

Do you want to make it difficult for the sponsor to practice restraint of tongue? What do you get out of it?

Do you find people are always getting angry at you? Do people explain to you why they or others are getting angry?

Warning: when you start doing inventories, you'll start getting sick of yourself and want to quit. Please don't. Does Step Ten help you with this? How?

Do you get that the Tenth Step is more than doing a mini Fourth Step Inventory? What else does the *Big Book* ask you to do?

When you look at Step Ten, do you see any of the earlier Steps? Which ones?

Do you practice self-restraint? Restraint of thought, tongue or email? Ever? Sometimes? Never?

Have you reached the point where you see that you, as well as those about you are often emotionally ill and frequently wrong?

Without looking at the *Big Book* or any place else, could you give a summary of what the Tenth Step tells you to do. If not, write it on a separate piece of paper and start doing it!

Make sure you do ten total Tenth Steps in the next few weeks. Show them to your sponsor and spend some time talking about them.

How good were you at '…resolutely turn out thoughts to someone we can help. Who did you think you could help and if you did?

How did you do at the 'Love and tolerance is our code.'

Look at what upset you and write a sentence or two on how you practiced love and tolerance.

'We (have) ceased fighting anything or anyone.' Write down exactly who or what you refrained from fighting. (We understand that we are not cured of alcoholism and acknowledge that)'… we have a daily reprieve contingent upon the maintenance of our spiritual condition.'

'We carry the vision of God's will into all of our activities, asking ourselves How can I best serve Thee-Thy will (not mine) be done.' No kidding-in all of our activities. Did you do this? Will you do this?

Do a check off. Write down yes or no, and if something came to you about God's will or how you could serve God (HP, authentic self, etc.) write that down as well.

We check to make sure that these thoughts go with us constantly, that we are God conscious. Did you check to see that? (A simple check with a yes or no).

STEP ELEVEN: Sought through prayer and meditation to increase your conscious contact with God, praying only for knowledge of His will or the power to carry it out.

Here comes another inventory. Please write it out, hopefully without having to check with the literature.

Do you see that your imperfections and poorly conceived actions are the foundation of spiritual growth and development? Do you understand that AA doesn't want you to leave off your daily life or your desires but to use them in the development of your relationship with God?

You can write a little about this please.

Why not do a little Eleventh step inventory, referring to admissions of wrong or amends you had to make. How good were you at thinking of others, or were you still stuck on yourself, selfish and self- centered as always?

How about the actions you took that were selfless and useful for others? If not, please write a reminder to perform some by the next day.

Did you think about what you could pack into the stream of life? Well, what did you come up with? Did you do some packing? Were you filled with worry, remorse and morbid reflection? So what did you do about it? I hope not wallow. If you did, I think of some ways to stop that kind of response. Maybe even ask your sponsor for some help?

What did you ask God to forgive you for?

Were you good about asking for knowledge of the corrective measures should be taken, without obsessing on what you should do to correct some situation.

This is the Program, folks. Each Step brings us closer to practicing the presence of God

If for some reason you don't ask for forgiveness or what corrective measures should be taken, you might try to ask first thing in the morning.

How about the morning; do you have your own routine? That, of course, is fine. I ask only that you write down what the *Big Book* asks you to do, and that you do it for thirty days.

If you're not sure of what to do, ask God (your Higher Power, your authentic self, etc.) for an inspiration, intuitive thought or a decision.

Don't nag God

Asking the same question over and over again must be very annoying for Him. Are you a nag?

Wait before acting

If some great insight you've received in prayer or meditation has far reaching consequences, do you check with someone else before acting on the thought? How about insights without far reaching consequences but some negative ones? Write about that a little.

Do you: '…pray that we will be shown all through the day what our next step is to be, that we be given whatever we need to take care of such problems.'

That doesn't mean that you pray all day long, by the way.

The *Big Book* reminds us '…that there is action and still more action that is necessary. The rest of the morning meditation is done according to the beliefs of the God of each person's understanding and is left to the choice of the practitioner of this Step. How good are you at this?

This is where outside help is essential. You and your sponsor or some other person can make a plan for improving your conscious contact with God.

Are you doing this? 'During the day we pause, when agitated or doubtful and ask for the right thought or action.'' We constantly remind ourselves that we are no longer running the show, humbly saying 'Thy will be done.'

Have you been doing Step Ten? Are you sick of yourself yet?

Principles of the Eleventh Step:

Your turn

STEP TWELVE: 'Having had a spiritual awakening as the result of these steps, we tried to carry this message to alcoholics, and to practice these principles in all our affairs.'

Please write a little bit about your personal spiritual growth

Your spiritual awakenings as a result of each Step

Step One: Your problem

What you learned. A spiritual awakening: Step Two: A Solution to your problem: What you learned:

Step Three: What you decided What you learned:

Step Four: What you had to do: What you learned:

Step Five: What else you had to do: What you learned:

Step Six: Seeing another problem: What you learned:

Step Seven: What you had to do about this problem: What you learned:

Step Eight: Getting going; more about what you had to do: What you learned:

Step Nine: Some hard choices: What you learned:

Step Ten: The route (or path) you took: What you learned:

A route is really a routine: What habitual behavior did you practice?

Step Eleven: What you have to do: What you learned:

Step Twelve: A three part solution to becoming happy, joyous and free: What you learned:

Where you are now? Is it good enough?

What do you have to do to improve your spirituality?

A few more Twelfth Step Questions

'The joy of living is the theme of AA's Twelfth Step, and action is its key word.' Have you had one spiritual awakening or many? Do you see them as a combined gift, part of your own making, and part from your Higher Power?

Please speak to your sponsor. It is probably better to save these questions for a time when you have a broken leg. (Just kidding) You might even have a Twelfth Step Study Group or Workshop or meeting where you discuss all of these questions.

Discuss your concept of a Higher Power? Do you think the Steps give you the ability to create any God you want? Why

Why do we 'turn over' our will and lives as opposed to give them? What is this process? The Step says it is a decision. How does the Third Step Prayer fit into this decision making process?

What were the things (plural) in you which brought you to physical, moral and spiritual bankruptcy?

Again, have you told yourself, God and another human being all of your character defects? If not, HERE IS THE TIME TO DO IT.

What are your character defects? Which have been removed and which lessened by this stage of your development?

Where are you in the removal process? (Of having your character defects removed.)

Is there anyone you cannot find yourself willing to make an amends to? How does the amends process relate to having peace and joy in your life?

Where do you fit in your world? In the center, the middle, or off to one side? Has your perception of the world changed as a result of these Steps? How?

Are you learning that what you think, feel and believe, greatly influences your reality? Give a few examples:

Where does restraint of pen, tongue and thought fit in to the process of living a joyful life (just kidding, too obvious but worth discussing one more time)?

My goodness, need we write an essay on the effects of having God in our lives? I think so. Talk about your personal experiences as well as what you have seen in AA and outside of it.

Are you carrying your message by your demeanor and actions? Do you remember that carrying the message is not only a matter of words?

Discuss further ways you can act to make your life more joyful.

Practicing these principles in all of our affairs

Have you had a spiritual awakening about which there was no question? Has that awakening caused major changes in your actions? Do you think it should?

Do you actually demand nothing in return when you do Twelve Step work? What do you expect? Is this ego? Think carefully.

Do you sense the presence of God and God's power enabling you to make a new beginning? Are you beating up on yourself for your failure to be more spiritual and more joyful?

Are you letting fears, self-judgment, traces of condemnation on the part of your parents, your *Church or your concept of God, prevent you from moving forward?*

WILAA: The process of change occurs over a period of time and sometimes means two Steps forward, one step back. The ego is very powerful, as are our fears. Sometimes we need help and encouragement to keep going. Sometimes we can't face our darkest secrets although we believe we have faced ourselves fully. It takes time and trust to do that.

Your sponsor is your greatest ally in moving forward as best as you can without engaging in rationalization and needless procrastination.

Go back over your life and think who might say you had hurt them and decide if you owe them an amends.

Make a list of all the ways in which you have changed-then make the list from the perspective of the meaningful people in your life-parents, spouse, lover, children, good friends, co-workers, if any, and sponsor (certainly).

If this does not convince you, ask God for help and guidance.

Reread the *Big Book*. Go back and do the Steps again, but differently-ask your sponsor for help in this matter.

Remember, always, that it is progress, not perfection. Please remember, also, that we're not doing the work so that we become emotionally healthy. That usually happens. Why are we doing this?

AA has taught me to be very practical here-no theory, no philosophy. Take a look at your actions in AA. It will help you see how you are practicing the principles of the Program, both in and out of the rooms.

Are you doing what you can to help new comers, speaking to them at meetings instead of your friends?

In an AA meeting do you feel that what you have to say is much more important than any of the other members of the group? Are you eligible for the humility award?

Do you give reassurance and support but do so honestly, not saying life is great when it really isn't? Do you cite all those great platitude like 'It's all good' and 'God doesn't give us more than we can handle.' I always wonder what planet people are on who say these things. Do you know why? When you speak (or share) at a meeting, do you carry the message? Are you talking of solutions or wallowing in your problems or resentments. When you speak of what is going on wrong in your life (in relation to the topic or what someone has said), do you talk about solutions?

Do you stick to your experience, strength hope, or are you giving opinions, thoughts and philosophy? Do you allow others to take your place if they are new and need service work?

Are you over managing things? Do you understand the difference between principal and agent, between carrying the message and feeling important because you are the messenger?

Are you clear that you became a messenger out of desperation and need, not because of any special knowledge, intelligence, insight, or other talent?

What do you do when your ego has taken over and you're back to trying to run things?

How about when you feel that the world, the group, your family and the stranger on the train, really need you, your advice and your directions?

Do you love all your life as well as that part where you are helping other alcoholics achieve sobriety? Are you bringing that same spirit of love and tolerance to your family members? At work? With friends? Can you bring a new spirituality to those about you without saying a word about spirituality or God?

Take a look over the Steps and see how practicing the suggestions contained in The *Big Book* and *The Twelve and Twelve* can lead to joy.

A simple example demonstrates this: I fearfully faced my powerlessness, fearfully saw that I was insane but could be restored to sanity and finally asked God to help me.

I saw how corrosive fear was in my life and how it beat me down, again and again-compelling me to make poor choices in all areas of my life, and precluding the possibility of any more than momentary happiness. Six and Seven is the beginning of asking God to remove this fear, while Eight and Nine take me further out of a fear driven universe. Ten propels me further on this path while the additional actions (and make no mistake, each time I move further from fear it is because of actions taken as a result of the Steps) of Steps Eleven and Twelve help me remove the lasting effects of fear in my decision making processes and in my responses to the environment.

I do not act or react but restructure my life so that fear is but an emotion to be acknowledged and dealt with.

No life replete with fear can be jubilant. Fear is a major impediment to a joyful existence.

Now do the same thing with selfishness, self-centeredness, anger, and resentment. It seems difficult but it's only a few paragraphs. You may want to do this when you have a lot of time.

WILAA: Living the principles is necessary if we want to carry the message-we are visual aids.

WILAA: Spirituality is a three minute share. (Do you observe this one?)

WILAA: Coffee makers make it. (How so?)

As you look at your life over these past years, can you see how your practice of the principles has affected those around you? How has it affected you? Talk about that.

Are you carrying the AA spirit into your daily life? What is that spirit?

Are you changing your values as you begin to see what is truly priceless? What do you value now that you did not before-not verbally but in actions and your emotional responses?

Did you trust your emotional responses? Do you now?

Are you truly prepared to accept what life hands you, not as a matter of resignation, but because of an abiding faith in God's presence?

If you don't believe in God, perhaps an abiding faith in reality, honesty and humility?

Does that mean that things might not go your way but you will continue to walk on the path of Godliness or goodness?

Where do you feel that you have the most difficulty in practicing the principles?

Are you saying the same things you said, either in your meetings or your life, when you came into AA?

Where have your beliefs changed? Think about the way you look at the Steps, people and life. Are you sharing differently?

When we do the Steps, read the *Big Book*, or the stories, we find that we see things differently. Do you have some examples of this?

What happens when you want to be taken care of but still insist upon having things your own way? Do you feel more connected to others, strangers as well as friends?

Okay, here's the biggie, talk about being dependent upon God and how this has increased since you've been working the Steps. How can you become even more dependent? How about if you're an atheist?

Do you know God's will now? Can you think of any guidelines to help? Of course, this doesn't mean neglecting any literature which helps make faith vital and alive.

Are you 'balanced' today, mind, body and spirit, secular and lay, family and AA, friends, relatives and meetings, spiritual growth and physical well-being? Talk about these and add some others to the list.

Would you say that recovery is the most important thing in your life? If not why not? (No right or wrong answer, but something to think about.) This is where balance and harmony really come in.

What are the fears you have today? How would you rate your spiritual condition? If you haven't done a spiritual inventory or done one in the distant past, this might be a good time to do the Spiritual Inventory in this book.

Do you have any regrets about not being a world historical individual? Rich? Famous? Sought after madly for your beauty, wit and personality?

Do you believe that you are a true leader of AA? How so or no?

Do you feel more comfortable in your own skin? Do you feel more comfortable when out and about in the world? In your home?

Serenity, courage and wisdom do not come easily. They come after time, a lot of energy and a lot of work. Talk a little about how there is more serenity, courage and wisdom in your life than there had been before.

Pretty awesome. The answers to all of our questions are in the *Big Book* and *The Twelve and Twelve*. We just have to know where to look. The answers to all our problems are there as well.

'With each passing day of our lives, may every one of us sense more deeply the inner meaning of AA's simple prayer…God, grant us the serenity to accept the things we cannot change, The courage to change the things we can, And wisdom to know the difference.

Do you notice that the Serenity Prayer is now in the First Person Plural? What do you think that signifies? I think it is important to talk about this.

CHAPTER THE LAST: AFTERWORD

I hope this book has been helpful for you. I am including some resources for further study. For me, the resources have been useful. They have served as a starting point of discussions with sponsees and others. Ultimately, and always, the beginning is always a gift from something outside of me and the gift of willingness to continue with the directions in the *Big Book*.

When I was learning how to waterski, my friend told me to wait for the boat to pull me up. I shouldn't stand up too quickly, because then I would fall over.

I dutifully waited for the boat to pull me up. I bent my knees and held the rope close to my chest. I found myself planed off, sitting down-waiting. It was kind of trick waterskiing.

I had to wait for the boat to pull me up but I had to stand up when the time came for me to stand up. AA is like that. We're given help but the time comes when we have to stand up ourselves.

Sometimes I just have to act. AA and the Steps help me act wisely and well but I have to act. Once I am giving the gift of sobriety, it is up to me to use it immediately That, too, is the urgency of now.

Resources: a mere beginning

You can find a wonderful history of AA written by Bill Wilson, and a lot of other interesting stuff as well. The history is a must. You'll find it at: http://www.a-1associates.com/aa/index.html

http://westbalto.a-1associates.com/LetsAskBill.htm

Go to iTunes-Podcasts-look up AA Speaker Tapes-there are hundreds of great AA speakers-all free.

Some great websites to download AA speakers

http://www.elmoware.com/spktapes.htm
http://www.aaprimarypurpose.org/speakers.htm http://www.xa-speakers.org/

Here is the famous Dallas group: http://www.ppgaadallas.org/ Never forget iTunes, particularly the Podcasts

Here is an AA history site: http://www.dickb.com/index.shtm

And here are some pictures of the people in the BB, etc.: http://aabbsg.de/aahistoryphotos/ Here is where you can find a very good *Big Book* Study: http://www.thejaywalker.com/

This is a new site (very hi-tech that I haven't checked out but it seems to have some good photos, etc.): http://www.aarootsrevival.com/

Step Study Guides: http://www.step12.com/

http://www.eskimo.com/~burked/history/tablemat html An interesting site: http://alcoholism.about.com/od/study/

www.bettyfordcenter.org/pdfs/alumniresources/STEP_STUDY_OUTLINE.doc

And one more: http://www.stepnahead.com/

Don't forget this gold mine of information. http://www.a-1associates.com/AA/Lets_ask_Bill.htm.

This is part of the West Baltimore Group, with the general website: http://www.a-1associates.com/AA/index.html (It might be worth going to some of their meetings if you're in the area.

The same for the Primary Purpose Group of Dallas. There are more of them all over the country.) Finally: http://silkworth.net/ (good stuff but may shut down if too much monthly traffic.

That's just a beginning. Each year there are many new websites to look at. This is one time when surfing the net is not idle activity.

A SHORT BIBLIOGRAPHY

You've probably read *Dr. Bob and the Old Times*, one of my favorites. *Pass it On* is another good one. Check out the entire list of AA approved books and literature. The pamphlets have tons of information. A good non-AA approved, but approved by lots of people in AA, is *Not God* by Kurtz. It is probably the best book written about the history of AA. E.

Larsen *Stage Two Recovery* is useful in early recovery, as *is Living Sober*. *Anne Smith's Journal* is very interesting. There are tons of books on meditation. *Physician of the Soul* gives some great short meditations. CD's afford much guided meditation practice and can be purchased on line. You can download guided meditations as well-which takes a lot of work because most of them are very short.

Here is a website where you can find all kinds of recovery books and other materials: http://www.soberrecovery.com/forums/alcoholics-anonymous/what-is-sobriety-56339.html

So go to it. The resources are at their most helpful when you're working with a sponsee and don't know what else you can say. I don't know if the sponsee will hear any of this better than anything you said, but at least you can feel as though you're doing something.

I hope this book has been a little bit helpful. Perhaps we shall meet each other as we trudge our road.

By the way, thanks for letting me share.

The *Wilaa's* one more time

WILAA: When someone tells me I don't understand, the odds are pretty good that I do.

WILAA: Sponsorship is all about the Steps

WILAA: Gratitude is an action word.

WILAA: Gratitude elevates the soul; a sense of entitlement destroys it.

WILAA: People who are intensely afraid of being abandoned often act in ways that make it impossible for other people to stick around.

WILAA: Anything that doesn't move me closer to sobriety takes me further away from it. I try to put recovery first. I have to be sure I don't get off track. I've seen too many people who could never make it back.

WILAA: Silence is golden except when it's yellow.

WILAA: The process of AA takes time. That doesn't mean we should dilly dally with our step work. I do it like the founders of AA did, and then go back, and go back, and go back. We trudge the road of happy destiny, although sometimes we do skip lightly down the yellow brick road.

WILAA: We may think we have stopped believing in the need for self-sufficiency but it returns to haunt us. There is constant tension between the necessity of believing in a power greater than myself and my compulsion to take over and do things right.

WILAA: My life must be in balance, sure, but more important, in harmony. Doing some things that give me pleasure, and that might be useful to others help me lead a harmonious life: I've learned how to practice the principles of AA in all of my affairs, and not make AA all of my affairs. I am, indeed, entitled to have a life.

WILAA: Part of my inventory is checking to see if I had spread chaos or joy, confusion or harmony.

WILAA: It's hard to carry 'the' message if you haven't done the Steps.

WILAA: Silence is golden except when it's yellow.

WILAA: 'It takes balls to stay sober,' says a friend of mine with fifty two years of sobriety.

WILAA: After I've gone through the Steps, my understanding of them grows.

WILAA: Patterns of behavior are more recognizable if we start with our early childhood and go forward, but whatever works is fine.

WILAA: Step Four enables me to look at myself clearly, feel my emotions in real time, and stop being a victim.

WILAA: Sometimes you have a sponsee who says she, or he, has nothing to put in the Fourth Column. She, or he, did nothing wrong. Lots of luck, honey.

WILAA: A sponsor can tell the sponsee not to let the one secret she can't tell, sometimes for valid reasons, prevent her from doing the rest of the Fourth Step. The sponsor can explain that people find that they tell things they'd never thought they would divulge to anyone. That's how it works.

WILAA: If you don't do a Fifth you'll probably drink one. I didn't do a good Fourth or Fifth Step in the beginning, but it was good enough.

WILAA: Dishonesty is not just about our drinking (or overeating, or drugging or excessive sexual behavior). It permeates every area of our existence. We learned that we didn't have a clue, no matter what our age or experience, as to our ability to recognize who was dangerous and what situations to avoid. We didn't know what we wanted, or if we did, were too afraid to go for it.

WILAA: Striving for perfection in all things can be an excuse for not doing anything.

WILAA: I guess that's why Step Six is only one paragraph in the Big Book. I take the step and move on. Even so, I want to keep on talking about it.

WILAA: Self-centeredness isn't thinking too much of myself. It's thinking of myself too often.

WILAA: An impaired mind cannot fix an impaired mind. How do you know your brain isn't functioning when your brain isn't functioning?

WILAA: Humility is just honesty in a more pleasant form.

WILAA: All my character defects derive from my inadequate relationship with God.

WILAA: We can't buy our own peace of mind at the expense of someone else.

WILAA: When making an amends I do not go with anger, but I also don't proceed with an attitude of shame. As a child of God I crawl before no man.

WILAA: The most effective beauty treatment is forgiveness-of others and yourself. The world becomes more beautiful and you do too.
WILAA: Whether believer or atheist, it's my task (1) to clean up the messes I've made and (2) to practice forgiveness. I'm not looking for it from anybody except from God

WILAA: When you don't know what to say, think Big Book. There's always something there.

WILAA: The feeling of setting things right stays with us long after the deed is done. We are truly getting rocketed into the fourth dimension.

WILAA: Part of my inventory is checking to see if I had spread chaos or joy, confusion or harmony.

WILAA: It's hard to carry 'the' message if you haven't done the Steps. That's one reason why it's good to do the first run through of the Steps right after you get sober.

WILAA: One thing I've learned about the Traditions; when they're not observed, the group tends to die, sooner, usually, than later.

WILAA: You can go to meetings any place in the world; they start on time, they end on time, they move along well and there is no violence. There is no president, sergeant at arms, armies, police and no organization. That's pretty amazing when you think of who the members of the organization are.

WILAA: The short form of Tradition Twelve is that I place principles over my personality.

WILAA: If someone is powerless over alcohol you can't ask them to try to stop drinking. What you can do is ask them to take positive actions.

WILAA: The process of change occurs over a period of time and sometimes means two Steps forward, one step back. The ego is very powerful, as are our fears. Sometimes we need help and encouragement to keep going. Sometimes we can't face our darkest secrets although we believe we have faced ourselves fully. It takes time and trust to do that.

WILAA: Living the principles is necessary if we want to carry the message-we are visual aids.

WILAA: Spirituality is a three minute share.

WILAA: Coffee makers make it.

Printed in Great Britain
by Amazon